CRITICAL DIALOGUES IN SOUTHEAST ASIAN STUDIES

Vicente Rafael and Laurie J. Sears, Series Editors

Imagined Ancestries of Vietnamese Communism: Ton Duc Thang and the Politics of History and Memory, by Christoph Giebel

Beginning to Remember: The Past in the Indonesian Present, edited by Mary S. Zurbuchen

Seditious Histories: Contesting Thai and Southeast Asian Pasts, by Craig J. Reynolds

Knowing Southeast Asian Subjects, edited by Laurie J. Sears

Making Fields of Merit: Buddhist Female Ascetics and Gendered Orders in Thailand, by Monica Lindberg Falk

Love, Passion and Patriotism: Sexuality and the Philippine Propaganda Movement, 1882–1892, by Raquel A. G. Reyes

Gathering Leaves and Lifting Words: Histories of Buddhist Monastic Education in Laos and Thailand, by Justin Thomas McDaniel

The Ironies of Freedom: Sex, Culture, and Neoliberal Governance in Vietnam, by Thu-hương Nguyễn-võ

Submitting to God: Women and Islam in Urban Malaysia, by Sylva Frisk

No Concessions: The Life of Yap Thiam Hien, Indonesian Human Rights Lawyer, by Daniel S. Lev

The Buddha on Mecca's Verandah: Encounters, Mobilities, and Histories along the Malaysian-Thai Border, by Irving Chan Johnson

Dreaming of Money in Ho Chi Minh City, by Allison Truitt

Mapping Chinese Rangoon: Place and Nation among the Sino-Burmese, by Jayde Lin Roberts

The New Way: Protestantism and the Hmong in Vietnam, by Tâm T. T. Ngô

Imperial Bandits: Outlaws and Rebels in the China-Vietnam Borderlands, by Bradley Camp Davis

Living Sharia: Law and Practice in Malaysia, by Timothy P. Daniels

Mediating Islam: Cosmopolitan Journalisms in Muslim Southeast Asia, by Janet Steele

The Crown and the Capitalists: The Ethnic Chinese and the Founding of the Thai Nation, by Wasana Wongsurawat

THE CROWN AND THE CAPITALISTS

THE ETHNIC CHINESE AND THE FOUNDING OF THE THAI NATION

WASANA WONGSURAWAT

UNIVERSITY OF WASHINGTON

Seattle

The Crown and the Capitalists was published with the assistance of a grant from the Charles and Jane Keyes Endowment for Books on Southeast Asia, established through the generosity of Charles and Jane Keyes.

This book was also supported by a grant from the Association for Asian Studies First Book Subvention Program.

23 22 21 20 19   5 4 3 2 1

UNIVERSITY OF WASHINGTON PRESS
uwapress.uw.edu

LIBRARY OF CONGRESS CATALOGING-IN-PUBLICATION DATA ON FILE
LC record available at https://lccn.loc.gov/2019018124

ISBN 978-0-295-74625-8 (hardcover)
ISBN 978-0-295-74624-1 (paperback)
ISBN 978-0-295-74626-5 (ebook)

COVER DESIGN: Katrina Noble
COVER PHOTOGRAPH: Memorial statue of King Rama VI, by Silpa Bhirasri (born Corrado Feroci), 1942. Lumpini Park, Bangkok, Thailand. Photograph by Adaptor Plug, 2009, Flickr.com.

CONTENTS

PREFACE

In the same way that it is physically impossible for one to get a comprehensive view of oneself without looking in a mirror, it is virtually impossible to get a comprehensive perspective on the history of the nation-state and nationalism through the mainstream narrative of nationalist history. This book therefore investigates the history of the nation-state and nationalism in Asia through the transnational perspective. The case study that lies at the center of this investigation is the evolution of the Thai nation-state from the mid-nineteenth century to the late twentieth century. Instead of relying solely upon Thai sources and secondary materials, it investigates the history of Thai nation-building from three main perspectives. The first, as reference and historiographical context, is the perspective of the Thai state through the different periods within this time frame. This part of the narrative is constructed largely on primary sources gathered from the National Archives of Thailand and an abundance of secondary materials—published research, books, journal articles, and graduate theses at the masters and doctoral levels—in both Thai and English.

The second perspective comes from the Chinese state and its communications with the ethnic Chinese community in Thailand during this period. The perspective of the Chinese state represents that of a competing nationalist movement that came into being almost at the same time as the earliest royalist-nationalist movement, led by King Vajiravudh in the early 1910s. The perspective of leading personalities in the ethnic Chinese community in Thailand shows a transnational community negotiating, compromising, and at times resisting the rising forces of nationalism that were constantly pressuring them to declare loyalty to one nation and to relinquish their ties with all the rest in their extensive and long-standing transnational networks. This alternative perspective is constructed from primary materials collected from the national archives of the Republic of China (Taiwan), the Academia Historica in Taipei, and secondary materials from Chinese-language newspaper articles, memoires, and memorial volumes published by leading individuals and organizations within the ethnic Chinese community in Thailand.

Finally, the third perspective is that of the powerful outsider—the colonial powers as represented by the British Empire in East and Southeast Asia. The British perspective as gathered from the Public Record Office at Kew Garden in London provides insight into the relationship between the British Empire and the Thai and Chinese governments at different points in time throughout the period in question. It also provides a comparative perspective since Britain was also struggling with the rise of Chinese nationalism as well as resistance from ethnic Chinese and Chinese communist insurgence in many parts of the British colonial empire in Southeast Asia. The British perspective also provides a useful comparative view from the standpoint of a Western/colonial power as opposed to the rising nationalist perspectives provided by state documents of both Thailand and China through much of the period.

Collecting and analyzing an extensive body of primary and secondary materials from three national archives and numerous library collections across the publishing universe of English, Chinese, and Thai languages allows for a broader and more comprehensive understanding of the transnational history of the founding of the Thai nation, which is the main focus of this book. Yet it creates more than a few complications in terms of theoretical frameworks, historical periodization, and at the most basic level, the systems of translation and transliteration. While the primary historical timeline in main narrative is that of Thai history, which is my principal area of investigation, this book employs the Gregorian calendar as is the common practice in academic publication in English. Hence, certain important historical incidents that are normally dated in Thai history in the Buddhist era or Rattankosin era are given as Common Era dates instead. For example, the Siamese Revolution is called the Siamese Revolution of 1932 (CE) instead of the Siamese Revolution of 2475 BE (Buddhist Era), and the foiled republican coup at the beginning of Vajiravudh's reign is the coup of 1912 instead of the coup of 130 RE (RE, Rattanakosin Era, begins with the establishment of the ruling dynasty). Romanization of proper nouns, when possible, follows the style employed by the named individual or organization. For common nouns or in cases where the original style is unknown, the Royal Thai General System of Transcription is used for Thai words, while Chinese terms are transliterated using the Hanyu Pinyin system.

As for theoretical frameworks, this study lies in between two important region studies—East and Southeast Asian studies. The employment of cross-regional primary and secondary materials yields analysis and inter-pretation that may not conform with certain established norms of interpre-tation. Chinese historians may find that some parts read like the Thai perspective on Chinese history, and Thai specialists might argue that parts read like the Chinese interpretation of modern Thai history. All in all, this is an attempt to construct a transnational/transregional history of the Thai nation-state with the understanding that East and Southeast Asia share an experience through the colonial period, the Great East Asia War, and the Cold War. As a comprehensive perspective on the history of nation-building could not be achieved solely through the investigation of national history, or even within the limitations of regional studies, comparative perspectives and contesting narratives from sources outside the immediate circle of Thai and Southeast Asian Studies allow for new interpretations and a more com-prehensive understanding, while being unfamiliar and even disconcerting at the earlier stages.

ACKNOWLEDGMENTS

This book has been more than a decade in the making. I would like to express my deepest gratitude to the following individuals and institutions without whose support the publication of this work would have been impossible.

First and foremost, I thank the Thai taxpayers who supported my work at the University of Chicago and Oxford. Most of what I have today as the tools of my trade as an academic was paid at a very high price by Thai taxpayers' money.

Prasenjit Duara has long been my mentor and still is my inspiration in doing border-crossing history to this day.

I learned much from Rana Mitter and am still deeply influenced by his work. He is the inspiration for this book.

I am forever indebted to the spectacular services of the three national archives I have relied upon for the primary materials in this book; the National Archives in Bangkok, Thailand, Academia Historica in Taipei, Republic of China, and the Public Record Office in London.

I am very grateful to my home institution, the Faculty of Arts, Chulalongkorn University, for having provided me with stable and secure employment for the past ten years. I owe all my generous colleagues at the Department of History for allowing me to take time off—not once but twice—to work on the research that was fundamental to the production of this book in two fellowships.

In particular, I would like to express thanks to the following colleagues and former colleagues at the Department of History, Chulalongkorn University: Chalong Soontravanich, Pipada Youngcharoen, Suthachai Yimprasert, Sunait Chutintaranond, Villa Vilaithong, and Bhawan Ruangsilp. I have learned much from all of you.

I was generously supported by a fellowship from the Asia Research Institute, National University of Singapore, between 2007 and 2008. During that year I received invaluable advice and encouragement from Anthony Reid, Geoff Wade, and Wang Gungwu. I also was very fortunate to befriend and learn much from fellow researchers at NUS during that year, including Hiroko Matsuda, Tuong Vu, and Pinkaew Laungaramsri.

In 2012–13, I was awarded another fellowship from Hong Kong Polytechnic University. I would like to express my sincere gratitude for the support of colleagues there, especially Huang Shuren, who was then the Dean of Humanities of Hong Kong Polytechnic University. The bulk of this book was written during that year in Hong Kong.

Through the past decade of working in Thailand, I have received much support from the Thailand Research Fund both in terms of providing research funding and connecting me with kind and supportive senior scholars in Thailand who have been extremely supportive of me and my work. I am deeply grateful for the friendship, support, and encouragement from Suwanna Satha-anand and Yos Santasombat, whom I have come to know, love, and respect deeply through the Thailand Research Fund.

I have been fortunate to receive much support and encouragement from leading scholars and authors in related fields both in Thailand and abroad. I am most indebted to the kindness and wisdom of Pimpraphai Bisalputra and Jeffery Sng, whose *History of the Thai-Chinese* has been such an inspiration for my own work on the history of the Chinese community in Thailand.

I have been greatly inspired by the works of Tani Barlow since my years as an undergraduate at the University of Chicago and have been very fortunate to meet her in person in the pantry of the Asia Research Institute at NUS in 2008. Ever since then Tani has been extremely kind and supportive. I am forever grateful to her not only for all that I have learned from her work and for giving me the opportunity to work with her, but also for being the best role model of how to survive and excel as a woman in such a male-dominated area of academia.

Thak Chaloemtiarana's *Thailand: The Politics of Despotic Paternalism* is definitely one of the most important works of the twentieth century. I owe much to him both in terms of the great wisdom and inspiration I draw from his works and for his kind advice and encouragement every time I run into him in person and through email. Craig Reynolds and Chris Baker are definitely two of the greatest historians of Thailand with whom I have had the pleasure of discussing my work. Both have been exceedingly supportive and encouraging through the decade-long process of getting this book published.

I would also like to thank my good friends from the University of Chicago—Kaveh Hemmat, Jeehee Hong, and Rivi Handler-Spitz—who have shared this journey with me from the very beginning.

I am grateful to Arnika Fuhrmann for her brilliant mind and her fearless approach to all academic endeavors related to Thailand. Without Arnika's insistence and challenges, this book would never have seen the light of day.

I am beholden to the four people who read my manuscript at the initial stages; my mother, Janice Wongsurawat; my colleague Carina Chotirawe and her mother; and the grand and illustrious double SEA-Write awardee, Veeraporn Nitiprapha. These are the four loveliest women in my life.

I have had the great fortune of having worked with some outstanding graduate students from whom I have learned much over the years. I thank my very first PhD advisee, Waraporn Ruangsri, whose dissertation on the caravan traders in the northern frontiers was truly inspirational for our shared endeavor of ever questioning and pushing the boundaries of the nation-state. I am grateful to Thep Boontanondha, whose MA thesis on the military image of King Vajiravudh encouraged me to look again and take the period of 1910s and 1920s more seriously. Without the works of these two brilliant minds, this book could never have materialized.

I am forever grateful for all the efforts and patience put into the production of this book from the editorial team at the University of Washington Press. It has been a great pleasure to work with Lorri Hagman. This book has also been immensely improved through the kind and constructive comments of the two anonymous reviewers. I thank them very much as well.

My deepest gratitude goes to the members of my family, who have been extremely loving and supportive, not only of my career and well-being but also of whatever they figured was what I considered important regardless of how nonsensical it might initially appear to them. I thank my siblings, Rosie, Winai, and John Wongsurawat, with all my heart.

This book is dedicated to my parents, Kovit and Janice Wongsurawat, my two greatest teachers of life.

Bangkok
January 2019

THE CROWN AND THE CAPITALISTS

INTRODUCTION

THE IDEA OF THE MODERN NATION-STATE AND NATIONALISM, which began to take root in East and Southeast Asia from the late nineteenth to the early twentieth century, in many ways favored bigger and more prosperous nations, and few even marginally successful modern Asian nation-states were established prior to the outbreak of the Second World War. One was China, whose resources and territories offered enormous economic potential; another, Japan, used military technology and economic performance to create a massive empire. The Kingdom of Thailand—or Siam, as it was known to the world prior to 1939—also succeeded in rapidly transforming itself into a modern nation-state, although it was neither big nor particularly prosperous nor much more technologically advanced than most of its neighbors in Southeast Asia.

Mainstream state-sanctioned conservative Thai histories credit the modernization policies and diplomatic skills of King Chulalongkorn (r. 1868–1910) and members of his royal government with leading Siam to modernity, while more progressive historians have argued that Siam in the earliest decades of the twentieth century was neither really modernized nor transformed into a modern nation-state like the Republic of China or Meiji Japan. In these more progressive narratives, Chulalongkorn is described as governing his own realm as if it were a colony and modernizing Siam as the British did in Malaya and the Dutch in the East Indies. According to this narrative, nation and nationalism did not become a fundamental part of Siamese governing policies, if at all, until the 1932 Revolution, which supposedly transformed the kingdom into a constitutional monarchy.

Recent historiography, shaped in the ideological context of the Cold War, has placed the development of Western-style liberal democracy at the center of Thailand's narrative and has told the story largely within the framework of the nation-state. However, that view underestimates the importance of transnational perspectives involving the colonial context, in particular, conditions created by Siam's long-standing relationship with China and the existence of a large and important Chinese diaspora community within Siam.

The court of Siam's Chakri dynasty, which has ruled Thailand since 1782 and survived as a sovereign government in the high colonial era, occupied an unusual position, with Siamese absolute monarchs in the late nineteenth and early twentieth centuries ruling Siam as colonial masters of their own self-colonized kingdom.[1] This was, at least in part, caused by trade agreements that colonial powers—namely, Britain and France—had forced Siam to sign beginning in the mid-nineteenth century. Colonial demands for free trade came with the imperative of extraterritoriality, which in turn made the establishment of a territorial nation-state impossible. How could the boundaries of a modern nation-state be absolutely defined when a large number of residents in that state possessed rights that transcended the boundaries of the nation-state and were beyond the judicial sovereignty of the national government? How could a modern nation-state be established in late-nineteenth-century Siam when a large portion of the population could not be coerced into accepting Siamese citizenship and relinquishing political ties with competing empires—either China or the colonial regimes of Great Britain and France? Because of this peculiar situation, the founding of the nation in Siam—later transformed into Thailand—relied to a great extent upon compromise with neighboring colonial powers and cultivation of strong business-political alliances with the extensive and influential network of transnational Chinese entrepreneurs.

After the first three reigns of the dynasty (Rama I–Rama III, 1782–1851), in which kings ruled within the economic context of the Chinese tribute system—presenting Siam as a tributary state of the Qing Empire and prospering as a loyal vassal within the Chinese trade universe—political and economic encroachment from European colonial powers transformed the scene completely in the mid-nineteenth century. Following the splendid success of the First Opium War (1839–42) and the ratification of the Treaty of Nanjing with China, the British delegate Sir John Bowring successfully convinced King Mongkut Rama IV (r. 1851–68) to sign the Bowring Treaty in 1855. The Bowring Treaty, like so many other "unfair"[2] treaties that would follow between European colonial powers and Asian kingdoms, was drafted in almost the exact same fashion as the Treaty of Nanjing—imposing an end to royal monopoly of international trade, a fixed tariff rate of 3 percent, and extraterritorial rights[3] for subjects of the colonial powers. Basically, it was a declaration that the center of the universe regarding trade and political power had been relocated from the Great Qing Empire to the British Empire.

The Siamese government under the leadership of Chakri monarchs from the late-nineteenth century through the first three decades of the twentieth century chose to endorse and encourage this semicolonial state imposed by the Bowring Treaty of 1855 with Britain and similar "unfair" treaties with other colonial powers. The establishment of extraterritorial rights through these treaties enabled Chinese entrepreneurs in Siam—the richest and most powerful among whom had managed to have themselves registered as British or French colonial subjects—to enjoy the extraordinary degree of freedom that came with being colonial subjects, by residing and engaging in business in a marginally independent state such as Siam.[4] Because the Siamese state had difficulty exercising judicial control over these subjects, Siam was attractive to the transnational Chinese as a base for conducting and expanding business.[5] At the same time, the fantastic growth of ethnic Chinese businesses based in Siam became the main driving force of Siamese economic growth and competitiveness in a region that was almost completely dominated by colonial empires. For this reason, the Chakri monarchs from the mid-nineteenth century on maintained a cordial relationship with leading Chinese entrepreneurs, bestowing on them courtly titles and ensuring continuation of their state contracts. As a result, Siam had a large and highly influential Chinese community.[6]

This peculiar symbiotic relationship between the Siamese royal government and the British colonial empire allowed the Siamese economy to remain competitive through the vibrant network of ethnic Chinese entrepreneurs based in the kingdom while permitting the British colonial powers to establish dominance over the vast universe of maritime trade from the South China Sea across the Indian Ocean without having to colonize every political entity in the region. However, it proved problematic when Siamese rulers confronted the task of building a modern nation-state in the early twentieth century. As Japan became a world-class superpower in its own right through the amazing victory in the Russo-Japanese War (1904–5) and China declared its rebirth as a modern nation through the founding of the Republic of China in 1912 (following the Xinhai Revolution of October 1911, which overthrew the Qing dynasty and ended the dynastic rule that had lasted over two millennia on the mainland), King Vajiravudh Rama VI (r. 1910–25) was struggling to transform Siam into a modern nation-state and establish some form of modern nationalism to ensure the survival of what was to become his royal nation and secure his political position as the royal head of state and absolute monarch.

The most fundamental task required of King Vajiravudh in establishing a modern nation-state in Siam was to envision a nation large and flexible enough to contain a sizable and highly influential transnational population—namely, the ethnic Chinese community in Siam. This involved not only defining and promoting the idea of a modern nation-state that allowed the transnational Chinese to remain transnational, but also allowing them to enjoy their colonial status and extraterritorial rights while continuing to flourish economically and contribute financially to the growth and development of the modern Siamese nation-state. Moreover, this novel idea of the Siamese nation-state as devised by Vajiravudh had to be credible and convincing enough to compete with the Chinese nationalist narratives promoted by both reform and revolutionary factions in Chinese politics, who wanted to gain as much support as possible from overseas Chinese communities for their political causes. Much of the history of the founding of the modern nation-state in Siam during the first few decades of the twentieth century therefore involved justifying the inclusion of Chinese colonial subjects in nationalism and nation-building as well as competing with the nation-state of their ancestral homeland—China—for the loyalty and devotion from this transnational population.

Much of the contest for political justification and the effort to win the hearts and minds of a transnational people residing in and contributing to the fledgling nation-state, starting with the end of Chulalongkorn's reign and continuing through Vajiravudh's reign, was carried out through what seemed like minor sociocultural battlefields, such as the establishment and reform of compulsory education; control of the media, especially the printing press; and the reorientation of the local economy so as to gain some degree of independence from both the British colonial structure and the ethnic Chinese trade network, which had come to enjoy a near monopoly of the Siamese economy nearly from the beginning of the Chakri dynasty. Unlike Japan, Siam under Chulalongkorn and Vajiravudh did not enjoy the level of military prowess that could enforce loyalty from its subjects nor did it possess the financial means to bribe anyone into submission. The art of enticing ethnic Chinese entrepreneurs to continue trading, investing, and reinvesting in Siam even after the kingdom had been overpowered by the colonial superpowers of the region—in this case, Britain and France—while reassuring the native population that it was in their best interest to remain docile and devoted to the Siamese crown despite appearing to be second-class citizens in their own land thus came to be key to the founding of the Thai nation in the earliest decades of the twentieth century.

This was how Vajiravudh's royalist nationalism came into being. The modern nation of Siam, according to Vajiravudh, was identical with the person of the monarch. This was justified by a historical narrative claiming that it was Vajiravudh's father, King Chulalongkorn, and his grandfather, King Mongkut, who saved Siam from the fate of being colonized by the Europeans. Hence, the monarch was the great protector of the nation. Consequently, loyalty and devotion to the monarch should be considered to be the same as loyalty and devotion to the nation. This was the fundamental definition of Vajiravudh's version of nationalism. While propagating this idea of royalist nationalism, he also promulgated the citizenship act, which transformed all Siamese subjects into citizens and demanded of them, in return for legal protection of their basic rights as citizens, loyalty to the nation and active participation in the king's nationalist movement.[7] Through this bifurcated policy implementation, Vajiravudh not only managed to create citizens out of his subjects but also created a loophole that allowed a significant number of colonial subjects to be included in and contribute to his national project. While Siamese subjects enjoyed rights as citizens, colonial subjects could continue to enjoy their extraterritorial rights and still be considered Siamese patriots through their support—mostly financial—of the monarch's various policies and royal initiatives. Essentially, it was a way of allowing colonial subjects to continue as a privileged class within the nation in exchange for their financial support—an unspoken form of taxes for privileged foreigners—while the majority of native citizens continued as second-class members of the nation-state in exchange for lower income taxes.

Scholarship on the transition from absolutism to the constitutional regime in Siam in 1932, which has concentrated on the domestic story of rising opposition to the monarchy, has missed the transnational perspective, in which much changed between the 1910s and the 1930s, particularly with respect to colonialism, extraterritoriality, and the situation of China. In fact, the founding of the Thai nation as a modern constitutional regime following the Siamese Revolution of 1932 was as much about solidifying borders and citizenship and transferring sovereignty from the person of the monarch to the national territories and citizens as it was about renegotiating the nation's relationship with neighboring powers, including both independent nations (China and Japan) and colonial entities—the likes of British Burma, British Malaya, and French Indochina.[8]

The biggest difference between the Siamese nation-state of Kings Chulalongkorn and Vajiravudh in the late nineteenth and early twentieth centuries and that of the revolutionary People's Party following the Siamese Revolution of 1932 was the latter's success in completely abolishing extraterritoriality by finalizing the revision and revocation of the numerous "unfair" treaties the Siamese ruling elite had signed with various world powers, starting with the Bowring Treaty of 1855. This was fully accomplished in 1938, resulting in restoration of Siam's full judicial sovereignty and the abolishment of extraterritoriality, as Siam became for the first time a territorial nation. This was a crucial stepping stone that paved the way to changing the nation's name from the Kingdom of Siam to Thailand in 1939.

The transformation of Siam into Thailand was not simply a name change. In fact, it symbolized a transformation in the entire concept of what the nation was within the geographical boundaries of what was once Siam and then became Thailand in 1939. New Siam, known as Thailand, no longer revolved around the person of the monarch. Unlike the Vajiravudhian nation, Thailand would not be defined as identical to the person of the ruling Chakri monarch. Thailand was to be defined by her geographical boundaries and the people who resided there, contributing to the national economy from within those boundaries. For the ethnic Chinese in particular, the main focus of this study, this was the watershed moment when they could no longer be Chinese and a subject of a European colonial power and serve the Chakri court while contributing to the building of the Siamese nation at the same time. They were forced to choose one citizenship and relinquish political ties with all others.

It therefore should not surprise anyone that the People's Party government under the leadership of Field Marshal Phibunsongkhram would decide to side with Japan when the Greater East Asia War arrived on Thailand's shores in December 1941.[9] The People's Party government, which ushered in the era of "Thailand" to replace "Siam," were anti-imperialists keen on reestablishing a modern nation-state founded upon its geographical territories and citizenry, thus replacing the old royalist model, which defined the nation as one and the same as the monarch. In achieving this, it was clearly in their interests to enter into an alliance with Japan, the superpower opposed to European imperialists and keen on putting the ethnic Chinese— who were the most powerful financial supporters of the old royalist regime—in their place.

Thailand's entry into the Greater East Asia War as an ally of Japan was an attempt to solidify the recently established concept of the modern nation-state of Thailand, confirming the territorial integrity of the nation-state by depriving the ethnic Chinese elite of extraterritorial rights they once enjoyed under the absolute monarchy and reducing the political influence of the monarch by declaring war with the European imperialist powers that had compromised and supported the Chakri monarchy to maintain their position of absolute power since the late nineteenth century. However, once Japan was defeated, this revolutionary vision of a nation symbolized by its people was unceremoniously pushed aside and replaced by a slightly updated form of royalist nationalism, this time sponsored by the US Cold War hegemonic influence in Southeast Asia.

The history of the founding of the Thai nation from the mid-nineteenth century to the conclusion of the Cold War in Asia in the late 1970s is closely intertwined with the changing transnational understanding of what the Thai nation stood for and which parts of the population were to be included in the national project through over a century of nation-building.[10] The Kingdom of Siam of the late nineteenth and early twentieth centuries was identified with the person of the monarch and functioned within the same framework as the British colonial empire, recognizing native and colonial subjects as part of the national project so long as they expressed loyalty and devotion to the king. The post-1932 revolutionary nation that was renamed Thailand attempted to deconstruct the British colonial structure, disassociated the nation from the person of the monarch, and managed to abolish extraterritoriality, which in turn redefined the nation as a territorial polity that included only the population within its geographical boundaries as citizens. Finally, in the postwar and Cold War Kingdom of Thailand, which remained a territorial nation with citizens identified by birth and residence within the national boundaries, the monarch was reinstated as the personification of the nation. In addition, the state's relationship with its ethnic Chinese community came to be strongly influenced by Thai-American relations and US strategic policies in the Cold War in Asia.

How does a nation redefine itself three times within one hundred years while not only maintaining its place among legitimate and credible nations but also managing to survive the severest of political threats, including colonial aggression, two world wars, and nearly half a century of the Cold War? This book investigates the constant struggle to dominate the Thai national narrative that pitted conservative royalists against a dissenting political faction within the context of the greater struggle of world powers in the international arena of global politics. At the center of this multilayered struggle and across the period of study (mid-nineteenth to late twentieth century), a key contributor at almost every level is the transnational Chinese diaspora of Southeast Asia, especially the ethnic Chinese community in Thailand. The chapters are thus divided according to the different aspects of this narrative of struggle for the Thai national narrative and for the hearts and minds of the ethnic Chinese in Thailand.

Starting from the struggle to establish national sovereignty in the area of modern education, chapter 1 explores the contest over provision and control of Chinese education in Siam and the development of state control over education, as well as the transformation of education from a localized private enterprise to one of the most efficacious tools of state propaganda and nation-building. This process was carried out through much of the first half of the twentieth century and was an uphill struggle against the Qing and later the Chinese Nationalist government's overseas Chinese educational policies, which were intended to make loyal citizens of the Chinese nation out of members of the Chinese diaspora in Southeast Asia.

Chapter 2 investigates the propaganda contest between the royalist Siamese government of King Vajiravudh and ethnic Chinese journalists in the realm of print media, particularly in Thai- and Chinese-language newspapers and periodicals. News articles and editorials of the 1910s through the end of the 1920s clearly expressed each author's understanding of what the nation was and what nationalism entailed. The debate shifted from whether the Chinese in Siam should be patriotic to Siam or China during Vajiravudh's reign to whether the Thai state should be anti-imperialist and support Japan or side with the Allied Powers in supporting the Chinese war effort during the Greater East Asia War.

Chapter 3 looks at the evolution of Thai economic policies from the absolutist era of Chulalongkorn and Vajiravudh, when the state made great efforts to conform to the trade structure of the colonial powers—especially the British world order as imposed by the "unfair" treaties—to the revolutionary government of the People's Party, which accomplished the abolition of extraterritoriality and attempted to wrest economic dominance in the domestic arena away from the ethnic Chinese entrepreneurial class and return it to native Thai citizens. The alliance with the ethnic Chinese capitalists was a crucial source of power and stability for the absolute monarch; this chapter shows how the revolutionary government targeted this alliance to neutralize the ancien régime.

Chapter 4 explores the multifaceted nature of the position of the Thai nation in the Greater East Asia War and how the relationship of the ethnic Chinese and Thailand with China played a key role at the most crucial

turning points of the war—from Prime Minister Phibunsongkhram's decision to enter into a formal alliance with Japan in 1941 to the Allied Powers
allowing Thailand to be counted among the victors of the Second World
War. The conclusion of the war set the stage for the return of royalist nationalism and the dominance of right-wing politics throughout the Cold
War era.

Finally, chapter 5 brings the concept of the modern Thai nation back to
the royalist narrative of King Vajiravudh, but within the neocolonialist context of the Cold War. Through the investigation of major historical developments, including two Chinatown race riots and the Cold War Thai
government's oscillating foreign policies concerning the kingdom's relations
with the People's Republic of China vis-à-vis the United States, this study
demonstrates how the idea of royalist nationalism, which has been conjured
up since the prewar decades of the twentieth century, evolved to survive and
flourish within the Cold War context of the territorial nation.

CHAPTER ONE

EDUCATING CITIZENS

Building a Nation

THE NINETEENTH CENTURY WAS NOT THE FIRST ERA IN WHICH political leaders of East and Southeast Asia had come into contact with delegates from the West. Neither was the colonial era the first time Asian states benefited from scientific knowledge introduced by Western powers. In fact, there are ample examples of contact with the West and introduction to various technological advances that came with European visitors to the three Asian nations that are the main focus of our investigation of nation-building in pre–World War Asia—Siam, Japan, and China.

King Narai (r. 1656–88) of Ayutthaya, one of the most famous monarchs of Siam prior to the establishment of the Chakri dynasty in the late eighteenth century, was curious about European scientific knowledge, especially related to astronomy, navigation, and map and calendar making. He employed a large number of foreign advisers and had a sizable European mercenary force as an integral part of his standing army. Oda Nobunaga (1534–82), an important warlord who was responsible for unifying Japan's fragmented feudal society into one polity under a political overlord, took as his friends and allies the Portuguese traders and Jesuit missionaries. Nobunaga was fascinated by Portuguese firearms and armor technology and employed both to his advantage in establishing his hegemonic position over the Japanese archipelago in the late sixteenth century. The Ming dynasty of early modern China was among the earliest Asian monarchies to employ large numbers of European experts, especially Jesuit missionaries, for their expertise in Western scientific knowledge and technology. Imperial rulers of the Ming benefited from European techniques in mathematics, astronomy, and the atmospheric sciences to correctly predict certain natural occurrences, which allowed them to perform ritualistic functions at appropriate intervals. This was of paramount importance for maintaining the credibility of the emperor's status as Son of Heaven in an empire whose economy was largely based on the majority of the population laboring in the agricultural sector.

The main difference between the introduction of Western scientific knowledge in Siam, Japan, and China in the sixteenth to eighteenth centuries and the situation in the mid-nineteenth century involved the political implications of this knowledge and the position of power of the Western empires vis-à-vis the Asian kingdoms. While the Europeans serving in the courts of King Narai or Nobunaga brought the latest advances in scientific knowledge and modern technology, they were simply employees of the local government, dependent on the patronage of their respective Asian monarchs. Their function was primarily to provide tips on technological advancements in the world to support the monarch's legitimacy and dominance over potential challengers in the domestic political arena. Foreigners presented in Asian courts in the nineteenth century, on the contrary, represented the expanding hegemonic power of European colonial empires and posed an obvious threat to the independence and sovereignty of the Asian monarchs of Siam, Japan, and China alike.

In the nineteenth century, the rulers of Japan, China, and Siam faced threats of colonization and even annihilation by European imperialist powers. China's Manchu court was desperate to salvage the Qing dynasty's political prestige following the catastrophic defeats of the Opium Wars, which essentially ended the tribute system and forced the Chinese empire to allow free trade and the presence of European political advisers, trade officers, and religious proselytizers.[1] Japan's Tokugawa Shogunate faced its demise soon after being forced to submit to US Navy Commodore Matthew Perry's gunboat diplomacy in 1853.[2] In Siam, King Mongkut Rama IV (r. 1851–68), credited as the father of modern Thai scientific investigation, perceived the grave and immediate colonial threat that lurked behind Sir John Bowring's request for a formalized trade agreement with Siam in 1855. Having witnessed the devastation of Qing imperial power after a humiliating defeat in the First Opium War, it was obvious to the Siamese ruling class that the only way to survive was to adjust to the new world order— which was that of the British Empire by the late nineteenth century—and try to catch up with what the West perceived as modern and civilized.

The application and proliferation of Western scientific knowledge in Siam—as in many other parts of East and Southeast Asia throughout the colonial era—were part of the ruling classes' ability to adjust and adapt to epoque-making transformations in regional and global power structures. Their strategies vis-à-vis Western learning and the global political evolution from the colonialism of the nineteenth century to the era of the nation-state in the twentieth century are reflected in the evolution of the state's educational policies from the mid-nineteenth century to the conclusion of the Greater East Asia War. The process of modernizing state education in Siam was therefore of critical importance to nation-building.

NATIONALIZING EDUCATION: TO ENLIGHTEN OR CONTROL?

Education is fundamental to the grand process of nation-building. The work of the twentieth-century British-Czech social philosopher and social anthropologist Ernest Gellner is useful here, though he never mentioned Thailand in his works, as he proposes that the nation-state came into being only through the establishment of a state-controlled modern educational system, following successful scientific and industrial revolutions.[3]

Gellner's analysis recognizes gradual stages of development from the period of the so-called scientific revolution of sixteenth- and seventeenth-century Europe to the industrial revolution that started in England in the eighteenth century, resulting in the flourishing of the nation-state and nationalism along with state-controlled systems of mass education. Gellner's sequential presentation is an interesting depiction of how—in the European context—scientific knowledge brought about an outburst of productivity and prosperity, which in turn established certain classes of people in positions of power. As the ruling classes acquired more political influence and secured increasing control over the masses, they seemingly provided a degree of scientific knowledge to the masses through systems of public education. However, Gellner believes that in most cases mass education serves as an ideological state apparatus to enhance state control over the population instead of being a sincere attempt to enlighten the masses.

The scientific revolution made way for new discoveries and inventions that would come to significantly improve the quality of life in human society with the arrival of the age of the enlightenment and later the beginning of the Industrial Revolution toward the end of the eighteenth century. Scientific knowledge led the way, encouraging scientists to invent, merchants to trade, entrepreneurs to invest, and finally, the ruling classes of the capitalist society to emerge by the dawn of the nineteenth century. To secure their position of power and economic dominance, the ruling classes then attempted to seize control of the unsystematic access to knowledge, which was once their gateway to dominance. Thus systems of state-controlled public education and laws related to compulsory education came into being as fundamental apparatuses employed by the ruling classes to maintain their superior position within the traditional class society. Gellner presents education as the most effective means of homogenizing a population and producing a perfectly blended culture and history for the nation-state. The state achieves this by employing standardized, state-authorized curricula in compulsory education to transform citizens into children of the state. Gellner alludes to Mamluk warriors—orphans raised and trained by the state to become military slaves—who became a dominant force in the Islamic world between the thirteenth and sixteenth centuries. He compares school children to Mamluks in their state-controlled, compulsory, en masse education. The amazing effectiveness of building national subjects through compulsory education could thus replace all other forms of traditional education—apprenticeships, guilds, and the passing on of skills within family trades from generation to generation. According to Gellner, compulsory education allows the state to pose as the source of all basic knowledge and training, firmly returning to the state the devotion and loyalty that was dispersed in other forms of traditional schooling. Mass education was indeed destined to play a crucial role in founding nation-states and fostering nationalist movements.

In mid-nineteenth-century Siam, King Mongkut supported the study of European science and culture (including foreign languages) with an acute awareness that Western scientific knowledge was no longer simply a curiosity that could be used to impress his own people and to reinforce his superior position vis-à-vis potential domestic challengers. Mongkut perceived scientific education as a device for safeguarding his kingdom's independence and sovereignty from rapidly encroaching imperialist threats from the West. This fundamental change in the strategic position of science and foreign languages distinguished the nineteenth-century monarch's fascination with Western knowledge from that of King Narai some two centuries earlier. By the reign of the fourth Chakri king, the long-standing political and economic dominance of China-centered commerce in Asian maritime trade was rapidly becoming a memory. King Mongkut faced a new hegemony from the West, expressed by the arrival, in force, of the aggressive power of the British Empire. His earliest educational reforms included Western scientific thought, suggesting that Siam's ruling class was beginning to acknowledge new global standards of knowledge.

King Chulalongkorn Rama V (r. 1868–1910) followed closely in the footsteps of his Western-oriented father, building on foundations of European knowledge and Western scientific modes of learning to modernize his kingdom. Finally, in a third generation of royalist nation-building, Vajiravudh Rama VI enhanced and expanded scientific learning, establishing a system of compulsory education intended to serve as the foundation for his nationalist policies in 1921.[4] In less than seventy years, three Siamese monarchs thus led the kingdom—with varying degrees of success and failure—through a simulacrum of the entire Gellnerian nation-building process, from the scientific revolution to the establishment of a state-controlled system of public education.[5]

The only problem with mapping Gellner's framework onto the history of modern education in Siam is the fact that, despite the institution of compulsory education in 1921, modern education at the primary level was not extended to the Thai masses until well after the Siamese Revolution of 1932. Much of what became the modern Siamese nation-state was modeled on the structures and policies of the colonial administrations of neighboring states in Southeast Asia. In the same way that modernized Bangkok was supposed to be only as modern as British-built Singapore or Dutch-built Batavia, modern education in Siam, which started for part of the public in the late nineteenth century, was largely intended for training officials to work in the newly modernized state bureaucracy, in the same manner that colonial powers established modern educational facilities in their colonies initially for the purpose of training colonial officers. When Vajiravudh started injecting nationalist propaganda into the national curriculum in the early twentieth century, it was not intended to indoctrinate illiterate peasants in the farthest reaches of his kingdom. What was the point of nationalizing public education if it was not intended to reach the masses?

This is where the critical role of ethnic Chinese and extraterritoriality come into play in the founding of the Thai nation. Throughout the era of the absolute monarchy, public education was intended only to train state officials in the same manner as colonial officers were trained in neighboring states. When public education was first offered during Chulalongkorn's reign, in the last decades of the nineteenth century, it was limited to a small section of the population. That is, the state did not need to provide education for all intended employees of its modernized bureaucracy. The top echelons of the ruling class—members of the royal family and nobility—were already sending their own children to private schools or even abroad to be educated in leading institutions in the West. Sons of rich entrepreneurs who worked closely with the court—most of whom were of Chinese descent—were also privately educated, either in Chinese schools, Western missionary schools, or even abroad for those of the richest and most influential business families. It also did not matter that people in the countryside continued to be educated in Buddhist monasteries, since most of them would never be involved in state administration. Consequently, through much of the nascent period of Siamese public education, the state was responsible for providing education to only a small number of mostly urban, middle-class commoners who were needed because the modern state bureaucracy had outgrown the supply of recruits from the feudal elite.

The limited modernization of public education began to face problems around the turn of the twentieth century, largely because of political developments in China. With the political turmoil in late-Qing China came the rise of modern Chinese nationalism. Renegade Chinese political leaders from both the reform and revolutionary factions started touring major overseas Chinese communities across the globe, starting with their closest strongholds in the southern seas. In their quest for support for their diverse political ideologies, most started calling for national unity among the Chinese diaspora. This in turn spurred nationalization of Chinese schools across Southeast Asia, where Siam housed one of the region's largest ethnic Chinese communities. Suddenly the Siamese ruling class could no longer trust Chinese schools to train state bureaucrats, as the schools had increasingly come to represent the interests of the Chinese state and propagated strands of Chinese nationalist propaganda—including antimonarchism, republicanism, socialism, and other strains that could be considered a threat to political stability and the well-being of the Siamese absolutist regime.

Seditious education from Chinese schools was only the beginning of the serious problems in Vajiravudh's grand plan of nation-building. While Chinese schools were becoming increasingly politicized, a new generation of the educated urban middle class—consisting of returned overseas students and those who had benefited from Chulalongkorn's limited yet effective first wave of modern public education—was on the rise and actively questioning and criticizing the absolutist regime through the already much more open system of publication and private education. The real motive for Vajiravudh's nationalizing of public education was to provide an alternative to antimonarchist and other seditious ideologies that were promoted through private education, thus maintaining a reliable system for training state bureaucrats without the government having to be the sole investor in modern education.

Vajiravudh's government continued to provide public education to support the preparation and training of commoners to serve in the ever expanding state bureaucracy of the modern nation-state. At the same time, the government encouraged the proliferation of private schools to provide education for the merchant class and bourgeoisie, who could afford to pay school fees and did not want to overcrowd the state educational system, which at the end of the 1910s remained limited to major port cities and still overcrowded and undersupplied. Yet the royal government needed to make sure it had the private schools under control—that the private schools were producing loyal citizens of good character and not being used as a breeding ground for rebels and revolutionaries or fifth-column nationalists supporting foreign governments. The Private School Act was promulgated in 1919, followed in 1921 by the Compulsory Education Act, ensuring that the central state had some degree of control over all forms of primary education across the kingdom. In other words, compulsory education was not so much about the state attempting to educate the masses as maintaining control over primary education, including keeping in check seditious monks who might spread antimonarchist materials in temple schools.

The Gellnerian framework must be adjusted to make sense of the limited nationalization of the educational system in Siam through the reigns of Mongkut, Chulalongkorn, and Vajiravudh. In Siam, building the nation through the nationalization of the modern education system was done not for the sake of enlightening the masses but to control the hearts and minds of the rising middle class, who were becoming increasingly important in the expanding state bureaucracy and many of whom were scions of the influential ethnic Chinese business community. Ironically, Gellner's original Mamluk analogy is probably more relevant to the Siamese case than to any of the modern European cases he cites in *Nations and Nationalism*. This is also why, when investigating the evolution of nationalized education in early twentieth-century Thailand, it is necessary to start at the first inklings of nationalist sentiment in late Qing and early Republican China.

CHINA AND OVERSEAS CHINESE EDUCATION IN THE LATE QING–EARLY REPUBLICAN ERA

The Qing court had no clear policy toward overseas Chinese before the turn of the twentieth century. The first concern for Chinese education in Southeast Asia came from the reformer Kang Youwei.[6] While in exile from China, Kang made several visits to overseas Chinese communities to rally support for his Association for the Protection of the Emperor (Baohuanghui). The association's primary objective was to regain political control of China and to reestablish the Guangxu emperor as the constitutional monarch, so as to continue the process of reform that had been broken off as a result of the Palace Coup of 1898.[7] Kang's idea for the improvement of Chinese education in the overseas settlements of Southeast Asia was highly nationalistic and, ironically, almost colonialist in character. In 1900 he embarked on a political tour in the southern seas, propagating the Three Protections slogan: "Protect the nation, protect the race, protect education" (Baoguo, baozhong, baojiao).[8] The basic idea behind this slogan was the belief that to protect the Chinese nation—which Kang envisioned as a constitutional monarchy with the Guangxu emperor as the political figurehead—Chinese people throughout the world needed to be "protected" so that they would remain true to the ethnicity and civilization of their ancestors. In turn, holding fast to their Chinese identity, they would contribute to the Chinese nation. The best way to accomplish this, according to Kang, would be through an educational system that enabled Chinese descendants to remain authentically Chinese, even though their families might have immigrated to Southeast Asia many generations before.

In his 1900 visit to Southeast Asia, Kang expressed shock and dismay that many ethnic Chinese people appeared to have abandoned the lifestyle of their ancestors, assimilating so completely into the local society that it was often difficult to differentiate the Huaqiao (ethnic Chinese) from the natives. Many among the younger generation no longer even spoke Chinese. Apropos of Kang's advocacy of constitutional monarchy, he applauded one mark of "Chineseness" that had survived in large commercial centers of Southeast Asia: the queue and the shaven forehead, traditional signs of submission and loyalty to the Qing dynasty. Kang urged ethnic Chinese communities to establish and improve their local Chinese educational system so that later generations would appreciate their national identity and be better able to contribute to the modern Chinese nation. To achieve this, Kang suggested that Chinese schooling in Southeast Asia offer not only subjects directly related to China but also studies popular in the West, such as geometry, biology, and physics. Perhaps the most intriguing among his proposals on education was his insistence that there be bilingual—Chinese/English—education for ethnic Chinese students in Southeast Asia.[9]

One very significant development was his call for recognition of a standardized Chinese language based on the northern Chinese Mandarin dialect, the official language of the Qing court. Standard Chinese was to be preferred over the various southern dialects—Cantonese, Hokkien, Teo-chiu, Hakka, and Hainanese—which had long been diversely employed as languages of instruction in traditional Chinese education in overseas communities of Southeast Asia. The new view effectively transformed the fundamental purpose of Chinese language learning across a significant geographical and economic area. Giving precedence to standard Chinese undercut the prestige of the dialects that had long divided and thereby supposedly weakened every overseas Chinese community throughout Southeast Asia. No longer was the primary purpose to acquire important basic language skills for conducting trade among business associates of the same dialect group. The study of a common language was urged, rather, as an affirmation of the bond existing among compatriots across boundaries, lineages, and hometowns. Through Kang's initiatives, Chinese education would, for the first time, serve overseas as an instrument of Chinese nation-building.

It appears that as a reformer and a leading modernizer, Kang Youwei, not unlike Siam's Mongkut and Chulalongkorn, realized that the dominant power in world trade and politics had shifted from China to England in the late nineteenth century. Mongkut had found it necessary to have his children learn English from an early age; Chulalongkorn thought it appropriate to have his sons educated in the powerful empires of Europe; Vajiravudh stressed the importance of English teaching in Thai schools. Kang also insisted on the need to educate ethnic Chinese in both the language of their ancestors and that of England, the new Western superpower of the twentieth-century world. The fact that Chinese schools in Southeast Asia did provide an effective bilingual Chinese/English education by 1900 later caused friction between the Thai and Chinese states. Siam, though smilingly deferential, clung stubbornly to her independence, a colony of neither China nor England. Kang's proposal for nationalist Chinese education in Southeast Asia provoked further reforms in the educational policies of King Vajiravudh. The king used Thai education as a driving force behind his own nation-building project. Standard Chinese was becoming the unifying language of both the Chinese business community and the rising Chinese nation. As this became clear, Chinese education was perceived as a threat to the Siamese ruling class. Not only was Chinese nationalism likely to embolden Siam's Chinese minority, but it might also encourage native Thais to resist the authority of their own government.

Shortly after Kang's 1900 visit to Southeast Asia, other Chinese political groups started to take a serious interest in Chinese education in Southeast

Asia. Having awakened to the urgent need for modernization, the post-Boxer Manchu court embarked on a last-minute effort toward modernization, adopting much of Kang Youwei's reform plan, which they had forcefully terminated only a few years earlier. One aspect of this attempt to modernize was a plan to recruit financial and technological support from overseas Chinese communities throughout Southeast Asia. Realizing that the ousted Kang Youwei had already made his mark in educational reform there, the Qing court was eager to get involved. They hoped to establish and improve Chinese schools in Southeast Asia according to their own ideas of what the modern Chinese nation and its citizens should be. Meanwhile, as Manchu agents were being sent to liaise with Chinese communities in Southeast Asia, the Revolutionary Alliance (Tongmenghui) under the presumed leadership of Sun Yat-sen was also becoming active there and competing for influence. By the end of the first decade of the twentieth century, there were ten Chinese schools in British Malaya and sixty-five in the Dutch East Indies.[10] One study of overseas Chinese political activities in Thailand suggests that between 1903 and 1908, Sun visited Siam at least four times. Partly as a result of his political activities there and shortly after his last visit in 1908, at least four Chinese schools, one library, and one oratory association were established.[11] Documents from both the Chinese Nationalist Party's (Kuomintang, KMT) Ministry of Foreign Affairs and the Ministry of Interior of the Royal Thai Government strongly suggest that the Revolutionary Alliance—and later, the Nationalist Party—disseminated revolutionary propaganda through these newly established schools and recruited support from both the students and parents' associations.

By 1912, Sun Yat-sen's revolutionary faction had been transformed by the success of the Xinhai Revolution and the establishment of the Republic of China. His was now the core group in the Chinese Nationalist Party. Despite being the last to arrive in the race for influence in Southeast Asia, Sun's Nationalists became the main political influence in forming the modern Chinese educational system in Nanyang. In the grand scheme of Nationalist administrative policies throughout the Republican era (1912–49), overseas Chinese education fit within the set of general guidelines concerning the administration of overseas Chinese communities. These guidelines included four major components: migration (*yi*), settlement (*zhi*), protection (*bao*), and education (*yü*).[12] The basic idea behind this quartet of policies was not drastically different from Kang Youwei's Three Protections program of the 1900s. Basically, the Nationalist government vowed to support the migration of Chinese citizens who wished to settle abroad in overseas Chinese communities. These settlers would enjoy the protection of the government of the Republic of China. Finally, the government would control and provide support for state-sanctioned Chinese schools in all such overseas communities throughout Southeast Asia. The aim of this policy road map was, of course, to help preserve the national identity and culture of future generations of ethnic Chinese people residing abroad, with the expectation that awareness of their Chineseness would shape them into loyal overseas citizens who could be counted upon to support the Republic of China.

Under present-day conventions of nation and citizenship, the overseas Chinese educational policies of both Kang Youwei and the early Chinese Republic appear misplaced and intrusive, to say the least, and in violation of the independence and sovereignty of the host nations. How could any government actively support the migration of its own people to a foreign country to live, generation after generation, and then expect their primary loyalty to remain with the old country, which they left so long ago? In retrospect, it is not difficult to understand how this could lead to serious tensions between the Chinese state and the governments of host countries. Siam in the early twentieth century, preserving its fragile independence at almost all costs, was trying to establish itself as a modern nation-state with modern citizens of its own. The educational policies established in overseas Chinese schools bear an uncanny resemblance to those of the schools of many European colonial masters of Southeast Asia. The colonial oligarchies had their own privileged educational systems, separate from native schools, for European children born or living in the colonies. The fundamental idea behind such policies was clearly to discourage integration or assimilation. These colonial arrangements typically led to discord between residents of different ethnic backgrounds. In this case, however, the particular nature of the Chinese population, culture, and nationalism in the early twentieth century has some bearing.

At the dawn of the twentieth century, the Chinese ruling class was just beginning to reluctantly make some adjustment in the time-honored, ethnocentric sense of its own identity. Until the devastating defeats of the mid-nineteenth-century Opium Wars, the most popular notion of Han Chinese society and culture was that China represented "all under heaven" (Tianxia) that was civilized. The Han had long congratulated themselves on their contrast to the nomadic herders of the north and the hill tribes and island dwellers of the south. A deeply ingrained sense of superiority was reinforced by mainstream Confucian values and by traditions of ancestral worship that forbade and condemned abandonment of the ancestral homeland. As a result, Chinese seafarers, maritime merchants, and itinerant laborers clung to China as their homeland. Their journeys overseas were often considered and expressed as temporary, not a permanent migration. This is why, at least up to the end of the Second World War, the most popularly employed term for the overseas Chinese was Huaqiao (literally, "Chinese [Hua] who sojourn"), that is, those who were residing abroad but would one day return to their homeland. Assimilation of ethnic Chinese communities overseas into their adopted societies had historically been discouraged among the Chinese.

Circumstances became more complicated when well-known advocates of reform, revolution, and nationalism in China such as Kang Youwei and Sun Yat-sen began their campaigns in Southeast Asia. They sought support abroad because any challenge at home to the power and legitimacy of Qing rule would have met with violent repression. At the same time, ethnic Chinese communities had come to dominate much of the Southeast Asian regional economy. Even within the framework of European colonial power, these industrious and flourishing communities became a highly dependable source of financial and technological support for building a modern Chinese nation-state. Their success was reflected in the slogans that dominated the modern Chinese political scene, such as "Overseas Chinese are the mothers of the revolution" (Huaqiao wei geming zhi mu).[13] Consequently, it is nearly impossible to make sense of Chinese nationalism in the early twentieth century without including the contributions of ethnic Chinese communities overseas, especially in Southeast Asia. These settlements came to represent a sort of "diaspora nationalism,"[14] a major driving force behind the establishment of China as a modern nation-state.

Early Chinese Republican policies concerning overseas Chinese education in Siam (as well as most other areas in Southeast Asia) were not a direct attempt at cultural colonization. Kang Youwei and Sun Yat-sen had no intention of imposing Chinese culture and education upon the non-Chinese natives of those countries. Nor was there any suggestion that these policies were aimed at territorial gain. A fundamental conflict between the Chinese state and the sovereign state of Siam arose from their clashing perception of citizenship. The young Republic of China had a large overseas population and a nationalist movement that, in some respects, arose from overseas bases. That nascent republic chose to recognize Chinese citizenship according to the *jus sanguinis* (right of blood) principle. Early twentieth-century Siam, by contrast, had no significant overseas population. Siam did have a large foreign ethnic population within its geographical boundaries, and its earliest citizenship laws cited the *jus soli* (right of the soil) principle. Hence, by the reign of King Vajiravudh, a significant number within the total Siamese population as well as a large number within the Siamese state bureaucracy were eligible for both Siamese and Chinese citizenship: Siam-born persons of Chinese ancestry.

THAI OVERSEAS CHINESE EDUCATIONAL POLICIES
UNDER THE ABSOLUTE MONARCHY

By the time Vajiravudh ascended the throne in October 1910, the Siamese court had entered yet another crisis concerning the legitimacy of the Chakri dynasty's absolute power within its realm. Of course, such crises were neither novel nor unique to the Siamese royal family. Both King Chulalongkorn and King Mongkut had experienced similar challenges. Both the Qing dynasty—in its defeat in the Opium Wars—and the Tokugawa Shogunate, in submitting to Perry's gunboat diplomacy, faced a crisis of confidence. During a period of intense European and American imperialism, the retainers and subjects of the Qing and the shogunate asked why they should accept the authority of those who could no longer safeguard the country from foreign imperialism. Mongkut and Chulalongkorn survived by presenting themselves as enlightened, civilized monarchs who acknowledged contemporary European models while investing in the changes necessary to keep Siam competitive in the regional and global economy of the colonial era. Their strategies sufficed, and their legitimacy was reaffirmed. The native Thai majority could get on with their lives, despite the disruption of modernization projects. Those shocks were preferable to the distress of being completely colonized by either France or Britain. The Chinese minority operating in and controlling much of Siam's economy could continue doing business with less state interference than ever, free to register as colonial subjects in partially independent Siam. In fact, the colonial powers now realized that conducting business on their own terms with this sovereign state was far more cost effective than taking over the kingdom by force. Under Vajiravudh, however, the question of legitimacy was restated in new terms. The challenging question during that first decade of the twentieth century concerned the need for an absolute monarchy in Siam. The old colonial perils no longer threatened, and local Chinese businesses were thriving because they enjoyed extraterritorial rights. To what end, then, was the rest of the Siamese population remaining subject to the Crown?

To make matters worse, Vajiravudh, who had been educated abroad from an early age, was not only unpopular among the high-ranking members of the royal family who had been highly influential in his father's court, but also had trouble gaining respect and cooperation from his brothers and half-brothers, many of whom were highly influential in the armed forces.[15] Feeling like an unaccepted outsider among his relatives and the highest echelons of court politics from his father's reign, Vajiravudh initially tried to rely more on trusted friends and appointed many ministers and courtiers from outside his extended family circle. This was possible thanks to Chulalongkorn's earlier expansion of the royal state bureaucracy to include a wider range of state officials, most of whom were not necessarily members of the royal family or even from long-established noble families. Vajiravudh's move to depend more upon the expanded modern state bureaucracy, however, also meant that he would need to rely more on the public educational system that his father had put in place to provide trained manpower that the existing nobility were unable to supply.

This leads to another problem related to the increasing trend toward sedition in private education in Siam due to the rise in political/nationalist consciousness of the ethnic Chinese and the politicization of Chinese schools. Early in the sixth reign, the loyalty of commoners in the state bureaucracy was called into question due to the increasingly seditious influence of private educational institutions—especially Chinese schools—as well as the proliferation of highly critical newspapers and periodicals (discussed in the next chapter). Less than two years into Vajiravudh's reign, there was a foiled coup attempt that included a plot for regicide. The plotters—most of whom were commoners educated through the modern public system and serving in the armed forces and more than a few of whom were of Chinese descent—had been influenced by the success of the revolution that had resulted in the collapse of the Qing dynasty and the establishment of the Republic of China earlier that year. It appeared that the only way out of this crisis of authority and leadership was to systematically discredit the Chinese Nationalist movement and exert greater control over the proliferating system of private education—especially that of the ethnic Chinese community. Vajiravudh applied himself to accomplishing these goals. He employed both rhetoric—through highly publicized propaganda pieces—and legislation, the most significant of which were the Private School Act of 1919 and the Compulsory Education Act of 1921.

Early in his reign, Vajiravudh had invoked the image of the Chinese secret societies, notorious for racketeering, smuggling, fraud, and other criminal activities through much of the previous reign. The king stated time and again that being Chinese indicated an inevitable and ruinous connection with the evil influence of secret societies: "Among the Chinese, there is a strange tradition. That is, they tend to be divided into groups and factions according to whichever secret society they happened to subscribe to. Moreover, each group or each faction will try its best to unscrupulously condemn its rival. Even if they must lie blatantly to discredit their opponent, they have no hesitation about doing so."[16]

Known as the Ang-yi, Chinese secret society gangsters raised havoc and caused so many disturbances that a law bearing their name and aimed especially at countering their illegal activities was promulgated in 1897.[17] Nonetheless, it became more difficult for the Thai state to pit the different groups within the Chinese community against each other when Kang Youwei made his nationalist educational proposal, and the idea of a national education in Mandarin Chinese for ethnic Chinese of all dialect groups started to gain support among the overseas Chinese of Southeast Asia.

Through the ideological rhetoric of Sun Yat-sen and other leading Chinese political figures, a vision of the modern Chinese nation began to take hold. Lines of division blurred and conflicts softened among the different groups of overseas Chinese. A more united people now tended to resist pressures from their host country or the domineering force of European imperialists in the colonies. Vajiravudh was aware of the development of these tendencies in Chinese schools in Siam. Nor was the secret society trope completely obsolete, despite the great changes in overseas Chinese education. The king chose to regard the likes of Sun Yat-sen as opportunistic criminals and the entire spectrum of Chinese nationalist movements as modernized versions of secret society gangs. This policy is most clearly reflected in Vajiravudh's response to the declaration of the Association [in Siam] of Chinese Students in support of China's May Fourth Movement, which was spearheaded in 1919 by students and intellectuals at Peking University against unjust treatment of China in the resolutions of the First World War: "This is the nature of the Chinese which cannot be easily cured. No matter what kind of association is established, it will always become a secret society, mostly specializing in extorting money. The Association of Chinese Students is no exception. Despite the elegant words of their manifesto, in the end they are no more than the instrument of a certain person or a certain group, intent on embezzling money from their compatriots."[18]

By thus branding the Chinese school students' support for the May Fourth Movement, Vajiravudh discredited all past, present, and future political movements by the ethnic Chinese in his realm as money-making scams of secret societies. Such statements were aimed, no doubt, at discouraging upper- and middle-class Chinese entrepreneurs—many among them the most important allies of the Chakri dynasty—from getting involved in these movements, which were potentially a threat to the stability and security of Siam's absolute monarchy. The critical tone of Vajiravudh's statement also repudiated any similar political movements in sections of Thai society that might have been influenced by what the king deemed seditious.

Vajiravudh's secret society characterization soon became popular among officials in his government whose work brought them in contact with the ethnic Chinese community and its educational system. Phraya Ratsadanupradit (Kaw Simbee Na Ranong), governor of Phuket and a celebrity in the overseas Chinese community in southern Siam, supported the king's campaign. He questioned the spread of Sun Yat-sen's "Three Principles of the People" (Sanminzhuyi) in many Chinese schools in Siam, saying that the Nationalist Party was behind it all. He also pointed with alarm to the fact that most of the parents, who had sent their children to these schools to learn Chinese for business purposes, were not aware that students were also being introduced to propaganda. Real problems were bound to arise. Instilled with republican ideals and values, the younger generation was on a collision course with core elements of Thai society: culture, tradition, and government.[19] Phraya Ratsadanupradit described how he had been trying to deal with the younger generation of Chinese in his locality:

> The Chinese in the province of Phuket continue to behave in their usual compliant manner. However, most of them have cut off their queues. At present, only miners, rickshaw pullers, and farmers still keep their queues. I have assembled them to explain that the word "kekmeng" should not be used anymore, since the revolution [in China] has already been successfully carried out. Whoever claims to be a "kekmeng," from now on will be considered a secret society member and will be arrested and punished by the government. I also forbade those who had already cut their queues not to make fun of those who had not yet done so. They must not coerce anyone into cutting their queue, either. Anybody who disobeys these instructions will be arrested and punished.[20]

Phraya Ratsadanupradit's statement presents an interesting categorization of the ethnic Chinese and the *kekmeng* (geming) revolutionary mentality.[21] That is, it was acceptable to be of Chinese descent so long as one was "compliant" with state authorities. Ethnic Chinese persons also had the freedom to keep or cut their queues, so long as they did not impose their choice on others. Notably, revolution was also acceptable as the reality of an important political development in China, but it had absolutely no place in polite Siamese society. Revolution had succeeded in China, but whoever continued to talk about such things would be considered secret society members and prosecuted accordingly. Vajiravudh promoted this view through his "anti-Chinese" writings. The idea was not to offend upper-class Chinese who were already supporters of the Siamese monarchy—such as Phraya Ratsadanupradit—but to persuade other ethnic Chinese communities to be "compliant" by distancing themselves from troublemakers.

Following Kaw's observations, a flurry of police reports throughout Vajiravudh's reign and at the beginning of Prajadhipok's concerned Chinese schools suspected of association with revolutionaries. The following excerpt is a typical example:

> Mr. Tam Chinsam attempted to establish an association for the overseas Chinese, but because the authorities did not allow him to do so, he cunningly applied for authorization to establish a night vocational school in the district of Phlapphlachai Road, Bangkok. However, this is not a real school intended for educating students in positive directions. This school is actually a secret society. He only used the name of the school to trick law-abiding overseas Chinese into thinking that his association had been sanctioned by the government. He frequently recruited members to his secret society [through this channel].[22]

It is interesting to note that, not unlike Phraya Ratsadanupradit's earlier warnings that law-abiding ethnic Chinese parents were being tricked into sending their children to antimonarchist Chinese schools, this report suggested that some ethnic Chinese were unknowingly joining Tam Chinsam's secret society, mistaking it for a legitimate Chinese vocational school. Other official reports suggested that Chinese schools, both in the capital and upcountry, were being used as headquarters for seditious organizations. From time to time, the arrest of ethnic Chinese "revolutionaries" led to the discovery of a secret cache of seditious literature in one Chinese school or another.[23] In rare cases, authorities caught a Chinese schoolteacher redhanded: seditious documents would be discovered in the school, in the teacher's office, and on the person of students fleeing the scene. In such cases, however, the police would later find that the individuals arrested did not have the documents required for serving as state-approved Chinese schoolteachers and that they were actually either agents of the kekmeng[24] or communists posing as schoolteachers. Consequently, the authorities would conclude that the ethnic Chinese students had been misled into attending classes taught by fake teachers and therefore should not be held accountable for their possession of seditious educational materials.[25]

Although King Vajiravudh may have appeared dismissive of the rising nationalist fervor within the overseas Chinese educational system, and some leading figures among his ministers tended to treat Siam-based Chinese revolutionary figures as small-time crooks, one should not underestimate the severity of the threat this issue posed to the security of the fledgling Siamese nation-state and the king's royalist nationalist movement. Not all members of the Siamese ruling class in the pre-1932 era agreed that simply discrediting antimonarchist Chinese schools and branding them secret societies would be sufficient to curb the revolutionary tide that was threatening the monarchy. Some prominent figures in the courts of both Vajiravudh and Prajadhipok pointed out how dangerous seditious Chinese education could be if antimonarchist ideology spread to the general public, especially the lower social classes. According to Phraya Thammasakmontri, the minister of education, Chinese schools should be made to teach Thai language, culture, and values, and teachers in Chinese schools, before being allowed to teach in Siam, should be approved by the Ministry of Education. The Thai government should, with utmost urgency, seek to ensure the loyalty of all Chinese schoolteachers. They should be citizens of the Thai state, not of the Republic of China. "In resolving [this problem] and preventing the danger that may arise from these schools, I think it is best to deal with the matter in the most immediate fashion. The longer time passes, the more numerous these schools will become. Their legacy will also become more deeply rooted. [The government] must be strict in eradicating the problem at its source. I do not agree with allowing the Chinese to change gradually according to their own willingness."[26]

In practice, however, Phraya Thammasakmontri's suggestion could not be easily put into practice. Such draconian measures could easily shut down Chinese education in Siam and be the cause of much protest among the ethnic Chinese—both the upper-class Chinese who supported the monarchy and the lower classes, who might already have been tempted by revolutionary ideas. Furthermore, the Siamese government at the time seriously lacked bilingual personnel who could be relied upon to monitor the activities of

Chinese schools. To resolve this ongoing problem in a more sustainable fashion, Prince Damrongrachanuphap, minister of the interior, suggested that the Siamese government establish its own, state-sponsored Chinese schools: "Why should we not consider Chinese as a language worth learning? I think that Thai people could benefit much from learning the Chinese language because it is used very widely. Moreover, according to Chaophraya Yomarat, it is, at present, very difficult to find a Chinese person who will do investigative work for the police. If more Thai people knew Chinese, this problem could be resolved. Also by allowing the establishment of Chinese schools, the government is doing the overseas Chinese a great favor."[27]

By establishing public Chinese schools, authorities could gain absolute control over the selection of teachers and textbooks, curriculum design, and all other aspects of Chinese education in Siam. Native Thai students would also be allowed to enroll and learn the language, enabling them to support authorities in their future dealings with the Chinese community. Better still, if there were state-run Chinese schools, the government could order the closure of the private Chinese ones found to engage in seditious activities without having to deprive the ethnic Chinese community completely of institutions of Chinese education. As enlightened as Prince Damrong's suggestion may seem, the royal court saw the proposal as outlandish. State-run Chinese language schools would require many more bilingual staff besides those already employed in policing and censoring Chinese teachers and educational materials. Courtiers of a high rank would have to receive a thorough education in China to prepare for their task, like those who were trained in Europe to manage the nation's new railways, telegraphs, modern medicine, the legal system, and so on. Siam's ruling class had for some time been resolutely distancing themselves from Chinese influence and things Chinese, determined to establish the kingdom as a modern state according to Western—especially British—standards. Indeed, this swing toward the West had been promoted since the reign of King Mongkut more than half a century earlier. Furthermore, encouraging non-Chinese citizens to learn Chinese might suggest to the unlettered masses that Siam was leaning toward China, a state that represented, among other royalist horrors, a republican revolution. Not surprisingly, Prince Damrong, one of Vajiravudh's most detested senior relatives, found his suggestion quickly dismissed.[28]

King Prajadhipok Rama VII, during his short reign prior to the People's Party Revolution of 1932, continued Vajiravudh's legacy of maintaining cordial relationships with upper-class Chinese entrepreneurs, while discouraging the lower classes from subscribing to antimonarchist Chinese teaching. References to the secret society threat continued to have an effect. As the tides of revolution became stronger in the 1920s, Prajadhipok made further attempts to influence Chinese communities and the Chinese educational system in Siam. Supported by the major dialect associations in Bangkok's Chinatown, he made well-publicized visits to the four most prominent Chinese schools to express his support for these loyal Chinese establishments. The prestigious royal visit was calculated to enhance the influence of these schools in Siam's Chinese educational system.

In a personal letter to his minister of education, Prince Thaniniwat, Prajadhipok expressed concerns about the increasing number of Chinese immigrants arriving in Siam. Ongoing political unrest in China meant that more Chinese women were coming as well. The king, fretting over declining Chinese assimilation into Thai society, imagined that Chinese men were now better able to find themselves a Chinese bride.[29] His concerns about the deteriorating Sino-Thai integration process due to the recent influx of female migrants reflects the increasing difficulty in curbing the rise of Chinese nationalist fervor. Negative propaganda seemed to have less impact, and Chinese interest in Thai public education showed no sign of increasing, though the campaign had been urged along for the past three reigns. As more Chinese migrants married within their old culture, the next generation of ethnic Chinese was less likely to use the Thai language, to practice Thai culture, or to adopt Thai traditions. The unassimilated would be more likely to attend Chinese schools, thereby missing out, to some extent, on the nationalist propaganda being channeled through Thai-language schools and newspapers.

Even so, there was little change in official policy toward Chinese education in Siam under Vajiravudh and Prajadhipok. There are a few plausible explanations for this quiescence despite all the heated rhetoric. First, the most concrete measures—the laws passed during Vajiravudh's reign, most importantly the Private School Act of 1919 and the Compulsory Education Act of 1921—were largely unenforceable. The Private School Act, drafted for the most part with the intention of exerting more control over the operations of Chinese schools—including setting high qualifications for teachers and headmasters and stringent requirements concerning the curriculum—could not be effectively enforced because the state lacked trained personnel capable of policing the Chinese educational system. Not only were there not enough officers to check frequently on every Chinese school. There were hardly any officers of the state who were fluent enough in Chinese to be able to effectively detect breaches of the Private School Act. Similar problems plagued the enforcement of the Compulsory Education Act. The state had neither the means nor the personnel to provide primary education for its entire population, so the idea of surveillance and policing to make sure that everyone received the minimum educational requirements was out of the question.

Another major obstacle in the educational nationalization project throughout the sixth and seventh Chakri reigns was the continued existence of extraterritoriality, which made serious persecution of colonial subjects who flaunted the law nearly impossible. Since operators of private schools, especially Chinese schools, were very often ethnic Chinese individuals who had been registered as colonial subjects, they were almost always protected from persecution under the Siamese judicial system. In more severe cases, it might be possible to close down the school, yet the individual who owned the school was often not punished. This person could then go on to start a different business or even open another school with impunity.

Finally, the royal government itself had since early on in Vajiravudh's reign come to rely more and more on the much expanded state bureaucratic system, which was being operated increasingly by educated commoners from beyond the limited circle of the royal family and old nobility. Because the Siamese state faced a continuing state of economic crisis through much of the sixth and seventh reigns due to both political turmoil in the global arena and poor policy decisions on the part of the Siamese ruling classes, both monarchs had no choice but to continue to rely heavily on the private educational system to supply the much-needed and constantly lacking trained manpower for modernized state bureaucracy.

This highly unequal system of an absolutist royalist regime that had to rely increasingly on commoners educated in potentially seditious modern private schools that could not be sufficiently controlled by the state was obviously unsustainable. And due to this unsustainable dependency, the absolute monarchy eventually met its demise in the Siamese Revolution of 1932. The new constitutional regime would strive to establish a more equal political system for commoners as well as push for expansion of compulsory education for the masses of Thai citizens throughout the kingdom. The new regime would find new solutions to resolve the existing problems, with varying degrees of success. The regional and global political context, however, continued to change rapidly, and Chinese nationalism remained a fundamental problem for educational policy. Ironically, despite having succeeded in terminating absolute monarchist rule and ushering in a new era of constitutional government, leaders of the People's Party continued to put education at the very foundation of their nation-building policy. They would find China, once again, to be a fundamental obstacle to their educational policies.

CHINA AND OVERSEAS CHINESE EDUCATION IN
THE LATE REPUBLICAN ERA

Overseas Chinese educational policies came to the forefront of Republican Chinese politics again in the early 1930s, following Generalissimo Chiang Kai-shek's consolidation of power as uncontested leader of the Nationalist Party and the Republic of China in 1927. This happened to coincide with the Siamese Revolution of 1932, which toppled the absolute monarchy and put in place a new regime under the new, supposedly preferred system of constitutional monarchy. This was a period of drastic shifts in educational policy. An abrupt change took place from royalist nationalist education aimed at cultivating devotion to the Crown to a territorial sort of nationalism aimed at developing the nation for the benefit of all citizens. China had made progress since the turbulence of the Xinhai Revolution. Major warlords had been more or less neutralized, and the most populated and economically vibrant areas of the country were again under the rule of the political party of the revolutionary founding fathers.[30] Whether the turn toward military dictatorship was a healthy direction of recovery remains a matter for debate. In any case, it was a brief period of relative peace before the calamity of the Greater East Asia War befell much of the continent. At this point, both "revolutionary" governments, Thai and Chinese, had an opportunity to come to a better understanding concerning the long-standing issue of overseas Chinese education in Siam. The Thai ruling class was no longer in constant fear of attempts to overthrow the monarchy,[31] and the Chinese state was momentarily strong and unified enough to push for real improvements in nationalist Chinese education overseas.

For various reasons, however, a revolutionary understanding between Chiang Kai-shek's Nationalist government and the revolutionary government of Thailand's People's Party was not achieved. Instead, Sino-Thai relations on the subject of overseas education declined, mostly due to a misunderstanding between the two governments and disastrous miscalculations on the Chinese side. Archival materials suggest that the Chinese Nationalists understood the People's Party Revolution in Siam to be not only pro-Republican but also inspired and influenced by the success of the Xinhai

Revolution and the Republic of China. This was probably largely due to the assumption that Siam's 1932 Revolution was somehow related to the foiled republican coup of 1912, which had obviously been inspired by the Chinese Revolution and had substantial connections with some leading personalities in the overseas Chinese community. After all, it was the government of the absolute monarch Chulalongkorn that had deported Sun Yat-sen for making antimonarchist statements at the final rally of his last visit in 1908. The establishment of a constitutional government in Siam was only a partial success in the view of the Chinese Nationalists, who now hoped to become the revolutionary coach for the People's Party. With a proper revolutionary education, the overseas Chinese in Siam could be the vanguard to assist the still wavering and hesitant Siamese people in completely overthrowing the monarchy and establishing a truly modern republic. The Republic of China was among the first foreign powers after the revolution to formally congratulate the People's Party government. Within months of that major political turning point in Siam, the Chinese Ministry of Foreign Affairs issued *Guidelines for Sino-Siamese Nationalist Movement (Secret)*. Significant parts of these guidelines clearly express the Nationalist Party's intention to involve itself in an antimonarchist revolution in Siam. The success of this anticipated second revolution in Siam would create a government fully supported by the Nationalist regime, making Siam a closer and more reliable ally of China than it had ever been of the United Kingdom, even under Oxford-educated Vajiravudh. The guidelines include:

A. Main points:
1) Organize an association of Sino-Siamese revolutionary comrades without discrimination on grounds of nationality. The group must not be divided into cliques and factions, and must not compete for power among themselves.
2) The high-level cadres of this Sino-Siamese association must be active members of the [Nationalist] Party and sympathizers of the spirit of the "Three Principles of the People," which will lead to the liberation of the Sino-Siamese people, the foundation of a "new international sentiment" and the transformation of [Siam] into a truly democratic nation.

. . .

6) Focus on the training of Sino-Siamese members to resist exploitation by the privileged classes.

. . .

8) Focus on researching the conspiracies of the privileged ruling classes and the true conditions of the oppressed masses that must be liberated.

. . .

C. Propaganda:

. . .

3) Translate and publish the theories and important works related to the Sino-Siamese nationalist liberation revolution.

. . .

D. Training:

. . .

3) Establish a Sino-Siamese nationalist movement as an organization for fostering and educating cadres and personnel. Eliminate the language barriers among the Sino-Siamese nationalities for the sake of the realization of a new international sentiment between the two nationalities.[32]

Whether the People's Party intended to completely overthrow the monarchy, the way they envisioned the monarch's post-revolution role and whether they succeeded in achieving the true objectives of the 1932 Revolution remain to this day matters of debate among historians. Nonetheless, one aspect of this political transformation is certain: although they were largely commoners, the core leaders in the People's Party had been educated in Europe, mostly on state scholarships. Unlike their predecessors in the failed revolution of 1912, who were heavily influenced by the ideas of Sun Yat-sen, the People's Party's vision of modernity and democracy was very European. Moreover, and perhaps more importantly, among the party's fundamental justifications for overthrowing the absolute monarchy was its claim to represent a truer form of nationalism. The revolutionary narrative of the People's Party criticized Vajiravudh's version of royalist nationalism and pointed out what they perceived as the failure of the absolute monarchy to safeguard the nation's sovereignty and the people's well-being. They insinuated that Mongkut and Chulalongkorn were so obsessed with safeguarding their own political power and position in Siam that they were too willing to compromise with European imperialist aggressors.[33] As a result, Siam suffered major territorial losses to British Burma and French Indochina. Coming into power while making such claims, it was unthinkable that the leaders of the People's Party could allow any foreign power to step in and direct the revolution.

If anything could be considered a major change in the Thai government's policies toward overseas Chinese education in the era of the People's Party government, it would be the intense escalation of state control and censorship of Chinese education in Siam. To the chagrin of Nationalist leaders, the Thai government continued to gravitate toward alliance with stronger and more influential imperialist powers such as Britain and Japan despite the revolution. In 1939, Siam officially became Thailand and moved toward a military alliance with Japan, despite being fully aware of Japan's invasion of China, which had begun early in the decade. In the face of these unexpected and unwelcome shifts in Thai foreign policy, the Chinese government had to adjust its expectations regarding Chinese education in Thailand. An amiable relationship with the new constitutional ruling classes was necessary to ensure the well-being of Thailand's large ethnic Chinese community. By the late 1930s, this overseas community had become a major source of both financial support and manpower for Republican China's war efforts. Only months before the Thai government officially entered into an alliance with Japan, Liang Qiwan of the Chinese Ministry of Foreign Affairs made a proposal: "One reason for the deterioration of Sino-Thai relations is due to the low level of education of most Chinese who migrate to Thailand. This makes them unable to understand Thai politics and also makes it impossible for them to foster valuable connections with the Thai upper class. . . . We must make long-term preparations to train diplomatic specialists to work in the field in Southeast Asia, especially in Thailand."[34]

This was a far cry from the *Guidelines for Sino-Siamese Nationalist Movement (Secret)* of the early 1930s. With Japan's expansion through the Greater East Asia Co-Prosperity Sphere gaining momentum, Chiang Kai-shek's China was too weak to influence, much less impose, any of its political ideology upon others, even countries that the Chinese might have traditionally perceived as vassal states, including Thailand. Especially after a formal alliance with Japan had been declared in December 1941, any efforts to promote Chinese nationalist education in Thailand had to be carried out in secret. A further report from the Sino-Thai Problem Discussion Group in April 1943 included a proposal from Wu Shichao, secretary of the Ministry of Overseas Chinese Affairs, on topics of concern in the education of Chinese immigrants in Thailand:

(1) Nationalism and the concept of society before self;

(2) Basic training in covert activities, so that overseas Chinese migrants could serve their country if need be;

(3) Methods of preserving the virtues that are admirable to others of the Chinese race;

(4) Training in economics and business administration;

(5) Training in conducting surveys, in organizing, and further training in new surroundings, according to the model of the New Life Movement.[35]

The Nationalist government continued to fully expect ethnic Chinese who had gone through the Chinese educational system in Thailand to remain strictly loyal to the Chinese nationalist cause. Such loyalty had to be secretly and subtly instilled, however, to avoid worsening Sino-Thai relations, which had been seriously compromised by the Japanese-Thai alliance. By the end of the war, the Nationalist government had prioritized compromise with Phibunsongkhram's increasingly hostile government in order to save some form of Chinese education. If Chinese education could be maintained, even in a greatly reduced form, ethnic and cultural ties between Chinese communities in Thailand—then the largest in Southeast Asia and in the world outside the mainland—and the Republic of China could be preserved. Such bonds of affection and allegiance meant that the possibility of financial and technological support for postwar reconstruction of China remained alive. To achieve this strategic goal, the Chinese government had to completely repudiate any intention of colonizing Thailand, either culturally through the existence of the large ethnic Chinese community, or territorially, if the Allied powers were victorious in the war. The Nationalist government's sole requirement was that the ethnic Chinese in Thailand—who, according to the Republic of China's law, were Chinese citizens—continue to have access to Chinese education according to their basic rights as citizens of the republic. This was a highly complex and politically delicate matter to negotiate with the Thai government, considering that Thai citizenship law at that point considered many in this group of ethnic Chinese to be Thai citizens. Nonetheless, Nationalist delegates continued tirelessly to insist on this concession: "Even if China could diligently develop her culture so that others would naturally turn to respect her, to engage in imperialistic plots against Thailand would only bring trouble for the overseas Chinese residing in that country. At present, China can hardly manage to govern herself and is still very dependent on other people. That China would have imperialistic aspirations toward Thai territory is truly an incomprehensible idea."[36]

The issue of maintaining Chinese education in Thailand probably contributed significantly to the generalissimo's decision to be first among the major Allied leaders to fully endorse the Free Thai Movement and Thailand's status as a wartime victim of Japanese imperialist aggression. It was a pivotal act that would later allow Thailand to be considered a member of the victorious Allied powers, despite having formally entered an alliance with Japan at the outbreak of the war.[37]

OVERSEAS CHINESE EDUCATION IN THE ERA OF THE PEOPLE'S PARTY

After the People's Party Revolution of 1932, despite the transformation of the kingdom's governing system and ruling regime, little seemed to have changed regarding the state's policies toward the Republic of China and the ethnic Chinese community in Siam. Led by the People's Party, a group consisting mostly of commoners, the new regime, with its new ideology, continued to lean heavily toward Anglo-European views of modernity and stronger foreign allies such as Britain and Japan. Many among the leaders of the constitutional regime of the People's Party held faithfully to Vajiravudh's legacy of distrust toward ethnic Chinese who insisted on maintaining their Chinese citizenship. The only major difference was that compared with the absolute monarchs like Vajiravudh who preceded them, the methods of the new constitutional government in controlling and discriminating against such individuals were far more severe, even draconian. Part of the reason for their extremism was the newly established regime's instability and insecurity. In the early years, leaders of the People's Party government were well aware of the strong support the monarchy had enjoyed from the upper echelons of the ethnic Chinese community. The royals had maintained a long-standing policy of rewarding those wealthy and powerful "good Chinese" and encouraging them to stay away from the "bad Chinese," personified by the secret societies. The lower echelons of the Chinese community did in fact pose threats of communist insurrection, which also tended to bring down reprisals from military leadership within the People's Party. Because of this conflicting structure of alliances, the new regime was more or less forced into a hostile position vis-à-vis the entire spectrum of the nation's ethnic Chinese population.

Worse still, the educational system, which should have been highly effective in cultivating loyal and capable citizens for new Siam, was but a sore reminder of the absolute monarchs who laid its foundation and ensured that what little was established would carry on the royalist brand of nationalism. Not surprisingly, the promotion of new education for the people figured prominently as one of the six principles declared as the fundamental policies of the first, post-revolution, People's Party government.[38] As Chulalongkorn and Vajiravudh had intended, the Ministry of Education was, more often than not, at the forefront of the People's Party's nationalist campaigns. The post-1932 constitutional government made clear very early on that it would not tolerate any foreign interference in Thailand's educational system. In 1935, the Thai government responded to the Chinese Nationalist government's inquiries concerning overseas Chinese education in Siam:

> On the question of education, no matter in whatever country, a country
> reserves the right within its territory to lay down the educational training
> methods for both boys and girls. It will not allow other nations to have
> special privileges to conduct such training in their own way. Even in
> China the position is the same. This general basis is also adopted by Siam,
> which reserves the right to establish education within the Kingdom based
> on such a policy; and to not allow other nations, irrespective of whether it
> is China or any other nation, to enjoy special privilege in this direction.[39]

This clear message resulted in the subsequent change in Kuomintang policy concerning overseas Chinese education. The new constitutional government, with its political control still far from secure and its position still at odds with that of ethnic Chinese of all socioeconomic strata, would crack down more violently than ever before on any attempt to infringe upon the government's independent sovereign powers to monitor and control important institutions in its realm—the educational system being one of the most jealously guarded.

The People's Party government abruptly found itself following in the footsteps of Vajiravudh's hard-line minister of education, Phraya Thammasakmontri. The Primary Education Act, one of the earliest pieces of legislation passed under the new regime, stated that Thai was to be used exclusively in instruction of all primary school children.[40] No exceptions were made for Chinese schools. In other words, instead of teaching in Chinese twenty hours per week, Chinese schools were suddenly unable to teach at all.

As might have been expected, the promulgation of the Primary Education Act precipitated an uproar in the ethnic Chinese community. Over 6,000 persons affiliated with Chinese schools and 332 members of the Chinese Chamber of Commerce in Siam signed a petition protesting the government's new educational policy and delivered it to the National Parliament. The government made some minor concessions. Primary school students in the first, second, and third years were allowed to have up to

7.5 hours of courses taught in Chinese each week, while fourth- and fifth-year students were allowed up to 12.5 hours per week. This was the established allowance made for foreign schools of other nationalities. Chinese schools, prior to this controversy, had been treated simply as extensions of Thai private schools. Unfortunately for the Chinese community, however, even these grudging concessions proved short lived. In 1935, the Thai minister of education suggested that unlike foreign schools of other nationalities, Chinese schools were more likely to cause problems. The ministry then attempted to revoke the Parliament's earlier allowances. This time it took a general boycott of Thai rice throughout southern China to persuade the Thai government to concede. In 1936, the Ministry of Education announced that it would once again allow Chinese schools to provide Chinese language courses, but only for 5.5 hours per week for lower primary school students, and 11.5 hours per week for upper primary school students.[41]

As the Second World War began to envelop Southeast Asia and the Thai government became increasingly pro-Axis, Chinese education in Thailand continued to be pared away. In 1939, the Ministry of Education issued new orders limiting the study of Chinese language to two hours per week for children of compulsory age (seven to fourteen years) and insisted that all other subjects provided in Chinese schools be taught in the Thai language, in the same manner as other Thai private schools.[42]

In addition to drastically reducing the number of hours allowed for subjects taught in Chinese, the Thai government of the post-1932 era sought to control and reform Chinese school personnel. The authorities did this by reviving the Private School Act, which had been on the books since 1919, but had been loosely enforced until then. This legislation established the basic qualifications for headmasters of all private schools, especially Chinese schools. All non-Thai teachers were required to pass the government's Thai language examination within a year and a half of being hired.[43] The headmasters of Chinese schools, who held the great respect and loyal support of parents, were known to be dedicated and accomplished scholars of the Chinese classics. Unfortunately, these masters of classical Chinese studies seldom knew the Thai language well enough to satisfy the standards of the Thai Ministry of Education. Focusing on meeting the highest standards of Chinese education, Chinese schools often employed teachers directly from China, and they typically began teaching without any knowledge of Thai at all. For them to pass the government's language examination within their first year and a half on the job was virtually impossible.

As intended, the enforcement of the Private School Act put an inexorable squeeze on the targeted schools. Some schools attempted to manipulate legal technicalities by hiring a Chinese headmaster to serve as chief administrator of the school and a Thai principal whose sole job was to deal with Thai authorities. Even so, there was no way to manipulate the language abilities of teachers. Hiring Thai teachers would cost the schools their credibility as institutions providing Chinese education. When ethnic Chinese parents could no longer depend on the quality of education from within their own community, they preferred to send their children to Chinese schools in Malaya or Singapore, or even back to China. Without the support of ethnic Chinese parents, it became impossible for Chinese schools in Thailand to carry on. Not surprisingly, between 1933 and 1935, when the government began to strictly enforce the Private School Act, some seventy-nine Chinese schools were closed for violating the law.[44]

The unpleasant effects on Chinese education brought by the swift and severe reforms enacted by the post-1932 constitutional government fell upon the scions of wealthy upper-class Chinese entrepreneurs, many of them leading members of the Chinese Chamber of Commerce and tycoons of the rice business. These distinguished citizens rallied, calling for petitions and instigating boycotts in response, but the government had more on its mind than insisting on Thai studies. The new regime's educational policy was aimed at preempting the dangerous potential of Chinese educational institutions being used as headquarters for communist organizations or underground cells propagating communist ideology among the children of working-class Chinese. Such proselytizing would challenge the stability and security of the new regime and drive Siam closer to prototypes of modernity that the ruling classes—from the courts of the absolute monarchs to the post-revolution cabinet—had long attempted to stifle, the Chinese Communist Party and the Soviet Bolsheviks being prime examples. Paranoia about the Chinese working class escalated when the militarist wing of the People's Party gained dominance and vented its long-standing suspicions about the left-wing connections of the party's civilian leaders, Pridi Banomyong in particular. Labor movements and communist sympathizers were more or less the natural enemies of leading militarists with fascist leanings such as Field Marshal Phibunsongkhram. By 1938, when Phibunsongkhram first became prime minister, the ethnic Chinese were already center stage in the government's anticommunist policies. Not surprisingly, ongoing scrutiny and strict control of overseas Chinese education were central to the government's campaign.

In practice, Chinese schools deemed supportive of communist activities, whether in organization or ideology, were monitored and systematically pressured. The Thai ruling class viewed Chinese schools with communist tendencies as a serious threat for three major reasons; (1) overseas Chinese education was being used to spread communist propaganda among Chinese youths; (2) Chinese schools were functioning as headquarters for overseas Chinese communist youth organizations; and (3) Chinese schools were being used to educate and train the revolutionary working classes. It is interesting to note that the first two reasons represent possible threats to the Thai government if the ethnic Chinese community were overrun by communist elements. As volatile as they may seem, these threats remained relatively contained within the Chinese community. The last item, however, represents a deeper level of fear. This threat was directed against Thai authorities should communist ideology be disseminated among the Thai general public.

Reports and government records documenting various police raids on Chinese schools and overseas Chinese associations during this period suggest that communist elements in the ethnic Chinese community did indeed attempt to disseminate propaganda through the Chinese educational system. In one raid on a Hainanese library association in September 1932, police found a wealth of communist literature, including a statement of organizational purpose of the Chinese communist movement in Siam. This latter piece of evidence stated clearly that "the purpose of the Communist Youth (C.Y.) organization, also known as the middle class students, is to encourage the revolutionary spirit of students and young workers."[45] The same document also provided suggestions on how to establish and operate a successful communist student association. Thai authorities were understandably alarmed by the discovery of these materials, which were printed in both Thai and Chinese. The content was clearly destined for far larger audiences than the youth of the ethnic Chinese community alone.

Aside from functioning as propaganda tools for the Chinese communist movement, these schools were also involved in the operation and development of certain communist organizations in Siam. A police raid on Chinese schools in Bangkok in December 1932 yielded many revealing documents concerning the plans and achievements of the Association of Young Workers of Siam.[46] These documents suggested that young ethnic Chinese workers should make an effort to further their education to better support the imminent communist revolution. Moreover, they should try to interact with school-age Chinese youths through "the establishment of various youth associations specializing in sports, games, drama, etc. as a way of disseminating communist ideology among the youth."[47] Chinese schools in Siam were thus being turned into a common ground where communist workers could meet and interact with students while furthering their intellectual capacity at the same time. Many Chinese schools were actively propagating communist ideology in their teaching materials, supporting the organization of communist student associations, and encouraging interaction between ethnic Chinese students and members of communist associations. Not surprisingly, many ethnic Chinese youths of this era became heavily involved in communist activities while still enrolled as students in Chinese schools.[48]

As Thailand moved steadily toward the outbreak of the Second World War in Southeast Asia and to its ill-fated formal alliance with Japan, state policies toward Chinese education became increasingly severe. Since the post-1932 constitutional government did not believe in the old absolute monarchy's strategy of awarding favors to royalist upper-class Chinese and harshly repressing seditious secret societies, more schools were shut down.[49] Teachers and students were more frequently incarcerated, and increasing numbers of Chinese educators were deported throughout the war years.[50] Both Thai and Chinese archival materials suggest that the Nationalist government attempted to salvage the situation by making various inquiries into the mass closing of Chinese schools and the arrest and deportation of school personnel. However, with the abundance of incriminating materials collected from the frequent raids on Chinese schools and Chinese associations, it was only too easy for the Thai government to explain their anti-Chinese charges simply as straightforward efforts to curb communist activities: "Chinese newspapers and Chinese schools have been closed [by the Thai government] in an attempt to curb rising communist activities. Should the overseas Chinese community elect a representative, or should the Chinese government choose to dispatch an envoy to Thailand, the Thai government would be willing to negotiate concerning other possible ways of resolving this problem."[51]

The Chinese Nationalist government, with its own impressive anticommunist credentials, could do or say very little when the Thai government pointed out that by closing down Chinese schools it was, in fact, supporting Nationalist efforts to eradicate Chinese Communist elements.[52]

ANTI-CHINESE EDUCATIONAL POLICIES AND THE ESTABLISHMENT
OF NATIONAL LEGITIMACY

There is a logical explanation as to why Western scientific knowledge did not become the fundamental theme of the Siamese state's educational policies starting with King Narai in the mid-seventeenth century. The reason was not, as historian Ian Hodges proposes, because that reign was "before the ideas that it [Western scientific knowledge] generated had either found their full expression or achieved widespread acceptance in Europe."[53] Western ideas were set aside because in the seventeenth century European standards of knowledge and civilization had yet to become the dominant order of the day across the Asian continent. It was not until the mid-nineteenth century, after a spectacular victory in the First Opium War, the grand opening of five treaty ports along the coast of southern China, and the consolidation of British rule in the South Asian subcontinent, that Sir John Bowring was able to convince King Mongkut that the British world order had successfully replaced the celestial order of the Qing dynasty even across the length of the South China Sea. These demonstrations of power fired up Mongkut's interest in Western scientific knowledge and transformed it into the driving force that would lead to major modernizing reforms in Siam's educational system in a way that could never have happened during Narai's seventeenth-century reign. The modernization and nation-building projects of the Siamese monarchies from Mongkut to Vajiravudh were essentially coping mechanisms of the ruling class in their struggle to survive the paradigm shift in global political and economic dominance from China to Britain. The modernization and nationalization of the educational system were fundamental aspects of both projects. The biggest obstacle happened to be the large and influential Chinese minority and the concurrent development of the overseas Chinese educational system.

The modernization of the Siamese educational system as a fundamental tool of nation-building was shaped by avoiding and overcoming obstacles raised by the particular needs and interests of the Chinese minority and Chinese education in Siam. The richest and most influential Chinese in Siam in the late nineteenth and early twentieth centuries were registered as colonial subjects, which put them beyond the control of the Siamese judicial system. They could not be forced into the state-operated Thai nationalist educational system. The royalist regime modernized and developed the Thai educational system, making it more attractive to the Chinese minority in various ways. The Siamese ruling class had been successful in manipulating the ethnic Chinese by playing upon the internal divisions and conflicts in their communities. The traditional divisions that defined Chinese by hometown, dialect, and lineage made it easier for Siamese authorities to constantly pit one group against the other, weakening any possibility of the Chinese community uniting and thereby gaining formidable political bargaining power.

This strategy became less efficacious toward the turn of the century, however, with the rise of Chinese nationalist sentiments, especially following the apparent success of the Chinese Revolution in 1911. With the rise of the Republic of China, the push for a united nationalist curriculum and a single language of instruction for Chinese schools across Southeast Asia gained momentum. For the first time in the history of the overseas Chinese in Siam, Chinese education appeared to begin to unite the diasporic community across old dialect divisions. Still hamstrung by issues of extraterritoriality, the absolute monarchy under Vajiravudh and Prajadhipok could only attempt to discredit popular Chinese nationalist movements, most commonly by branding them criminal enterprises like the secret society gangs that terrorized Bangkok's Chinatown through much of the nineteenth century. Their other strategy was to convince upper-class overseas Chinese capitalists that they could continue to benefit from the crown's favor by distancing themselves from "bad Chinese" who were involved in republican nationalist propaganda through the Chinese educational system.

Not much could be done to clamp down on seditious Chinese educational institutions in Siam until extraterritoriality was abolished, which became possible soon after the establishment of the first Siamese constitutional regime, born of the 1932 Siamese Revolution. Interestingly and to the great disappointment of the revolutionary Chinese Republican government, the People's Party's constitutional regime, though fundamentally antimonarchist in spirit, was even less tolerant of nationalist Chinese educational policies that appeared to have been traversing Thai national boundaries for so long. Having successfully done away with extraterritorial limitations, the Thai constitutional government appeared to be more interested in taking complete control of the educational system within its realm than going a step farther to completely overthrow the monarchy and establish a republic, which was the direction the Nationalist regime would have preferred. According to the revolutionary People's Party regime, the new Thai nation and Thai nationalism were to be strong and independent of foreign influence, with the monarch having a minimal role in politics. They thus made no allowances for any contesting nationalist propaganda flowing through the educational system. Moreover, should the new constitutional Thai state develop in the direction of any foreign power, it would most definitely take cues from the most powerful among the empires of the East and West, namely Britain and Japan, and not the perennially divided and struggling Republic of China. The overseas Chinese educational system in Siam in the years leading up to the outbreak of the Second World War was both a threat to national security and a major obstruction to the development of Siam into a new, politically and economically powerful nation-state of Thailand.

Thailand's ethnic Chinese minority had substantial status and a critical role in the nation-building process of the modern Siamese state. The educational system developed by and for overseas Chinese communities was one of the most deeply rooted and well-organized foreign educational systems in the modern history of Thailand. Consequently, the ethnic Chinese minority made up a significant portion of the country's literate public and the intellectual middle and upper-middle classes. One thing that should be evident from the conflict in Sino-Thai nationalist education of the late nineteenth and early twentieth centuries is that the Thai ruling class, in establishing a modern nation-state and its own nationalist movement, would have to come to terms with the power to survive and thrive of this problematic transnational community. How a new and vigorous alliance was eventually configured extends beyond the propaganda war in the educational systems to other areas, especially newspapers and other print media.

CHAPTER TWO

PUBLISHING NATIONS

The Media and Elite Propaganda

THE GREAT IMPORTANCE OF THE PRINTING PRESS AND THE establishment of printed vernaculars in the rise of modern nationalism is well known. The advent of print technology, together with the forceful tides of capitalism, propelled vernacular languages to replace Latin and Greek as the official languages of modern nation-states. In the European context, this print-capitalism combination provided new ideological bonds for the bourgeoisie that were even more powerful than the kinship and matrimonial bonds of the royals. Print culture, by gradually standardizing the written form of vernacular languages, allowed publics with mutually unintelligible accents or dialects (and alphabetic writing systems) to begin to communicate more easily to and for "imagined communities."[1]

With the rise of print capitalism came the popularized modern newspaper—a marvelous invention that allowed news, information, and ideas to spread through the populace at great speed, something rarely witnessed before the dawn of the Industrial Revolution. A shared, printed vernacular language became emblematic of cultural unity and contributed to the imagined racial and historical unity that is the very foundation of the modern concept of the nation-state.[2] Nations were being born out of a newly conceived linguistic sameness created on printed paper. By the late eighteenth century, however, the printing press had also become one of the major driving forces behind many of the world's most famous revolutions, including China's.

The concept of print capitalism provides a useful theoretical framework for analyzing how the development of the printed media through various forms of publication in Siam of the late nineteenth and early twentieth centuries eventually contributed to the founding of the Thai nation.³ If simple print capitalism is a one-dimensional emergence of an imagined national community from the shared experience of a reading public in one limited geographical area—reading the same published material, then psychologically establishing together one imagined community—the Thai situation requires a three-dimensional perspective that incorporates at least three geographical settings and three sets of publishers and readers, resulting in three competing visions of the hybrid imagined community.

Siam's first known newspaper, the *Bangkok Recorder,* began publication in 1844 under the American missionary Rev. Dan Beach Bradley. Its circulation was extremely limited, both in terms of readership, which included almost exclusively the top echelons of the Bangkok elite, and in duration, lasting less than five years. Only in the early twentieth century, during the reign of King Vajiravudh Rama VI, did published journalism begin to flourish in Thai society. The sixth king should not, however, receive all the credit for ushering in the age of print capitalism and, in turn, Thai nationalism, as much of mainstream state propaganda narrative has assumed.

One important aspect of the contribution of the published media to the founding of the Thai nation that has not been sufficiently explored in earlier works is the Chinese-language community publication known as *Qiaokan* (literally, Emigrant Newspaper). This type of publication initially functioned as a vehicle for maintaining contact between the ancestral homeland—typically in faraway hamlets of southern China—and overseas communities throughout the world. The information exchanged usually included mundane subjects concerning the well-being (or lack thereof) of the home community in China—who gave birth, who built a new house, whose son is marrying whose daughter, and so on—and the activities of the sojourning community overseas: business and political developments, career accomplishments, generous donations to the homeland, and the like. The main purpose was simply to maintain familial and social ties between the hometown in China and the migrant workers, entrepreneurs, and adventurers in overseas Chinese communities so as to ensure that the steady stream of remittances would continue despite the long years, even generations, of geographic separation between migrants and their hometowns. At a very basic level, we could perhaps consider this shared published material as the foundation of a sort of transnational imagined community perceived as united and connected in some ways even though in reality the members reside on opposite shores. At this point, the imagined community was mostly founded upon bonds of kinship and ancestral ties. It was very much a commitment based on Confucian filial piety, more like a sworn brotherhood or secret society than any political organization that could develop into a nation-state, as suggested in Anderson's original model. Siam, being one of the largest outposts of the Chinese diaspora in Southeast Asia throughout the nineteenth century, was one among the many bases of this sort of newsletter-based imagined community.

As new Chinese migrants to Siam from the mid-nineteenth century on become more established in the host country, a number of community-based Chinese-language newspapers began to develop. Around the turn of the century, a second set of imagined communities came into being when competing political factions in China—the declining Qing dynasty, the reformers under Kang Youwei, and the revolutionaries under Sun Yat-sen—set off in search of transnational allies and sponsors in the numerous and prosperous Chinese diaspora communities of the southern seas. Each faction then managed to make contact and eventually co-opt one or more of the local Chinese-language newspapers as their political mouthpiece in each host community in Southeast Asia. A new imagined community was then formed with the idea that each overseas Chinese community read a Chinese-language newspaper that published news from the mainland and kept them connected with the Chinese nation-state. That the Chinese community in Bangkok read the same news about what went on in mainland China in the same printed Chinese text made Bangkok Chinese an integral part of the national community of China.

Enter Vajiravudh, Oxford-educated crown prince of Siam, who returned home in 1902, fully westernized and a proud anglophile by his own right, and succeeded his father as King Rama VI in 1910. Vajiravudh had been greatly impressed by the democratic culture of cherishing freedom of expression and protecting the free press of Western superpowers that he had encountered in his many years studying abroad. Perhaps more importantly, the king was made aware early in his reign of the far-reaching influence of the Chinese-language press upon many sectors in his own kingdom. Seeing the rise of Chinese nationalism and its many forms of propaganda as a rising threat to the security of his own position, and perhaps with a degree of pride in his own writing ability, the king became the first monarch to write his own propaganda pieces and have them published in his own daily newspaper. Vajiravudh's initial assumption of the benevolent role of champion of the free press was not only about fashioning his reign after the enlightened monarchs of the modern West; it was also a way to get involved directly in the propaganda war with what Vajiravudh might have perceived as competing ideologies that threatened the well-being of his absolutist regime—Chinese nationalist propaganda, bolshevism, republicanism, and so on. With the monarch directly involved and regularly contributing articles to the daily newspapers, the budding journalistic circles in the Siamese capital became increasingly vibrant. Journalists, with both supportive and contesting views vis-à-vis the monarch, enthusiastically contributed to one fiery debate after another. Soon an argumentative exchange emerged between the monarch and a few daring ethnic Chinese journalists opposed to the king's seemingly incessant attacks on the Chinese nation and the overseas Chinese community in Siam.

Vajiravudh's direct and rigorous involvement in public debates through articles published in daily newspapers both served the monarch's propaganda purpose and helped stabilize the political standing of those daring journalists who were challenging him within the ethnic Chinese community in Thailand at the time. The king enjoyed a reputation as a champion of the free press, while the ethnic Chinese journalists enjoyed heightened popularity as strong leaders and defenders of the overseas Chinese community in Siam. The rising Thai-educated middle class in the kingdom's few urban centers, who had witnessed the exchange between the monarch and Chinese journalists, recognized the possibility of a shared public space in which they too could exchange views, suggestions, and criticisms concerning society, politics, and even the monarchy. Probably unintentionally, Vajiravudh had opened the floodgate of public opinion through his supportive stance and direct investment and involvement in the public media. Consequently, this group of urban, educated middle-class Thais who came to imagine a shared national community through a free press would become the driving force popularizing print media and expanding its reach to a Thai audience throughout the kingdom.

EARLY OVERSEAS CHINESE PUBLICATION

Throughout the world, Chinese immigrants' newsletters were the progenitors of overseas Chinese newspapers. First and foremost, they served Chinese sojourners abroad. They also served the ancestral hometowns with which those faraway scions forever strove to reconnect. Filial sons and virtuous fathers in the Confucian tradition were never supposed to abandon the tombs of their ancestors. To help preserve that sacred bond, newsletters were published and circulated in hometowns in southern China and ethnic Chinese settlements overseas. The sojourners were kept well informed about circumstances back home: the well-being of wives and children, neighborhood facilities or lack thereof, the latest village gossip, the most eligible future daughters-in-law, and other news. Likewise, families back in China read about the progress of their relations overseas, their work and businesses, funds being remitted home regularly to better the lives of families, and how they were helping to develop their hometowns in China. In the late nineteenth and early twentieth centuries, many such sojourners, especially in Southeast Asia, settled down and started new families in their host countries. Even so, the special connections, sentimental and practical, with the ancestral homeland, honored and never forgotten by the newsletters, remained strong, as did the steady stream of remittances that continued to flow back to China from abroad, generation after generation.

Bits and pieces of early publications from the ethnic Chinese community of Siam remain in the National Archives in Bangkok and in a few private collections of the major dialect group associations. However, no studies of these scattered materials in the Thai context match the thoroughness of research on overseas Chinese communities in North America. Even so, from the few available fragments, combined with later investigations on overseas Chinese publications,[4] it appears that publications in the Chinese community of Siam, as in other Chinese diasporic communities throughout Southeast Asia in the nineteenth century, were mostly concerned with issues also found in such communities elsewhere. Most frequently featured were current affairs in Bangkok's Chinatown and southern China, travel and remittance services, and business developments in the Chinese overseas entrepreneurial network throughout the Asia-Pacific region. What is most interesting from the perspective of a study of nationalism and nation-building is that earlier publications circulating in Chinese communities in Siam tended to focus on maintaining relationships with the ancestral homeland. That homeland was usually somewhere in southern China—mostly Guangdong and Fujian. The scope of those affectionate ties never extended to greater China, as in the wider Qing Empire, or even to the early Republic of China.

Early publications in overseas Chinese communities around the world—Siam being a prime example—came into being as a way to maintain bonds that were far more substantial and personal than any ties of imagined national solidarity. The newsletters that preceded overseas Chinese newspapers were published in standard Chinese script intelligible to Chinese everywhere, regardless of their dialect. However, each newsletter catered to a specific hometown-based readership bound together through a local dialect and the services of the remittance network active in that particular area of southern China. This regionalism was not only a serious obstacle to establishing any functional form of Chinese nationalism. It was also, more often than not, the major cause for competition as well as jealousy and contempt in the overseas Chinese community.

OVERSEAS CHINESE NEWSPAPERS AND NATIONAL POLITICS

Toward the last decade of the nineteenth century, periodicals and newspapers in Chinese communities in Siam became a crucial tool for communicating developments in Chinese national politics. From the perspective of most of the readership of the overseas Chinese press in Siam, this was by no means a natural course of development. The poor Chinese laborer in Bangkok, through the hardship of his work and the difficulties of remitting money to his family in China, did not suddenly become politically conscious and start calling for Chinese newspapers to become involved in building up the Chinese nation. On the contrary, the transformation of neighborhood journalism and newsletter-type publications into politically conscious overseas Chinese newspapers trumpeting Chinese nationalism occurred in a top-down manner. Leading political figures from the mainland visited Southeast Asia to meet and recruit influential persons in the overseas Chinese communities.

A decision was made at the local level to become political allies and support a particular political ideology through the circulation of a newspaper established especially for that purpose. Not surprisingly, the politics of Chinese newspapers in Siam mirrored almost exactly the numerous conflicts and chronic disunity of Chinese politics at the turn of the century. Despite having moved beyond competitive hometowns and dialect cliques, Chinese newspapers in Siam in the nation-building era continued their factional ways. By then, however, disagreements had been elevated to the level of national politics instead of simple hometown feuds. The sense of solidarity and comradery that was supposed to arise from the shared experience of a population reading the same printed information, as elaborated in Anderson's concept of print capitalism, therefore became a three-pronged contest of national belonging.

Chinese nationalist leaders among the ethnic Chinese in Siam attempted to use their publications as mouthpieces for the policies of the Chinese Nationalist Party (Kuomintang) and to encourage support for the Republic of China on the mainland. Thai-language newspapers, a few of which were subsidized by the Ministry of Interior and from the royal coffers, spread royalist-nationalist propaganda in support of King Vajiravudh's nation-building policies. Finally, the working class and the progressive Chinese who were residing and making a living in Siam but found no place in the conservative state-supported publications of both China and Siam chose to establish their own socialist/progressive publications to support the anti-imperialist and anticapitalist agenda of the less affluent working-class sector of the Chinese community in Siam.

ZHENG ZHIYONG

The first major political movement to successfully adopt a Chinese newspaper in Siam as its propaganda mouthpiece was Kang Youwei's reformist movement. The *Enlightened South Daily* (Qinan ribao) was established to support the reformist cause in 1906 with financial support from Zheng Zhiyong (1851–1935), one of the most influential figures in the Chinese community in late nineteenth-century Siam. An overseas Chinese from Chaozhou and a French subject, Zheng Zhiyong is better known as Yi Ko Hong (Chaozhou dialect pronunciation of Er-ge Feng, Second Brother Hong).[5] He was believed to be among the leading masters of the Siamese chapter of the Triad Society (Sandian Hui), which was among the most influential secret societies of the Chinese community in Siam.[6] Deeply involved in the underworld economy of the Chinese community, Zheng also contributed significantly to many public services. He was among the founders and most generous sponsors of the Poh Teck Tung Foundation, which provided soup kitchens for the poor and homeless. Even today, this charity arranges funeral services for unclaimed dead. Zheng also sponsored construction of one of the first modern roads in Bangkok, Techawanit Road, which carries his royally bestowed Thai surname. He was well liked in the court of King Chulalongkorn Rama V and was awarded the title of Phra Anuwatrachaniyom for his services in lottery tax farming.[7] At the peak of his career, Zheng was the owner of the largest gambling establishment in Bangkok. He continued to enjoy the favor of the crown into the early years of King Vajiravudh Rama VI's reign.[8] Zheng's support for Kang Youwei's reformist cause could be considered a reflection of his political inclination toward the royalist stance and the initial success of Kang's propaganda machine in Southeast Asia. On the other hand, it could also have been a strategic move to solidify Zheng's relationship with the Siamese court in an era of political turmoil. The *Enlightened South Daily* was received warmly by the Thai crown, which looked askance at the rising republican tendencies in many parts of the early twentieth-century world.

Zheng's relationship with the Siamese court continued, with occasional ups and downs, long after the collapse of Kang's reformist movement. *Enlightened South Daily* closed soon after the rise of the Republic of China in 1912, but Zheng remained active in Chinese community politics in Siam and supported various other newspapers. It was widely known that he tended to support movements and publications that would not offend the sentiments of Siam's ruling Chakri dynasty. For example, there was a major clash between General Yuan Shikai's government and the Nationalists soon after the establishment of the Chinese Republic. At that time, Zheng defected from the declining reformist camp to support Yuan's authoritarian regime. It was well known that Vajiravudh, the reigning Siamese monarch, favored Yuan over Sun Yat-sen, because Yuan's authoritarian rule and dynastic ambitions were, according to Rama VI, living proof that liberal democracy was not suited to Asian societies. Zheng's support for movements and publications favored by the ruling powers of both Siam and China was a strategy designed to safeguard his position amid the turbulent politics of the Chinese community of his day.

Zheng's penchant for frequently changing alliances and redirecting financial support for overseas Chinese publications makes it clear that even in the era of nationalist politics, overseas Chinese newspapers and the decisions and favors of their Siam-based sponsors were not determined by the ideologies of the leading political factions in China. On the contrary, conflicts and factions in Chinese politics may have been manipulated to serve the purposes of local political cliques attempting to maintain dominance in much smaller overseas Chinese communities. In the overseas Chinese communities of Siam, Zheng Zhiyong's history of strategically shifting alliances is a prime example. As Zheng's case suggests, Chinese Nationalist politics may have had much less influence on the development and direction of Chinese newspapers in Siam than did Siamese politics or the political relations between the Siamese state and its ethnic Chinese population.

XIAO FOCHENG

The Revolutionary Alliance under the leadership of Sun Yat-sen was another force in Nationalist Chinese politics that managed to align itself with an influential figure in the Chinese community and to establish one of the most influential Chinese Nationalist newspapers in the history of Siam. Toward the end of the first decade of the twentieth century, Xiao Focheng's *Sino-Siam News* (Huaxian xinbao) emerged as the leader in this field, with readership cutting across nearly all sections of Siam's highly dynamic Chinese community. *Sino-Siam News* quickly and decisively displaced *Enlightened South Daily*, reflecting the declining power of Zheng Zhiyong. The competition between Chinese language newspapers mirrored closely the fortunes of Siam's prominent ethnic Chinese politicians. It also paralleled, quite accurately, the rise and fall of contending political factions in mainland China. As Kang Youwei's reformist movement lost steam and Sun Yat-sen's revolutionary politics gained momentum, Xiao Focheng (1864–1939), the owner and editor of the most prominent Chinese newspaper in Bangkok's Chinatown, replaced Zheng Zhiyong as the most influential figure in that community.

A Malay-born, British-registered baba, or Straits Chinese, Xiao was more widely recognized as Siao Hutseng in official Thai documents and ethnic Chinese circles.[9] He was a fifth-generation descendant of Fujianese migrants to Malacca. Shortly after his birth, his father relocated the family to Siam and made a fortune in the rice milling industry. Well-schooled and fluent in both Thai and Chinese from a very young age, Xiao soon made a name for himself as columnist and editor of various publications in both languages. Soon after the inception in 1905 of the Revolutionary Alliance, Xiao pledged his allegiance and became one of Sun Yat-sen's most trusted associates in Southeast Asia. Xiao was the main host for Sun's four visits to Siam during the first decade of the twentieth century. There was little doubt that in 1907, when Xiao announced the publication of *Sino-Siam News*, this Chinese newspaper would serve as the main mouthpiece for Sun's revolutionary/Nationalist movement. Positioning itself in opposition to Zheng's *Enlightened South Daily*, toward the end of the first decade of the twentieth century, *Sino-Siam News*'s political stance often directly confronted Zheng's reformist/royalist agenda. The following excerpt is a typical example of the radical nationalist rhetoric Xiao often employed in *Sino-Siam News* in the years leading up to the Xinhai Revolution: "Now the Manchurians are worried that Chinese people will reclaim the national treasures from their hands. Moreover, they do not want Chinese people to have equal rights with Manchurians. Why would they allow for a constitution? If there were to be a constitution, Chinese people would definitely not remain subservient to the Manchu. The only reason why they [the Qing government] mentioned the drafting of a constitution is to fool the Chinese into ceasing revolutionary work."[10]

During the final years of the Manchu regime, *Sino-Siam News* regularly covered the military advances and victories of the revolutionaries while minimizing their drawbacks and failures.[11] Such reports were in stark contrast to the frontline news from Zheng's *Enlightened South Daily*, which proclaimed only the weaknesses and defeats of the revolutionaries.[12] When the Qing dynasty was eventually overthrown and the Republic of China created in 1912, Xiao's faction gained the upper hand in the overseas Chinese political scene, and *Sino-Siam News* displaced *Enlightened South Daily* as the leading news publication of the Chinese community in Siam.

Though Xiao was a prominent supporter of Sun Yat-sen when the Qing dynasty fell from grace and the Chinese Republic was established, it is important to note that his enduring prominence in the Chinese community in Siam was also due to his cautious and tactful relationship with the Siamese ruling class of his time—most notably with the king, Vajiravudh. Compared to Zheng, the lottery tax farmer, Xiao was better educated, more modern, and an altogether more sophisticated politician. Xiao realized that to survive and prosper in his dominant position in the ethnic Chinese community under the Oxford-educated monarch, it would no longer be enough simply to express loyal support for the Siamese crown. One also needed to be aware of political trends and be ready to position oneself as a useful alliance. Xiao was well aware of growing discontent among the middle and lower rungs of Siamese civil and military personnel. Substantial evidence shows that the failed republican revolution in Siam in 1912 was inspired in part by the propaganda disseminated through Xiao's publications. This alone should have put him at odds with Vajiravudh's court, yet he managed to turn circumstances to his advantage. Aware of the king's admiration for the British free press and of his aspiration to establish such an institution in Thai society, Xiao dared to engage in public debates with the monarch through articles in the Thai-language version of his newspaper—the *Sino-Siam Daily* (Chino-Siam warasap). Under the pseudonym Atsawaphahu, Vajiravudh regularly published articles highly critical of the Chinese revolution and its supporters in the royally sponsored broadsheet *Nangsuephim Thai*. Just as frequently, Xiao would argue back on behalf of Chinese revolutionaries in articles highly critical of Atsawaphahu's baldly anti-Chinese stance. At the same time, Xiao always clearly emphasized that while revolution was the only alternative for China after centuries of the oppressive Manchu rule, Siam, by contrast, had a long history of wise and benevolent monarchs and no need to strive for revolution. The following are typical disclaimers penned by Xiao and published in *Sino-Siam Daily*:

Kings of the Manchu are enemies of the Chinese. Hence, we have attempted to eliminate them. However, the kings of Siam have been kind to the Chinese. Therefore, we adore them. Even though our revolution will finally overthrow the Manchu king according to our wish and will successfully establish the republic, if there were even one Manchu king as merciful and wise as the late king of Siam [King Chulalongkorn], we would willingly invite him to become our president.[13]

In this day and age, all of us are happy with our lives [so] we should not waste our time thinking of a parliamentary system or any such nonsense. [We] should continue to make our living honestly and try with all earnestness to find a way to compete with foreigners in crafts and commerce. Do not let them take advantage of us. If all this could be achieved, it would be the best thing possible.[14]

In this way, Xiao avoided dangerous accusations that his pro-Chinese revolutionary publications were indirectly encouraging a revolution in Siam. As a journalist and editor well respected by progressive intellectuals of his day, his voice in support of the existing political system lent credibility to the regime of the absolute monarch. Perhaps most significantly, Xiao's open debate with Atsawaphahu through their respective newspapers helped to realize Vajiravudh's dream of having some semblance of a free press in his kingdom. After all, where could the press enjoy more liberty than in a country where journalists could openly debate with the monarch in the daily papers?

In fact, Xiao Focheng's shrewd support for Vajiravudh's political position not only gained him the enduring regard of the monarch but also boosted his political standing in Siam's resident Chinese communities. While the editor and the king engaged in fierce public debates in strings of ferocious articles posted in their respective newspapers, Xiao was privately receiving subsidies from Vajiravudh's government for the Thai-language version of his newspaper. In return, Xiao provided intelligence about changing circumstances and developments in influential circles in Chinatown. He was the one who informed the court that Zheng Zhiyong planned in 1913 to sell the Chin-Siam Shipping Company (Borisat Ruea-me Chin-Siam) to Canton's municipal government.[15] This was arguably an extremely damaging piece of intelligence, for it resulted in Zheng's fall from grace at Vajiravudh's court. Even though the Chin-Siam Shipping Company was legally Zheng's to sell, it was the only shipping company flying the Siamese flag and registered with the Siamese government. Selling it was interpreted as a severe setback to Siam's status in the world of international trade. Having no flag-carrier, the kingdom once again had to rely solely upon foreign vessels to transport its products and personnel. The complicated significance of this transaction was, of course, not lost in Xiao's report to Vajiravudh's government, and Xiao quickly overtook Zheng as the most admired and influential personality in the Chinese community during Vajiravudh's reign.

It is amazing that the rise and fall of each Chinese newspaper, along with its ethnic Chinese owner, correlates not only with political developments in mainland China but also, perhaps even more so, with the ability of the papers' owners to remain in favor with the ruling powers in Siam (or Thailand) in each era. The secret society godfather, Zheng Zhiyong, was eventually outwitted and outmaneuvered by the conniving intellectual journalist Xiao Focheng, who better understood the need to manipulate, by traditional expressions of devotion and loyalty to the crown, the Thai nationalist movement that was so important to the monarch. Following Xiao's damaging report on Zheng's sale of his shipping company, information concerning Zheng's substantial regular donations to his ancestral hometown in Chaozhou was leaked to the court. The king learned that Zheng had invested substantially in the land of his ancestors, thereby, in a sense, slighting the people of his benevolent host country. Nationalism had become the fundamental concern of the ruling monarch, and it was no longer enough for a wealthy Chinese entrepreneur to express his loyalty by offering valuable gifts and expensive fanfare, if he was simultaneously donating heavily to support the betterment of his ancestral hometown in China. Vajiravudh began to demand that his ethnic Chinese allies invest more in the kingdom and people of Siam. By 1917, Zheng had fallen from favor, and soon the last remnant of the tax-farming system, the lottery farm, was abolished, and a nationwide ban on private gambling dens was imposed. Unfortunately for Zheng Zhiyong, they were the main cash cows of his business empire. Vajiravudh's government had let the axe fall on the secret society master. By the end of the reign, Zheng was well on the way to bankruptcy. When he passed away in 1935, his possessions were sold to compensate creditors. His family mansion was confiscated as state property and eventually converted into what is today the Phlapphlachai Police Station.

THE CHINESE CHAMBER OF COMMERCE

To run a successful Chinese-language newspaper and gain power and influence within the Chinese community in early twentieth-century Siam required more than the friendship of top Chinese revolutionaries and the regard of King Vajiravudh. The fundamental support that allowed those newspapers to survive and prosper actually came from their subscribers. Of course, it was necessary to please influential figures and successfully navigate political trends, as the examples of Zheng Zhiyong and Xiao Focheng illustrate. Even so, the support of a substantial block of readers was still essential to the success of any paper. Since most people in the Chinese community in Siam were immersed in trade and commerce, the newspaper most likely to become influential was the one issued by the Chinese Chamber of Commerce.

The Chinese Chamber of Commerce-CCC (Zhonghua Zongshang Hui) in Siam came into being in 1908 with the formal approval and recognition of the imperial government in Beijing.[16] The founders were the wealthiest and most respectable entrepreneurs of Bangkok's Chinatown. That they chose to register their organization with the Qing court indicates their conservative, pro-establishment tendencies. They were wary of Kang Youwei's reformist propaganda and Sun Yat-sen's revolutionary ideas. Despite not being particularly involved in political trends, the CCC's strong pro-establishment stance allowed them to perform a vital function in Sino-Siamese relations of this era. Their respectable status was appreciated by the Siamese socio-economic elite, and they had been formally recognized by Beijing, which allowed the CCC to act as the de facto Chinese consulate in Siam at a time when formal diplomatic relations had not yet been established between the two countries. This semi-diplomatic status eventually became an important asset for members of the CCC. It allowed them to become more directly involved in trade and diplomacy at the state-to-state level and enhanced their prestige in the Chinese community of Siam. A common newspaper editor like Xiao Focheng or even a secret society boss like Zheng Zhiyong could not attain this kind of distinguished social status.

The CCC was invested in maintaining a status quo of political stability that would allow their businesses to thrive in both China and Siam. They were willing to engage internationally recognized governments regardless of political ideology. In this respect, the CCC was one of the most adaptable of all ethnic Chinese organizations in Siam in the early twentieth century. They were willing to support and represent Yuan Shikai's government, even after he outlawed the Nationalists and banished Sun Yat-sen. This brought the CCC into conflict with Xiao Focheng, who was, toward the end of his career, among the most prominent, die-hard Tongmeng revolutionaries. However, the CCC, secure in its official recognition and support, almost always had the upper hand in any conflict arising in the Chinese community of Siam. The establishment of the first CCC-sponsored newspaper, the *Milky Way* (Tianhan bao) in 1913 did give rise to one notable squabble. From its very inception, *Milky Way* had threatened the dominance of Xiao's *Sino-Siam News* in Chinese media circles in Siam. With their formidable resources and connections, the CCC's *Milky Way* could easily outpublish and outcirculate *Sino-Siam News*. It was well within their power to drive Xiao completely out of business. The threat was pressing enough for Xiao to spell it out in his report to Vajiravudh's minister of interior, Chaophraya Yomarat:

> Most importantly, at the present, the CCC in our country [Siam] has
> established a new newspaper for circulation in Bangkok. This paper is
> called *Milky Way* and is the most widely distributed in Bangkok at
> this time. It has as many as four or five editors. They [CCC] registered
> the paper with the French Embassy, assigning a certain Mr. Cheng, a
> French-registered Thai man, as the manager of the paper. This was done
> so that the paper could avoid the restraints of Thai law. . . . You probably
> already know the intentions of the CCC. I am certain that this newspaper
> will soon be picking fights with the *Sino-Siam News* over the matter of
> Sino-Thai politics. I know very well that, at the moment, I am in need of
> an assistant and cannot afford to increase the pages of my paper because I
> lack sufficient printing blocks. The ones that I have are so worn out that
> the printed characters are hardly legible. I am lacking in all things needed
> for competing with my rivals.[17]

It is ironic that Xiao mentions how the CCC has "registered the paper with the French Embassy, assigning a certain Mr. Cheng, a Thai man registered with the French, as the manager of the paper" so as to "avoid the restraints of Thai law." Xiao himself was registered as a British subject, and his establishments enjoyed similar advantages of extraterritoriality. If his report was intended to evoke sympathy and increase the subsidy Xiao was receiving from the crown, it was probably not successful. *Sino-Siam News* continued on a path of steady decline for the rest of the decade and was shut down in the 1930s, not long after the end of Vajiravudh's reign. Xiao himself faded from the political scene in Siam as he became more involved in politics on the mainland. In 1924, he was appointed chairman of the Nationalist Party branch in Siam. In 1926, he became director of the party's Overseas Department.[18] After that, he spent more time in China until he was appointed chairman of a campaign to sell government bonds in Siam. Xiao held this position from the outbreak of the War of Resistance in 1937 until his death in the summer of 1939.[19]

The CCC continued to dominate the Chinese publishing scene in Siam through much of the 1920s. Then, in 1925, a new charismatic figure emerged in the ethnic Chinese political arena in Siam. Chen Shouming (1904–45) was born in Chaozhou and educated in Shantou and Hong Kong.[20] He migrated to Siam, where he made his fortune in what had become the typical local Chaozhou business route—operating rice mills, banks, insurance firms, shipping companies, and so on. In 1932, Chen Shouming became the youngest ever chairman of the Chinese Chamber of Commerce in Siam. In that same year, Chen further extended the influence of the CCC by accepting from the Nationalists the position of the Republic of China's trade commissioner to Siam. Chen, the chairman of the CCC, now also had the power to approve or deny entry into China of merchandise or cargo coming from Siam valued at over two hundred Chinese Nationalist dollars.[21] With its chairman serving as the Chinese Republic's trade commissioner in Siam, the CCC was functioning very much like the Chinese consulate it had always aspired to become. To promote his own agenda, Chen established the *Overseas Chinese Daily* (Huaqiao ribao), which soon overtook *Milky Way* as the CCC's official mouthpiece. In keeping with the CCC's pro-establishment stance, *Overseas Chinese Daily* had slightly favored Chiang Kai-shek from its inception in the early 1930s. The newspaper belonging to the Nationalist-appointed trade commissioner to Siam and supported the generalissimo's government as well as most of the Nationalist Central Committee's agenda, despite the internal conflicts that had plagued the party since Sun Yat-sen's death in the mid-1920s.

The CCC's pro–Chiang Kai-shek stance no doubt contributed to the ongoing feuds among contending power groups within the Nationalist government, especially the protectors of Xiao Focheng's legacy. They continued to uphold Xiao's political ideology, publishing right-wing Nationalist agendas in overseas Chinese journalistic circles in Siam. It is generally understood that this group evolved around the core leadership of the Chaozhou Association in Bangkok under the highly influential rice milling and shipping industry tycoon and multiple-term chairman of the Chaozhou Association, Yi Guangyan.[22] Yi was a close associate of Xiao and followed in his footsteps, supporting the Nationalist right-wingers, first under the leadership of Hu Hanmin, and later under the Guangxi clique. Like Xiao, Yi opposed Chiang Kai-shek's dictatorship and made known his dissatisfaction with Commissioner Chen's apparent attempt to monopolize political influence in the Chinese community in Siam. Yi Guangyan (1879–1939) carried on his legacy through the publication of *Siamese Capital Daily* (Xianjing ribao), which propagated the Nationalist right-wing agenda up to the outbreak of the Second World War in Thailand.

Despite the imminent threat of a common enemy—Japan, which had been invading Chinese territories since 1931—the conflict between the two nationalist papers, *Overseas Chinese Daily* and *Siamese Capital Daily* , and their owners, Chen Shouming and Yi Guangyan, persisted with great intensity through much of the 1930s. Some scholars have suggested that this ongoing feud eventually led to the tragic death of both leaders. Yi was assassinated in 1939, shortly before the war came to Thailand, and Chen met his demise in a similar manner in 1945, right at the conclusion of the Second World War. The tragic demise of both Chen and Yi, and the end of the Chinese-language newspapers that carried their legacy, bore so many similarities that it makes the study of overseas Chinese history of this particular period seem ironic, poetic, and even uncanny. Despite the demise of both Yi and *Siamese Capital Daily* in the late 1930s, a new newspaper took its place under the name *Central Plain Newspaper* (Zhongyuan bao). However, shortly after Japanese forces occupied Thailand, *Central Plain Newspaper* was seized by Japanese authorities and appropriated as the primary local mouthpiece for Japanese war propaganda in the Chinese language. Not surprisingly, it was also the only Chinese-language newspaper to remain in operation throughout the Pacific War. Since most of the staff members at *Central Plain Newspaper* were old hands from *Siamese Capital Daily* and former associates of the Chaozhou Association, rumors circulated through Bangkok's Chinatown that Yi's powerhouse and the newspaper that was meant to carry on his and Xiao's legacy had sold out to the Japanese.

Chen's *Overseas Chinese Daily* did not suffer the awkward fate of *Central Plain Newspaper*; like all other papers, it was shut down by authorities in the years leading up to the war. With the assassination of Yi, Chen, by default, became the most prominent leader of the ethnic Chinese community in Thailand during the war years. Chen was in a difficult situation. He had to negotiate with Japanese forces occupying Thailand for the sake of his own well-being and that of the ethnic Chinese community. At the same time, he had to facilitate his community's underground anti-Japanese activities. It was an unenviable position, risking execution by Japanese authorities for sabotaging their war effort but also facing assassination by patriotic ethnic Chinese for his apparently treasonous collaboration with the enemy.

It appears that in the end it was the latter that caught up with him. Like Yi Guangyan, Chen was assassinated, his illustrious career as entrepreneur and community leader violently cut short.

LEFT-WING CHINESE-LANGUAGE NEWSPAPERS

There were major moderate or right-wing newspapers closely tied to dominant figures in the Chinese community in Siam from the first decade of the twentieth century to the outbreak of the Pacific War. There were also, during the same period, well-known radical or left-leaning papers circulating among Chinese readers. Though never dominant in the political sphere, these other newspapers also played important roles in this turbulent period for the overseas Chinese of Thailand. Some had been involved in promoting underground anti-Japanese activities since the early 1930s. Some supported the propagation of communist, socialist, or anarchist agendas. A few supported the development of art and culture in the ethnic Chinese community, bringing about a golden age of overseas Chinese literature in Siam in the early 1930s. All these activities contributed significantly to the relationship between the Chinese community and the Thai and Chinese states. They also influenced the perceptions and understanding of the general public about this ethnic community and its flourishing press in the early twentieth century. In terms of anti-Japanese activities and the spread of communist propaganda, on the other hand, the voices of these radical and left-leaning papers would trouble relations between the ethnic Chinese community and the Thai military government throughout much of the Cold War era.

Among the most prominent of the so-called progressive newspapers was the *Chinese People's Newspaper* (Zhonghua minbao). It was first published in 1912 and continued in print until 1928; it was thus exceptionally durable, considering that the average run of most of its contemporaries did not exceed a decade. *Chinese People's Newspaper* was among the late investments of the former Bangkok Chinatown godfather Zheng Zhiyong, after *Enlightened South Daily* was sidelined by Xiao Focheng's *Sino-Siam Daily* and the reformist faction that Zheng had been backing failed to prevent Sun Yat-sen's revolutionaries from overthrowing the Qing dynasty. Aside from being more critical of Nationalist policies compared to most major Chinese-language newspapers in Siam of the 1910s and 1920s, *Chinese People's Newspaper* made a name for itself by supporting local overseas Chinese literary circles. In the early 1920s, the first serialized overseas Chinese novel, *The Mingming Bird* (Mingming niao) was published in book form after enjoying great success as short serialized episodes in *Chinese People's Newspaper*. The novel recounted the life story of an overseas Chinese who grew up in Burma, highlighting his suffering and his resistance to the forces of feudalism and Confucianism. It was received with heartfelt enthusiasm by the younger generation of ethnic Chinese in Siam. Starting from the success of serialized novels in *Chinese People's Newspaper*, the 1920s witnessed other best-sellers in Siam's ethnic Chinese community, such as *Sound of the Love Song* (Lafu ge sheng) and *Love God* (Ai shen).[23] This era also gave rise to a heated debate in these circles as to whether the novels of this diasporic community should be "looking toward the country of origin" (*mian xiang zu guo*) or "focusing on the here and now" (*ci shi ci di*).[24] Thus one party claimed that regardless of where overseas Chinese literature was actually written, the subject matter should always reflect the reality of life on the mainland. Another faction argued that overseas Chinese literature should reflect the realities of the temporal and spatial contexts experienced in overseas communities.

A sophisticated debate formed in these overseas circles. Thai authorities had never taken any notice of these untranslated Chinese novels, which were published specifically for the ethnic Chinese community. Since they were presented as fiction, they were not seriously monitored. Government documents from the National Archives in Bangkok provide no evidence of debates related to popular Chinese fiction published at this time. Literary criticism among Siam's local Chinese readers suggests that despite the strong influence of Chinese politics and the Thai state's seeming ignorance of Chinese literary trends, those on both sides of the debate were strongly committed. The propaganda of the Chinese and the Thai states aside, these novels make clear that not all ethnic Chinese were convinced that they would one day return to their ancestral homeland. At the same time, however, neither were they willing to completely forget China to invest absolutely in Siam in the 1920s. Safely presented in fictional form, these clear indications of sentiment could be freely expressed and serialized in newspapers. The novels' popularity suggested that their content resonated with readers of the Chinese community. These indicators from the mass media may even be more revealing than editorials, since serialized novels were not as closely monitored by state authorities.

The golden age of serialized novels in *Chinese People's Newspaper* was short lived. By the late 1920s, with the expanding Japanese dominance in the Republic of China's northeastern regions and rising fears of imminent Japanese invasion, political factions and cultural movements in all areas of the ethnic Chinese community in Siam were forced to unite behind the anti-Japanese cause. Literary expression during the prewar years focused on patriotism and national salvation. *Chinese People's Newspaper* joined in anti-Japanese activism, publishing feverish patriotic propaganda and advertising boycotts of Japanese goods and businesses. This activism put the paper at odds with Siamese authorities, who were trying hard to keep the country out of the intensifying Sino-Japanese conflict. Eventually, *Chinese People's Newspaper* was shut down, most likely for publishing the following paragraph in June 1928: "People whose hearts are dead like to act against the norm and dishonor all Chinese people. The more this is discussed, the more hatred [I] feel. Beloved compatriots, Zhang Zuolin was assassinated because he was a traitor. In the same way, anyone else who attempts to sell his country must also be eliminated. Beloved countrymen, let us kill enemies of the nation that are far away from Beijing, and let us eliminate enemies of the nation that are closer among us."[25]

This was clearly in response to the news that a train explosion had killed the Manchurian warlord Grand Marshal Zhang Zuolin earlier that month. The writer confidently assumes that the assassination occurred because Zhang was a traitor to the Chinese nation. Soon after the article appeared in *Chinese People's Newspaper*, a series of death threats and assaults were carried out against ethnic Chinese merchants who had been trading and transporting Japanese goods in Siam. With the closure of *Chinese People's Newspaper*, the politics of Chinese newspapers in Siam became increasingly polarized. By the early 1930s, the pro-Nationalist press, particularly *Republican Daily* (Minguo ribao), nearly monopolized the publication of mainstream serialized novels. Established in 1935, *Republican Daily* made a name for itself through the publication of specialized arts and literature editions—*Hesitation* (Panghuang) and *The Prairie* (Pingwu)—and a literary theory edition, *The Wild* (Tianye).[26]

The 1920s also witnessed a flurry of radical left-wing publications. A few of these newspapers, though short-lived, made a significant impression on the political scene of that era. The most notable was Tan Zhensan's *Sojourners' Voice* (Qiaosheng). Tan was a colorful character who frequently found himself at odds with Siamese law enforcement in the early twentieth century due to his radical political perspectives. Considering the social norms of the day, *Sojourners' Voice* was no less outrageous than its creator, advocating everything from radical feminism to the organization of a May Day parade through the streets of Bangkok's Chinatown. The publishers received frequent warnings from authorities and were often criticized by established mainstream publications like Xiao Focheng's *Sino-Siam News*. Tan was registered as a Dutch subject, so *Sojourners' Voice* enjoyed extraterritorial privileges, like most of the major Chinese newspapers mentioned earlier in this chapter. Even so, left-wing publications tended to be more vulnerable to state prosecution than their pro-establishment counterparts. Radical leftist newspapers were not shy about attacking even European imperialist powers and their rapacious capitalist agents, many of whom were perceived to be among the root causes of China's decades of humiliation and suffering. *Sojourners' Voice* was forced to close its doors in 1926, after Tan was deported for his involvement in a series of protests against Britain's involvement in the May 30 massacre of Chinese demonstrators in Shanghai in 1925.[27]

The ethnic Chinese leftist press had neither the wide-ranging influence nor the longevity of the more conservative mainstream papers of Bangkok's Chinatown. Left-wing newspapers tended to be more heavily involved in political movements, fighting for China's national salvation with anti-imperialist movements, boycotting Japanese goods and businesses, engaging in fund-raising activities, and so on. It was precisely their wholehearted involvement in these matters that led the authorities to waste no time in shutting them down. Nonetheless, the fact that they were terminated so quickly may suggest the threat felt by Siamese authorities. The voices of such publications did not go unheard in Siam's ethnic Chinese community during this turbulent and vulnerable period.

KING VAJIRAVUDH'S MEDIA CAMPAIGN: THE ABSOLUTE MONARCH IN THE NEWSPAPER

King Vajiravudh Rama VI was the first Siamese monarch to take full advantage of the news media in the early twentieth century. Strengthening the spirit of Siamese nationalism was the fundamental goal of his reign and the focus of his media campaigns. He was, with good reason, less interested in countering the Chinese nationalist sentiments that were rising in the journalistic circles of that era. The feverish Chinese nationalist sentiments being stirred up during Vajiravudh's reign were published in Chinese and had little or no immediate impact on the non-Chinese majority. Furthermore, Siamese people generally—then as now—had little or no interest in reading. Vajiravudh's concern with publishing was aimed first and foremost at winning the support of Siamese and ethnic Chinese elite classes, those actively involved in the public sphere, and the ever-growing educated urban middle class. The public expression of Chinese nationalist sentiments generally remained confined to Chinese-language publications. Chinese nationalist campaigns were no threat because they were published only in Chinese. The king cared little whether the Qing dynasty would be overthrown by the Xinhai Revolution or whether Sun Yat-sen or Yuan Shikai became president of the Chinese republic. As long as the news and accompanying propaganda were circulated only in the Chinese-language press, this stream of controversy and discord did not threaten the stability of his realm. It was only when well-educated Chinese ("Sino-Siamese") publishers like Xiao Focheng began putting out Thai-language editions, cultivating Thai readers, and claiming credibility for their views about Siam that the king became concerned and felt the need to publicly express his dissent.

Throughout his reign, Vajiravudh faced difficulties in gaining the respect and winning the cooperation of the upper echelons of the Siamese aristocracy. This was primarily due to an unfortunate dislocation in Chulalongkorn's reform of the succession system that brought Vajiravudh to the throne in the first place. The king's support for the free press in Siam was not merely a fashionable move to demonstrate how thoroughly modernized the Oxford-educated monarch was. The free press was supposed to provide an alternative platform upon which the king—like any other literate person in his realm—could put forth his ideas and receive feedback from the reading public, most of whom belonged to the educated urban elite, including the uncles and brothers in his royal cabinet whose relationship with the young monarch was deeply problematic from the beginning of his reign. As it turned out, however, some of the most responsive readers were members of the local ethnic Chinese community.

VAJIRAVUDH AND XIAO FOCHENG

In recent decades, Vajiravudh has come under harsh criticism from historians and political scientists for being racist or, more specifically, anti-Chinese. The criticisms are well grounded in newspaper articles, short stories, novels, plays, and operettas penned by Vajiravudh himself, which describe the Chinese in less than admiring terms. Most notable among the king's anti-Chinese oeuvres is *Jews of the Orient*, first published in the royally sponsored *Nangsuephim Thai* newspaper in 1914.[28] Published under the monarch's favorite pen name for sociopolitical critiques, Atsawaphahu, the piece makes a nasty comparison between the ethnic Chinese in Siam and the Jews in Europe and warns of the perils that await the nation should

Thai people continue to allow the Chinese to dominate their economy. The following excerpt illustrates this theme:

> The Chinese did not come with the intention to settle down in [any foreign] land, and refuse to become true citizens of other countries. They always feel like speakers of a foreign language. Although some try to assimilate, the secret society leaders do not allow them to do so. It could not be denied that they generate wealth from the land, but it should not be forgotten that they also transport that wealth out of the country. As for the part that they must spend in their host country, they try their best to spend as little as possible. The food and utensils they consume in everyday life are also imported from China. Since this is the case, the Chinese must be considered as those who siphon the wealth of their host nation [to their country of origin]. They are like vampires that suck human blood.[29]

Such diatribes have earned him the disfavor of many in international academia. On the other hand, his words have been taken out of context and remarks he made that were friendly to ethnic Chinese in Siam not credited.[30] To be sure, anti-Chinese material does turn up frequently in Vajiravudh's prolific writings. However, a closer study of the reign, the context and consequences of the king's anti-Chinese campaigns, and the monarch's actual policies regarding the ethnic Chinese reveals that his harsh public statements were accompanied by restraint and even kindness in action.

Throughout Vajiravudh's reign, there was little policy or legislation to back up the king's incendiary rhetoric against the ethnic Chinese community. No Chinese schools or Chinese newspapers were shut down. Xiao Focheng, who dared to contradict and criticize the anti-Chinese writings of Atsawaphahu in his Thai-language newspaper, *Sino-Siam Daily*, continued to publish freely, and the king protected him from prosecution. In 1915, Prince Thewawong, the minister of foreign affairs, proposed that Xiao be deported from the kingdom because his inflammatory criticism of Atsawaphahu's writings and his staunch support for the republican cause in China posed a serious threat to national security.[31] Vajiravudh responded in a tone that is both sympathetic to and protective of the Chinese journalist: "[Xiao Focheng] is only Chinese by trade. That is, he earns his living by being a Kuomintang leader. However, he personally does not regard himself as Chinese at all. He has no serious ties in China, neither home nor possessions there. Also, his wife is genuinely Thai. If he were deported from Siam, for whatever reason, he would definitely fall into grave difficulty."[32]

It remains unclear whether the monarch was aware of Xiao's close ties with a few of the top Nationalist leaders. Nonetheless, when all aspects of the crown's relationship with this ethnic Chinese leader are taken into consideration, it is clear that Xiao was much more useful to the king as an outspoken journalist than he would be as a martyr to legal prosecution or deportation.

Vajiravudh lashed out against the ethnic Chinese in his newspaper articles because Xiao Focheng had crossed the critical language boundary: he had started publishing *Chino-Siam Daily*, a Thai-language version of the *Sino-Siam Daily*. Expressed in Thai, Xiao's political perspectives—which Prince Thewawong considered seditious and threatening to national security—started reaching Thai audiences. Although readers of Thai-language newspapers represented a small fraction of the kingdom's total population, those readers made up the majority of the ruling class—many of whom were already dissatisfied with the young monarch and his "peculiar" British plays and games.[33] There was already much evidence to confirm that the plotters of the foiled 1912 coup had read and been influenced by the political ideas circulating in Xiao's Thai-language publications. Even so, Vajiravudh chose not to ban the *Sino-Siam Daily* or deport its owner-editor. Such draconian measures would only have made the king appear autocratic and repressive, and would have driven potentially seditious publications underground, making them more difficult to control. The best approach, it seemed, was to engage in open debate in the newspaper. By doing so, Vajiravudh presented himself as an enlightened monarch and a champion of the free press. He also gained an extended platform from which to discredit Chinese revolutionaries and refute their ideology. Moreover, Atsawaphahu's fiery and public journalistic attacks reminded Xiao to be discrete and respectfully cautious. In his political arguments in the press, he repeatedly supports the monarchy, always including a disclaimer insisting that revolution is only suitable in the Chinese context: Siam is already good as it is, and it would be a complete waste of time for Siamese people to even think of changing their country's political system.

Vajiravudh's successful policy regarding the Thai-language publications of Chinese journalists also included buying them off and pitting one Chinatown power clique against another. Xiao Focheng was paid by the court to spy on and report the plans and activities of the top echelons of the Chinese community in Siam. He tipped off the Crown to the plans of secret society boss and reformist Zheng Zhiyong to sell a majority of shares in his shipping company to the municipal government of Canton. Zheng was discredited by this leak and undermined by his rival. Vajiravudh's stron-gest impression about his kingdom's ethnic Chinese was that "they tended to be divided into groups and factions" and that "each group or each fac-tion will try its best to unscrupulously condemn its rival."[34] It was in the monarch's best interests that the Chinese in his realm remain divided and continue to bicker among themselves. Hence, Xiao continued through most of Vajiravudh's reign to receive subsidies in return for inside infor-mation on developments in ethnic Chinese political circles. Of course, the court did not act on every accusation Xiao made against his competitors. The Chinese Chamber of Commerce, for example, prospered in ethnic Chinese political circles without posing any threat to the Crown. They were allowed to slowly put Xiao out of business without any hindrance from authorities. The newspaper industry in Siam was at a fledging stage in the early twentieth century, its readership limited to small circles of well-educated urban residents. The Chinese-language press had an even narrower reach. Ethnic Chinese journalists, secretly subsidized by the court, continued to publish opposing views to discredit each other. There was little Chinese-language publications could do to threaten the political well-being of the absolute monarchy as a whole. Journalists like Xiao Focheng who decided to switch to Thai-language publications were discredited by Vajiravudh's declamatory rhetoric or fell in line in the face of tempting government subsidies.

CONTESTED NATIONALISMS IN THE THAI PRINT MEDIA

Surprisingly, the initial struggle between the monarch and Chinese pub-lishers to seize the Thai press as a propaganda mouthpiece for their preferred brand of nationalism—republican Chinese versus Siamese royalist—instigated a wider debate in Siam on sociopolitical issues as well as what the modern nation and nationalism should mean from the perspective of the Thai public.

Printed materials from the end of Vajiravudh's reign in the 1920s to 1932—including satirical essays, cartoons, caricatures, and editorials—present views of society and politics differing from that of the monarch. Such materials show that monarchs of the Chakri dynasty—specifically, Mongkut, Chulalongkorn, and Vajiravudh—were not the only contributors to the idea of Siam as a modern nation-state. There were many competing views on what the modern Thai nation should look like and which defini-tion and direction for Thai nationalism could be agreed upon. At least for much of the 1920s, sociopolitical debates in the journalistic arena in Siam extended beyond the monarch and Chinese entrepreneurs and journalists. Although not all of the contributors can be definitely identified, the tone and language used in the articles as well as the topics discussed aim to attract the interest of the Thai general public. Some articles are severely critical of the monarch—especially Vajiravudh—and some oppose the influence of the ethnic Chinese community in the Thai economy and even refer to their ability to bribe high-ranking officials of the court.[35]

The assortment of critical publications in circulation between the beginning of Vajiravudh's reign and the Siamese Revolution of 1932 indicates the exchange of ideas about society, politics, and the monarchy of a community of urban-educated Thais through the printed media. That they were not all banned or censored or completely destroyed by the absolutist state—in as much as there could remain a whole archive of them for research nearly a century later—is in itself impressive. The fact that they came into existence following the earlier journalistic debate between Vajiravudh and the ethnic Chinese press, and that a significant part of their social criticism concerned the privileges of foreign publishers who were protected by extraterritoriality, suggests that this latest public sphere of Thai journalistic circles—a new imagined community arising from yet another incarnation of print capitalism—was instigated and greatly influenced by the propaganda contest between Siamese and Chinese nation-building forces of the early twentieth century.

THE CONUNDRUM OF VAJIRAVUDH'S ANTI-CHINESE RACISM

Aside from *Jews of the Orient*, the sixth king wrote many other fictional and nonfictional pieces criticizing two important groups in the Chinese community: those registered as colonial subjects and those who appeared to support Sun Yat-sen's republicanism. The tone and language of the king's rhetoric in these works are undeniably racist. How, then, could there have been an underlying alliance between the monarchy and the ethnic Chinese entrepreneurial class?

There are a few explanations. First, the ethnic Chinese are a diverse group including people who themselves or whose family came to Siam at various times and who belong to different social and financial strata, work in different professions, maintain different sorts of relationships with mainland China, and subscribe to different ideologies. Vajiravudh aimed his racist criticism at two subgroups: rich colonial subjects and poor political activists. Chinese colonial subjects, on the one hand, tended to belong to the upper middle class or upper class, with more career opportunities and more chances for social mobility due to their privileges as colonial subjects. Chinese republican nationalists, on the other hand, ranged from dock workers to schoolteachers and newspaper editors. Less privileged than the first group, they often had stronger political convictions, which could lead to radical activities with serious political implications. The two groups' relationship with neighboring colonial powers also differs significantly. While Chinese colonial subjects enjoyed a certain degree of protection in accordance with their extraterritorial rights, Chinese republican nationalists were considered dangerous elements by most state authorities.

Secondly, Vajiravudh's hostility toward these two groups had different motivations. He inveighed against the Chinese colonial subjects out of frustration at not being able to control them due to their extraterritorial rights. By contrast, the working-class Chinese republicans could possibly be controlled through the Thai judicial system or in cooperation with neighboring colonial powers. Yet there was a risk that their ideas and example could influence the native population and eventually result in some sort of republican-inspired political uprising against the monarchy in Siam. Essays such as *Jews of the Orient* can be seen as challenging the "good Chinese" to prove their loyalty to the crown by avoiding the typical Chinese behavior described in the article. For instance, they could donate more money to support royal projects, thus proving that they were not "vampires" that sucked the lifeblood out of the Siamese economy without giving anything back in return.[36]

Finally, as in many other respects, the situation in Siam was not so different from that in neighboring colonial territories. Colonial regimes often maintained a special relationship with their ethnic Chinese population because of its economic importance, elevating the sociopolitical status of the Chinese elite, yet at the same time adopting extremely racist attitudes toward the Chinese as a whole. Vajiravudh's anti-Chinese nationalism was inspired primarily by the Victorian British model, in which anti-Semitism was a widespread trend.[37] In the hierarchy of the colonial world, even though the Chinese were often preferred to local natives for certain positions of importance in the economic arena—tax farmers, trade agents, and so on—the relationship between even the elite Chinese and their colonial masters was far from equal. There had always been a pronounced racist divide between the governing class of white European imperial subjects and the ethnic Chinese colonial subjects.

Vajiravudh saw himself as equivalent to a European colonial master, not an Asian variant. The Surname Act was accompanied by a long treatise penned by Vajiravudh himself explaining that the Thai surname (nam sakun) was in the tradition of modern nations such as Great Britain and not the same as the Chinese tradition of clan names, which, according to the monarch, represented the culture of a much more primitive society.[38] Late in 1917, when the Siamese government finally agreed to send troops to participate in the First World War, the monarch went to great lengths to make sure that his officers were not mixed in with the troops of laborers from China and Indochina. Siam was contributing to the war as a modern sovereign nation on a standing equal to France and Britain, and its soldiers should not be treated the same as colonial conscripts or Chinese coolie laborers.[39]

In sum, many factors lay behind Vajiravudh's infamous anti-Chinese writings. They challenged insecure Chinese businessmen to donate more money to prove their goodwill to the Crown. They were part of a divide-and-rule approach designed to gain popularity with the impoverished masses by demeaning the national creditors who were the ethnic Chinese. They emulated racist trends in contemporary British politics while setting his royal government apart as the superior masters of their Chinese capitalist cronies, similar to how the colonial hierarchy was constructed in neighboring European colonies in Southeast Asia. Most importantly, however, the extreme anti-Chinese narrative did not negate the possibility of a mutually beneficial alliance between the Crown and the Chinese capitalist.

POST-VAJIRAVUDH MEDIA CONTROL

If Vajiravudh's manipulation of the free press could be considered a relative success in terms of undermining the unity and political influence of the ethnic Chinese press, the same could not be said of his attempts to win over the upper echelons of the Siamese ruling class through his prolific literary output. By the conclusion of his reign in 1925, dissent was boiling up among senior members of the court and in the armed forces. The prolonged economic depression that followed the Great War made matters even worse at the end of the reign of a monarch who had so frequently been criticized for his lavish spending. Vajiravudh's younger brother, Prajadhipok, ascended the throne as King Rama VII at a time when the monarchy's popularity was perhaps at its lowest point in the kingdom's modern history. Prajadhipok aligned himself with a strongly conservative government made up mostly of his uncles and half-brothers, and made clear to the publishing community from very early on that his reign would not be nearly as permissive as that of his late brother.[40] Almost immediately, *Sino-Siam Daily* and *United Sojourners' Newspaper* (Lianqiao bao), another left-leaning publication, were investigated and ordered to temporarily cease publication due to their provocative reports on British involvement in the May 30 massacre of Chinese demonstrators in Shanghai.[41] Soon after, *Sojourners' Voice* was ordered to close its doors for publishing an anti-Western article.[42] In most cases, the closures were temporary, and leading papers, such as *Sino-Siam Daily*, were allowed to resume publication after a suspension. Nonetheless, state monitoring of Chinese publishers became much more intense. As political instability in Siam increased along with the threat of Japanese political and economic dominance in China, the publishing industry in Siam lost support in the ethnic Chinese community. Xiao Focheng decided to relocate and in 1930 accepted a political position in China, resulting in the final closure of *Sino-Siam Daily*.[43]

Although Prajadhipok was not nearly as forward looking as his brother in terms of tolerance for the free press, it is important to note that the most draconian practices of press censorship and the darkest times in the history of Chinese publication in Siam came after the People's Party Revolution of 1932. That seizure of power was, ironically, supposed to transform the kingdom into a constitutional monarchy governed by a parliamentary democratic system.[44] It was, however, part and parcel of a general intensification of anti-Chinese policies from the mid-1930s to the conclusion of the Second World War. On the one hand, the more repressive policies might be attributed to the usual repercussions of a major regime change, in which the newly established government is unstable and easily threatened by remnants of the old regime. There was some official paranoia in regard to upper-class ethnic Chinese, who had long cultivated intimate relations with the old regime. On the other hand, it is important to note that one of the first and most notable achievements of the People's Party government was their successful negotiation with major powers of the early twentieth century to abolish extraterritorial rights for colonial subjects in Siam. Consequently, owners and editors of Chinese newspapers, most of whom had enjoyed privileges and protection all through the reigns of Vajiravudh and Prajadhipok as a result of their colonial status, could be more easily prosecuted and penalized in the Thai judicial system. In other words, unlike the monarchs, leaders of the revolution had no legal reason to exercise restraint in their control over the foreign language press in Siam.

Heavy-handed censorship and mass closings of Chinese newspapers in the late 1930s could also be attributed to the Thai government's relations with Japan, as Thailand responded to increasing Japanese influence in East and Southeast Asian regional politics in the years leading up to the outbreak of the Pacific War. The country was also gripped by a second wave of Thai nationalism that accompanied Premier Field Marshal Phibunsongkhram's rise in 1938. Repression of local ethnic Chinese, the influence of Japanese imperial power, and the nationalist policies of the field marshal all made the late 1930s and early to mid-1940s one of the darkest and most difficult periods in the history of overseas Chinese publishing in Thailand. By August 1939, all but one Chinese-language newspaper—the *Central Plain Newspaper*—had been permanently closed down by the government. Two years later, Japan began its occupation of Thailand. By early 1942, *Central Plain Newspaper* had been absorbed to become yet another voice in favor of the Greater East Asian Co-Prosperity Sphere.[45]

Another interesting aspect of the history of publication in Thailand during this second era of nationalism is the fact that not unlike the earlier campaigns of Vajiravudh, nationalist campaigns in the era of Prime Minister Phibunsongkhram did not rely heavily upon print media to diffuse propaganda to the masses at the grassroots level. To be sure, Luang Wichitwathakan, the People's Party's ideological mentor and Phibunsongkhram's chief propagandist, was heavily influenced by Vajiravudh's nationalist propaganda, as presented through Atsawaphahu's regular sociopolitical critiques in *Nangsuephim Thai*: "About twenty years ago, when China had just changed its political system, I was [only] fifteen years old. However, I enjoyed reading Atsawaphahu's debates against articles published in the *Sino-Siam Daily*. I read them over and over until I could almost remember every single word of Atsawaphahu's arguments."[46]

Like Vajiravudh, Luang Wichitwathakan was aware that Thailand's active reading culture was mostly limited to the urban educated upper and middle classes. However, the nation's system of compulsory education represented an ideal delivery apparatus for the nationalist message, which could be communicated by word of mouth to every member of every class in every corner of the kingdom. Just as Vajiravudh had made use of songs and plays, the new regime harnessed nonliterary forms of cultural media in its campaign. Thailand of the Phibunsongkhram-Wichitwathakan era experienced a powerful wave of cultural propaganda—including plays, songs, dances, and radio shows—all carrying strong nationalist messages. Another important piece of cultural propaganda during this period involved the Cultural Mandates of the State, a set of state-sanctioned cultural norms and values decreed by the government. These mandates were to function in the same way as customs and traditions. There were no official penalties for not abiding by them, yet one might be shunned in polite society or cease to advance in one's profession by failing to act according to these state-established national values. Considering that customs and traditions are normally established in a society over time, issuing the Cultural Mandates of the State was the government's way of creating instant customs and traditions. Altogether, twelve such mandates were declared between 1939 and 1942 (table 2.1).

Although none of the mandates explicitly targeted the Chinese community, some affected the ethnic Chinese more than other segments of society. The third, for example, required that all citizens of Thailand have names that were meaningful in the Thai language. Thus the majority of ethnic

TABLE 2.1. Cultural Mandates of the State

No.	Date	Matter(s) of concern
1.	June 24, 1939	Renaming of the state from Siam to Thailand, the citizens from Siamese to Thai, and the nationality from Siamese to Thai
2.	July 3, 1939	Protection of the state from dangers that may occur
3.	August 2, 1939	Naming of Thai individuals
4.	September 8, 1939	Paying homage to the national flag, the national anthem, and the royal anthem
5.	November 1, 1939	Encouraging Thai people to consume goods that originated or had been assembled in Thailand
6.	December 10, 1939	Lyrics and melody of the national anthem
7.	March 21, 1940	Encouraging Thai people to cooperate in state-building
8.	April 1, 1940	The royal anthem
9.	June 24, 1940	Thai language, Thai alphabet, and civic duties
10.	January 15, 1941	The clothing of Thai people
11.	September 8, 1941	The daily routine of Thai people
12.	January 28, 1942	Aid and protection for children, the elderly, and the handicapped

Source: Charnvit Kasetsiri, *Political History of Thailand, 1932–1957* (Bangkok: Thammasat University Press, 2001), 199–200.

Chinese who had acquired Thai citizenship had to abandon their Chinese names and officially change to names with proper meanings in the Thai language. The fifth attacked the Chinese custom of importing consumer products from China. The ninth limited the use of Chinese as the language of instruction in Chinese schools. Other mandates allowed for the promulgation of further anti-Chinese laws and regulations. For instance, the second mandate supported Phibunsongkhram's declaration that certain strategic military areas were off-limits for foreigners—the vast majority of whom were ethnic Chinese who still maintained their Chinese citizenship. The seventh mandate encouraged Thai nationals to enter professions traditionally dominated by ethnic Chinese, such as food vending and animal slaughter.

The mainstream narrative on the history of the ethnic Chinese in Thailand highlights Vajiravudh's reign and Phibunsongkhram's prewar and wartime regime as two peaks in anti-Chinese policies of the Thai state. There is sound evidence to support this line of reasoning. As mentioned, Vajiravudh's influence on Wichitwathakan's propaganda is evident, even self-proclaimed. In the context of both domestic and global politics, it is obvious that the intended purpose of this anti-Chinese rhetoric in the time of Vajiravudh and Phibunsongkhram was more nuanced. The propaganda machines of the Phibunsongkhram government reproduced and publicized much of what is known today as Vajiravudh's anti-Semitic or anti-Chinese propaganda in all forms—newspaper articles, essays, plays, operettas, short stories, and so on—to reach the masses more effectively, especially in the period leading up to and beginning Thailand's official involvement in the Second World War. Thus a notorious piece such as *Jews of the Orient* might not have been written with a mass audience in mind when it was first published in 1914.

Vajiravudh penned anti-Chinese pieces to challenge the Chinese business elite to prove their loyalty to Siam and devotion to the Siamese monarch. Not only did he publish endorsements of and thank-you messages to Chinese tycoons, who then donated generously to royal projects, but Vajiravudh even allowed Xiao Focheng to engage him in a protracted public debate concerning the logic, reasoning, and propriety of what many viewed as the king's journalistic attacks on the ethnic Chinese. The spirit of Vajiravudh's challenge is very different from Wichitwathakan's public statement that the Thai government might need to consider dealing with the "Chinese problem" in the same way the German Nazi government was dealing with the "Jewish problem."[47] While Wichitwathakan was influenced by Vajiravudh's comparison of the Chinese in Siam to the Jews in Europe, the context in which he alluded to this comparison was very different from that of 1914, when *Jews of the Orient* was first published. In Wichit-wathakan's time Thailand was about to enter an alliance with Japan in the Second World War. Japan was not only a major ally of Nazi Germany, which was deporting Jews, but also the most formidable enemy of China. While Vajiravudh's attacks on the Chinese could be seen as an unethical and irresponsible money-making scheme, Wichitwathakan's anti-Chinese propaganda during Phibunsongkhram's regime was a demand that the Thai public rise up against a minority that was ethnically and culturally linked with an enemy nation.

A THREE-DIMENSIONAL IMAGINED COMMUNITY EMERGING FROM THE COLONIAL ERA

The print media contributed significantly to building the modern Thai nation-state. The concept of an imagined community coming into being through the rise of print capitalism is relevant in the Thai case from the 1910s to the conclusion of the Greater East Asian War. However, the Thai nation-state, unlike classical European examples and other regions of Southeast Asia, embarked on the treacherous nation-building journey as a marginally independent kingdom at the tail end of the colonial era, when her immediate neighbors had already been colonized by Western imperialist empires.[48] Consequently, the imagined community that was to become the Thai nation did not come into being in a vacuum, but arose amid the collapse and rising of old and new empires all around.

Like the beginnings of nationalist education, nation-building through the print media in Siam began as a response to the rise of Chinese nationalism in the early twentieth century. The nationalizing trend of Chinese newspapers in Siam in turn prompted Vajiravudh to become the only Thai monarch to throw himself into the highly publicized arena of journalistic debate and propaganda. The fiery debate that followed in daily newspapers circulating widely in the capital inspired the educated Thai urban middle class to become more involved and invested in voicing their views through the print media. This inspiration is evident in the proliferation of Thai-language newspapers and the rise of polemical essays, editorials, cartoons, and caricatures published in daily papers and periodicals from the early 1920s up to the Revolution of 1932. Vajiravudh's use of print media to propagate his royalist nationalist ideology and to attack the competing views of ethnic Chinese journalist intellectuals opened up a new space for public debate that allowed even more diverse ideas concerning the modern Thai nation-state and nationalism to develop and proliferate. This new public sphere facilitated the building of the new Thai nation of the People's Party following the overthrow of the monarchy in 1932.

Perhaps the greatest irony of print capitalism's relationship to the Thai nation is that the freedom of expression that had allowed the press to become such a powerful nation-building apparatus came to an end soon after the establishment of the more egalitarian modern nation-state that so many in the fledging Thai journalistic circles of the 1920s had aspired to. The freedom of expression that allowed cartoonists to publish images of the royalist ruling class (including Vajiravudh himself) as monitor lizards was specific to the colonial era.[49] Popular publications in early twentieth-century in Siam were almost always owned, at least in name, by individuals registered as colonial subjects. Consequently, the publications enjoyed a certain degree of protection based on the extraterritorial rights of their owners. Even if, as often was the case, the Siamese ruling elite desired to shut down a publication or persecute the owner of a blasphemous newspaper, it was often not worth the trouble. Hence, once the absolute monarch was overthrown and the revolutionary regime managed to establish a supposedly more egalitarian, territorial nation-state by abolishing extraterritoriality, there remained no external powers to keep them from shutting down publications and persecuting journalists they deemed a threat of their rule.

The colonial era in which the last absolutist monarchs of Siam—Chulalongkorn, Vajiravudh, and Prajadhipok—came into being, rose to power, and declined was highly hierarchical. Yet, amid its inequality and unfairness, there was a degree of freedom and flexibility not found in the more egalitarian, constitutional regime of the People's Party. Journalistic freedom of expression, freedom to travel across borders, and free trade benefited certain privileged classes throughout the colonial era. These classes and their freedoms would also encounter major transformations in the new territorial nation of post-1932 Siam. People were freed from the whims of the absolutist elite only to be constrained by challenging conditions for business in the capitalized world of the mid-twentieth century.

CHAPTER THREE

ECONOMIC THAI-IFICATION

Dismantling the Crown and the Capitalists

THE TERM *ECONOMIC THAI-IFICATION*, WHICH DESCRIBES A harsh attempt at social engineering by the Thai government from the late 1930s through the Second World War, assumes that the Thai economy prior to Phibunsongkhram's era had been dominated by the ethnic Chinese.[1] The first Phibunsongkhram administration attempted to undermine ethnic Chinese control of the Thai economy to pressure this influential minority to stop resisting assimilation.[2] Thai-ification of the economy was launched via a series of blatantly anti-Chinese policies. For example, a number of professions that had been popular among Chinese migrant workers were suddenly reserved for Thai nationals. Then, toward the end of the Second World War, anti-alien strategic areas were established on short notice, forcing Chinese nationals to evacuate all major urban centers in Thailand. Such measures were intended to pressure the Chinese in Thailand to assimilate, giving up their Chinese citizenship and becoming Thai citizens. By pushing local Chinese entrepreneurs out of the picture, the state also hoped to encourage non-Chinese Siamese to try their hand at commerce.[3]

Although the so-called economic Thai-ification process failed to transform the Thai economy, it did make life difficult for the ethnic Chinese in Thailand, who found ways—mostly through bribery, systems of nominees, and the shadow economy—to circumvent the clumsy obstacles fabricated by nationalist state policies. Once the war ended with the defeat of Japan and the demise of the Phibunsongkhram wartime government, most anti-Chinese regulations and policies were discontinued. Ultimately, ethnic Chinese dominance of the Thai economy remained relatively intact.

There are problems, however, with characterizing the economic reforms during the prewar and wartime Phibunsongkhram regime as "Thai-ification." Most prominently this terminology suggests that this was a nationalist policy that struck back against foreign aggressors who tried to manipulate and control the Thai economy. However, so-called Thai-ification of the economy was in fact part of a wider policy framework of the People's Party regime to identify the nation and establish a nationalist narrative that did not revolve around the monarchy. Hence, the dismantling of ethnic Chinese dominance in the economy had much more to do with dismantling the dominance of the old royalist elite that made up the other half of that formidable alliance, rather than being an attack on external powers—either the Chinese state or the numerous colonial empires present in Southeast Asia at the time.

At least since the ruling Chakri dynasty came into existence in 1782, the ethnic Chinese had constituted the merchant class for Southeast Asia. Prior to the Opium Wars—the Bowring Treaty of 1855 is the apt historical marker in the case of Siam—the Chinese served as the Crown's agents in the China trade through the tribute system.[4] After the Opium Wars forced the opening of British treaty ports in China and the Bowring Treaty ended the Siamese crown's monopoly of international trade, the ethnic Chinese switched to serving in Thailand as agents of the British, and many registered as colonial subjects so as to enjoy extraterritorial rights in Siam. Yet the courts of the nineteenth- and twentieth-century Chakri kings—Rama IV through Rama VII—continued to employ ethnic Chinese to serve the court in various economic-related functions. In fact, the Chakri court benefited from both its submission to the British Empire's domineering influence in trade and politics across the Indian and Pacific Oceans and its time-honored alliance with the Chinese business elite, who were, by the dawn of the twentieth century, even better equipped to serve the court in its dealings across the South China Sea and beyond through their newly acquired colonial subject status.

A major achievement of the People's Party regime was negotiating the abolition of extraterritorial rights in 1938. Phibunsongkhram's economic reform policies did not set out to bring British colonial trade dominance in the Far East (with its network of colonial Chinese traders) to its demise, as the feverishly anti-imperialist nationalist propaganda of Wichitwathakan suggested. What was really going on was an attempt to dismantle the ethnic Chinese advantages linked with the old colonial system so as to weaken the economic dominance of the old elite, which relied on this formidable alliance between the royalists and the Chinese entrepreneurial classes. Economic Thai-ification was therefore primarily a domestic struggle in which the revolutionary constitutional regime attempted to seize economic dominance from the already greatly weakened monarchists. Surprisingly, despite their political dominance as well as absolute control of the military in the domestic arena, the People's Party under Phibunsongkhram ultimately failed to steer the economy away from the control of the royalist-Chinese Alliance. This failure eventually resulted in the fall of the People's Party and the royalists' return to dominance after the Second World War and continuing throughout the Cold War period.

EMERGING FROM A CHINA-CENTERED ECONOMY

In Siam, as in much of the rest of premodern peninsular Southeast Asia, the key to acquiring and maintaining political power had been the ability to collect, increase, and control scarce manpower. Among Siam's most effective methods of managing this was the corvée labor system, which had stabilized Siamese feudal society since at least the highly commercialized period of the mid-eighteenth century. All male commoners of working age (ages fifteen to seventy) were required to perform public service during designated periods every year or at other times required by the state. Such work included building infrastructure—roads, canals, city walls, and so on—as well as military service. The period of service varied according to various socioeconomic and political circumstances. A man could be liable for up to six months of service each year, serving one month on, one month off, to allow him to tend to his fields and family. The corvée system not only provided the state with regular access to free labor for state projects but also helped the state control the movement of its subjects. Men who owed service under the corvée system had to stay at fixed homesteads and be available at all times in case of emergencies, enemy invasions, or natural disasters. Since the state paid no wages for corvée labor, male subjects were supported by their families—mostly women, children, and elders, who were not subject to the corvée draft. Because agriculture was the primary occupation, the corvée system tied the bulk of the population to the land.

The corvée system did not encourage working-age males to engage in private services that would involve much traveling, let alone leaving the poorly defined boundaries of the realm. Hence, from at least the late Ayutthayan period, the livelihood of the vast majority of Siamese subjects was farming. The better educated and better connected could seek to enter the ranks of officialdom. However, one caste was conspicuously missing from this corvée-shaped labor system. There were no merchants or tradesmen— the entrepreneurial class that makes up the core of the middle class in most societies—despite Siam's location in the middle of peninsular Southeast Asia, the crossroads of some of the most lucrative trade routes of the eighteenth century. It is not surprising that Chinese sojourners, who had long been involved in maritime trade in this region, would step in to fill this vacuum in the Siamese socioeconomic system.

Allowing the overseas Chinese to serve as the merchant class in Siam benefited the ruling class as well as society as a whole, allowing the people to enjoy the goods and services provided. Chinese merchants living and doing business in Siam were well connected with the ethnic Chinese maritime trade network, which extended throughout the Asia-Pacific macroregion, enabling them to bring to Siam a wide range of goods from all over the world. These Chinese merchants shared excellent investment opportunities with members of the court who had had the foresight to recruit them. Chinese agents were also crucial in conducting the Siamese court's tribute missions to China. Until the mid-nineteenth century, the China trade was one of the most lucrative of the Siamese crown's enterprises. In terms of political stability and state security, allowing the ethnic Chinese to roam the kingdom while natives were tied to the land under the stringent requirements of the corvée system was much safer than the other way round. Not only were the Chinese a minority, they were also foreigners with no substantial family or social ties across the general population. There was little chance that they would instigate major disturbances or stage a rebellion, unlike what could happen if native subjects were allowed the same freedom.

In 1768, following the devastating Siamese-Burmese War, which left Siam's old capital of Ayutthaya in ruins, King Taksin reestablished Siamese dominion in Thonburi. As a man of Chinese extraction and a former courtier, he was able to rely heavily upon Chinese networks as he rebuilt the kingdom. Thonburi was to succeed Ayutthaya as one of the most popular and prosperous port cities in the southern seas. Trade would generate wealth for the reconstruction of the Siamese empire, and political and economic stability was ensured with the ultimate approval of the Qing emperor. The new king invested heavily throughout his reign in an attempt to gain acceptance from the Chinese imperial court. Without the approval of the Qing emperor, his regime would not be considered fully legitimate by the international trade standards of the time. This would be a disaster, as merchants from Siam would not be able to fully participate in China's lucrative tribute-trade channels. Taksin managed to gain this approval only toward the end of his reign. The Chinese emperor's approval was so important that when the king's chief lieutenant, Chaophraya Chakri, deposed Taksin and established himself as King Rama I of the Chakri dynasty, the new king adopted Taksin's Chinese clan name, Zheng, and presented himself as Taksin's son-in-law and heir. By claiming this family connection, the new reign did not have to independently acquire trading privileges from China.

The success of Chaophraya Chakri's strategy enabled the kingdom to enjoy a thriving position in the Chinese tribute trade from the late eighteenth through the early nineteenth century. Much of the construction and reconstruction of infrastructure, as well as numerous battles with domestic insurgents and neighboring military powers, was funded with revenue generated from the China trade and from taxation of overseas Chinese individuals and enterprises. Prince Jessadabodindra, who succeeded his father, King Loetla Rama II, to reign as King Nangklao Rama III, oversaw the court's China trade, which made him enormously influential and powerful, although he had been born of a minor consort. Prince Mongkut, his half-brother and the son of the queen, the more obvious heir who eventually became Rama IV, entered the monkhood, where he remained for more than two decades, discretely awaiting his turn.

King Nangklao (r. 1824–51), who came to power through his influence in the China trade, eventually decided that Siam should rely less on that trading network and more on domestic taxation as the main source of public revenue. This was partly due to the rise of British influence in the region and the first inklings of the Qing dynasty's deterioration after the reign of the Qianlong emperor (r. 1736–95).[5] Mostly, however, it was because the king knew full well that nobles overseeing the court's investments in the China trade were making much more money from the trade than what was being reported and deposited in the Crown's coffers. Nangklao developed another tactic of financial administration from the Chinese model—tax farming—as the main mode of generating revenue for the state. This system, which was said to be highly effective in China and had also been adopted by the Dutch in parts of their East Indies colony, involved auctioning off the right to collect taxes on behalf of the state. The tax farmer was mandated to collect a particular kind of tax on behalf of the state and to fulfill the quotas agreed upon with the state in the original bidding process.

When first instituted, tax farming was good business for both the state and the appointed tax farmers. The state treasury enjoyed much higher and more reliable returns than had been collected through the official bureaucracy. In the late eighteenth and early nineteenth centuries, the court lacked sufficient well-trained agents to carry out large-scale operations. Tax farmers made high profits from the surplus beyond the quotas established in the initial bidding. Moreover, and perhaps more importantly, tax farming was often associated with access to a potential monopoly on the products or services involved in the particular tax farm. When one producer possessed the right to collect taxes on all other producers of the same product, the competition was sure to be squeezed out. Consequently, owners of the most lucrative tax farms often doubled as the sole producer or provider of the product or service for which they owned the right to tax. Tax farming benefited those at the top of the socioeconomic hierarchy while short-changing common consumers and stifling potential business competitors.[6]

As in contemporary European colonies in Southeast Asia, under this system the tax farmers were almost always ethnic Chinese. Moreover, the main consumers of the products and services that generated the greatest revenue also happened to be Chinese. Opium, liquor, the lottery, and gambling dens were dubbed "Chinese vices" in the early nineteenth century and were the most lucrative tax farms. These fertile fields generated up to 50 percent of state revenue in the reign of Rama III.[7] Although the Siamese economy of the late eighteenth and early nineteenth centuries was dominated by the ethnic Chinese, this did not appear to be a problem for the Siamese ruling class. The state-dominated tribute trade with China and the tax-farming system kept the economic and political environment stable and ensured a generally amiable relationship between the nobility and the Chinese entrepreneurial class. By the end of Nangklao's reign in the mid-nineteenth century, the support of Chinese merchant lieutenants had become an essential part of Siamese upper-class culture. Many of the leading Chinese tax farmers acquired prominent positions in the court, and some even managed to form substantial kinship ties by offering their sisters, daughters, and nieces to prominent Siamese nobility as wives and concubines.

MODERNIZING AWAY FROM CHINA

The Siamese ruling class had long prospered comfortably within the China-centered system of international trade and commerce. Building on connections with China's imperial tribute system, the Chakri dynasty, relying on its own Chinese middlemen and representatives, carried on a flourishing trade with the Qing empire until the regional power structure began to show signs of an approaching upheaval. The First Anglo-Burmese War broke out in March 1824, only months prior to the ascension to the throne of Prince Jessadabodindra, himself a masterful old hand in the China trade. Almost immediately after his coronation, the new king was contacted by the British, who requested Siamese support in providing supplies and granting the right to pass through Siam during their conquest of the Burmese kingdom. This was the first sign of a fundamental shift of power that was already under way in the region. Quite suddenly, Burma, which had been Siam's arch rival among the kingdoms of peninsular Southeast Asia, was under serious threat from British colonialist expansion. The Burmese, who had conquered Ayutthaya twice (in 1569 and 1767), would no longer be a threat to Siamese political stability. They were being subjugated by the British, not by the Great Qing Empire, which in the late eighteenth century had made four failed attempts to subdue Burma. Jessadabodrindra, now King Nangklao Rama III, supported the 1824 British campaigns with Siamese fleets and elephants.

In 1826, the first Siamese-British accord, the Burney Treaty, was concluded with British envoy Henry Burney. This treaty was considered a complete failure by many British colonial administrators in the Far East, as it ceded great benefits to Siam. However, the Burney Treaty paved the way for British access to free trade in Siam. Major stipulations of the Burney Treaty included the acknowledgment of British rule in Penang. It recognized Siamese rule in the four northern Malay states—Kedah, Kelantan, Perlis, and Terengganu—as well as the British right to trade freely in those states without Siamese interference. The treaty also gave the British a substantial reduction in import taxes through the establishment of a single duty system based on the measurements of the beam of the cargo ship.[8] Perhaps more importantly, the Burney Treaty served as a wake-up call for the Siamese ruling class, indicating that future threats to the kingdom would no longer come in the form of traditional warfare with Burmese lords. Instead, they would be facing the expansionist aggression of European colonial powers. By now it was apparent to all that the center of influence in the global system of trade and commerce was shifting from China to Britain.[9]

The turning point that signaled Siam's course of modernization away from China was the signing of the Bowring Treaty by King Mongkut Rama IV of Siam and the British envoy, Sir John Bowring, governor of Hong Kong, on April 18, 1855. Unlike the Burney accord, the Bowring Treaty was a full-fledged unequal treaty, similar to the Sino-British Treaty of Nanking (Nanjing), which followed the First Opium War. It included all the hallmarks of an unfair agreement backed by badly disguised gunboat

diplomacy—extraterritoriality, unlimited access to travel and trade throughout the kingdom, and a British-approved flat rate (3 percent) for all custom
duties. The mainstream state-approved nationalist version of Thai history
often portrays the Bowring Treaty as the West's first assault on the kingdom's pride and sovereignty. Much importance and lamentation is devoted
to the Siamese state's loss of judicial authority to try British subjects under
Siam's legal traditions as a result of extraterritorial agreements. Another
bitter cut was the end of the crown's discretionary freedom to levy customs
duties, a long-standing privilege also cut short by the treaty.

However, those most affected materially by the new economic order
imposed by the Bowring Treaty were the ethnic Chinese merchants and
entrepreneurs who had enjoyed near-absolute dominance of the Siamese
economy for centuries prior to 1855.[10] While the Bowring Treaty ended the
largely symbolic power of the court to control international trade and judicial administration, it also reduced the many unfair advantages enjoyed by
the Chinese over the British. The termination of the Siamese court's monopoly on international trade had a severe impact on leading Chinese entrepreneurs because the Chinese were no longer the only foreigners allowed
to travel and trade freely throughout the Siamese kingdom. In practice, it
was always the Chinese who served as the court's agents in conducting trade
with foreign lands to the east of Siam, including the lucrative China trade.
The Bowring Treaty facilitated a freer and fairer trade environment that
could benefit the kingdom and its people in the long term, and the new wave
of competition led to important economic reforms in Siam at the turn of
the century. The tax-revenue collection system was centralized, and corvée
conscription of labor was ended. These changes, which were painstakingly
undertaken with the support of the crown, reflected the collective aspiration of the ruling class that Siam should remain competitive and compe-
tent in the face of the rapidly modernizing world economy and British
colonial dominance in the Far East.

The British-dominated world order that followed the Opium Wars called
for centralization of state power within the few regimes that were still, and
aspired to remain, marginally independent at the height of European colonization. The feudal regime of the old China-centered world order—with a
king or shogun relying upon the fealty of local and regional lords who
enjoyed direct control of the economy and manpower within their own
realm—could no longer survive amid the constant threats of expansion,
annexation, and gunboat diplomacy of European colonial powers.[11] In Siam,
a few essential feudal practices that had worked splendidly during the first

three reigns of the Chakri dynasty fell into decline or self-destructed by the end of King Mongkut's reign. The tax-farming system, which provided numerous opportunities for leading Chinese entrepreneurs to monopolize products and services directly connected to their tax farms, had given rise to extensive and intertwined clientele networks of Chinese capitalists and Siamese aristocrats. This resulted in extensive favoritism and corruption. In many cases, the same tax-farming families with aristocratic relations were continuously awarded farming rights, despite having repeatedly failed to make the quota promised in the original bid. Consequently, tax farmers and their aristocrat patrons became increasingly wealthy while the state treasury slid into decline. Circumstances such as these often led to further abuses of power and influence among the dominant figures in an increasingly tightly monopolized domestic economy. Black market trading and racketeering were commonplace, while Chinese secret society gangsters enjoyed increasing protection and patronage under the decentralized tax system.

The corvée, which provided conscripted manpower for the service of high-ranking aristocrats, had also become a threat to the stability and security of the Crown. The clientele of high-ranking nobility and influential Chinese tax farmers gained economic and political influence, while the Crown and the central government became weaker in the face of the mounting external pressures of imperialist aggression. It is not surprising that King Chulalongkorn Rama V, among his earliest attempts to centralize power and forge a modernized Siamese nation, moved toward concurrent reform and centralization of his tax-revenue collection and manpower management systems.[12]

Chulalongkorn continued his father's legacy of modernizing and anglicizing the Siamese economy in a direction both away from the old China-centered paradigm and toward centralization and the establishment of a modern Siamese nation-state. He embarked on a quest to centralize the tax-revenue collection system by establishing the Auditing Office, a central government agency that would in time take over the responsibility of tax collection from private tax farms. This was accomplished in 1873, almost immediately after the young monarch reached maturity and acquired the legal right to rule without a regent. In 1877, the king commenced the long and treacherous process of abolishing the corvée system. He instituted a practice of regular allowances for aristocrats instead of supplying them with the manpower that had been their due under the traditional system. Chulalongkorn's initiative to encourage free labor to support the modernizing economic and political systems met with skepticism as well as opposition from conservative nobility who lost their political clout when they lost access to free manpower.

Three decades were required to completely do away with this feudal manpower management system. In 1877, the first round of military conscription inducted all the remaining corvée draftees into the Royal Armed Forces.[13] The Siamese government's reform of tax-revenue collection and labor management dealt a major blow to leading Chinese entrepreneurs whose fortunes had been derived mostly from trade and labor privileges under the old systems. Many illustrious families went into decline as tax-farmer patriarchs descended into bankruptcy, spending their descendants' inheritance to pay off debts to the state.[14]

However, this decisive swing of the Siamese economy from the old Chinese-controlled tribute system to a modernized, anglicized version under British dominance was by no means the end of ethnic Chinese influence in the kingdom's economy. The policies of King Mongkut and the reforms of King Chulalongkorn had little, if anything, to do with racial preferences. Their reform policies were not aimed at despised ethnic Chinese entrepreneurs, but were required for the Siamese ruling class to hold on to some degree of sovereignty at the height of the colonial period. The monarch, as chief executive, needed to increase his control over tax-revenue collection and manpower management in the realm. The ethnic Chinese were not ostracized but were pressured to adapt to the new centralized system. The king employed quite a few British economic and financial advisers, yet the senior officials in this area of the court were still mostly of Chinese descent.[15] Leading ethnic Chinese aristocrats who had served directly under the monarch prior to the reforms continued to thrive in Chulalongkorn's court throughout his reign. Once again, the Crown's attitude toward the ethnic Chinese issue appeared to be economically driven.

Not all ethnic Chinese entrepreneurs who had enjoyed dominance in the Siamese economy prior to Chulalongkorn's reforms managed to adapt or survive unscathed under the new economic and political structures of the age of modernization. Many dissented, and they expressed their opposition to reform policies in various ways. Among the more notorious cases were secret society bosses who had once thrived under the patronage of aristocrats and tax farmers of the old system. Under the new regimen, they attempted to maintain their dominance in the Chinese community through black markets, racketeering, and various other criminal activities. Secret society disturbances became so prevalent in 1897 that a specific antiracketeering law was promulgated—the Ang-yi Act. Chulalongkorn instituted stern policies to centralize power and silence dissenters who still clung to practices from the premodernized feudal era. At the same time, however, the monarch's government was severely handicapped by the stipulations of unequal treaties with European colonial powers, especially in matters related to extraterritoriality. Many Chinese opted to register as European subjects so as to remain out of reach of what was often perceived as a brutal and backward judicial system. Extraterritorial rights allowed ethnic Chinese businessmen more stability, security, and freedom from the possibility of being harassed or extorted by overzealous or corrupt Siamese officials. Those who were prone to run into conflict with government policies—including professionals such as Chinese journalists, educators, and trade unionists—enjoyed greater leeway, and more often than not, better career success, when protected by extraterritorial privileges.

From the perspective of the Siamese state, however, those who registered as colonial subjects identified themselves as not being truly loyal to His Majesty's regime. Chulalongkorn's centralized government faced several outbursts of ethnic Chinese opposition to reform. The most notable protest was the Great Chinese Strike, which targeted the last of a long series of tax reforms. It was organized in 1910 by secret society bosses still active despite the promulgation of the Ang-yi Act.[16] By acts of civil disobedience such as these, Chinese colonial subjects gained notoriety, which cast some aspersion on ethnic Chinese generally. Their resistance made them appear untrustworthy and ungrateful. Despite having made their fortunes in Siam, they did not hesitate to take advantage of the unequal treaties and to exploit the limitations of Siamese judicial sovereignty by claiming extraterritorial rights. This bitterness toward ethnic Chinese exploitation of extraterritorial rights became one of the major issues at the root of what has often been categorized as King Vajiravudh's anti-Chinese nationalist campaign.

DOCUMENTED DOMINANCE OF UNDOCUMENTED CHINESE NATIONALS

A statement by the Republic of China government in 1943 assesses the "problem" of ethnic Chinese assimilation in Siam from the point of view of the Chinese state, which had aspired to garner as much financial support from wealthy overseas compatriots in Siam as possible:

> Because the overseas Chinese in Siam are very hard working, they have gained a firm standing in all areas. The major industries, such as the

production of rice, timber, sugar, jute, coconut, and rubber, are controlled by the overseas Chinese. . . . The Siamese government has
taken precautions through various policies. First, they lure [Chinese
migrants] to marry [native women]. Then they employ the educational
system to encourage assimilation and promulgate laws to control [the
overseas Chinese community]. . . . There is a large number of overseas
Chinese children born in Siam to Siamese mothers. This type of
overseas Chinese children receives education through the Siamese
system and their ties with the ancestral country are being increasingly
weakened as time passes by.[17]

The Chinese sojourners, who had "gained a firm standing in all areas" of
industry, including Siam's most prominent products in the first half of the
twentieth century, were identified by the Chinese state as being Chinese.
The Chinese government's perception of the overseas Chinese in Southeast
Asia added a new dimension to the already complicated international relations in the region.

In the early decades of the twentieth century, from the perspective of the
Siamese government, ethnic Chinese residing in Siam could be divided
roughly into three groups: Siamese subjects or citizens of Chinese descent;
Chinese subjects of European colonial powers; and subjects or citizens of
the Chinese state ruled by the Qing and, subsequently, by the Republic of
China. Thai archival materials from the reign of Chulalongkorn Rama V
to Prajadhipok Rama VII reflect these classifications, as do British documents concerning Siam during the same period. These complications were
created by extraterritorial rights, which constituted a particularly onerous
burden for Siam in the unequal treaties imposed by European colonial powers from the late nineteenth century until well after the conclusion of the
First World War. According to Chinese documents, however, it would
appear that the government of the Republic of China, from at least the early
1920s through the end of the Second World War, did not recognize any such
system of categorization for ethnic Chinese in Siam. Regardless of their
status as Thai citizens in the eyes of the Thai state or their registration with
European consulate authorities as colonial European subjects, the ethnic
Chinese were perceived by the Chinese state as belonging to the Chinese
nation and constituting part of the citizenry of the Republic of China.

The Chinese government of the early twentieth century was aware of the
existence of these other, internationally recognized, systems of categorization. Several wartime documents of the Nationalist government mention

that registering as European subjects allowed ethnic Chinese in Siam with extraterritorial rights to conduct business more effectively. The Chinese government also saw that it might be necessary for these ethnic Chinese to attempt to adopt Thai citizenship to continue doing business in Thailand under Japanese occupation. It was clear that these sojourners in Siam felt a responsibility to support the Chinese war effort and to help carry out modernization and postwar reconstruction projects. The Chinese state—especially the Nationalist government under Chiang Kai-shek—saw ethnic Chinese of any legal status as legitimate targets for Nationalist propaganda and recruitment in support of the Republic of China from the late 1920s to the conclusion of the Second World War.

This all-inclusive embrace of the ethnic Chinese in Siam by the Nationalist Chinese government contradicts the conventional understanding of the economic and political history of Siam and of the Southeast Asian region as a whole during the early twentieth century. Businesses sometimes registered as Thai or European, even if the owner or management happened to be of Chinese descent—which was the case for most major commercial enterprises in Siam up to the end of the Second World War. This overlap has obscured the fact that some of the earnings from such enterprises were likely to have been siphoned off to support the Chinese state. Such financial support would have been mostly clandestine and could easily have escaped documentation. The extent to which the overseas Chinese of Southeast Asia—regardless of their legal status as subjects or citizens—contributed financially to various causes of the Chinese state is revealed in Chinese archival documents from the early twentieth century.

Following the catastrophic Boxer Rebellion, the Qing court abruptly abandoned its traditional hostility toward imperial subjects overseas, especially the multitude of overseas Chinese in Southeast Asia. In their eleventh-hour efforts to modernize the empire and salvage what was left of Manchu political control, the Qing court relented in regard to its longstanding condemnation of the overseas Chinese of Southeast Asia. By the summer of 1903, it had become clear that the Manchu government was expecting guidance and support from wealthy ethnic Chinese communities in the southern seas for its various modernization projects. In the autumn of that year, Zhang Bizhi, among the best known of the Nanyang-based business tycoons, was summoned for a second time to an audience with the empress dowager. He was called upon to amplify his vision for a modernized China and to provide practical suggestions on how that dream might be realized. At least in its initial stages, the plan seemed fairly simple. Overseas Chinese investors, mostly from Southeast Asia, would be granted monopolies in the development of key industries such as mining and railways. Most of the funding needed for these modernization projects would be invested by the overseas Chinese themselves. They would keep the profits if these ventures proved successful in the long term.[18] It has been estimated that during the last decade of Qing rule, the annual remittance to the southern provinces of the empire coming from overseas Chinese could have surpassed ¥100 million.[19]

After the final collapse of Qing rule in 1911, the various power factions that loosely made up the establishment of the new Republic of China continued to preach the urgent need for modernization in China. Although the ratio of overseas Chinese financial support to other foreign sources varied in the different political cliques of the early Republican era, it was generally perceived that overseas Chinese funding, though not always sufficient, was the safer loan. After all, the Republic of China recognized the overseas Chinese as its own citizens, and therefore capital investments from these transnational migrants could hardly be considered foreign.[20] During the first decade of the republic, despite the constant turmoil of political disunity, a sizable stream of remittances continued to flow in from ethnic Chinese communities throughout Southeast Asia. Tables 3.1– 3.4 estimate the amounts and sources of remittances from ethnic Chinese in Southeast Asia, as recorded in two major port cities in South China— Xiamen (Amoy) and Shantou (Swatow)—in the first decade of the twentieth century.

The amount of remittance from Southeast Asia increased through much of the Republican era, despite the state's frequent political upheavals and chronic economic woes. This growing investment indicates the success of the Chinese state's policy of encouraging nationalist support from the ethnic Chinese in Southeast Asia, regardless of their legal status. Research data collected by a Japanese state agency through the Second World War show that remittances from Southeast Asia, especially those that came into China through Shantou, appeared to peak at significant turning points in the war.[21] These spikes in investment occurred, for example, at the time of the first major invasion by Japanese troops in Manchuria in 1931, in the period leading up to China's formal declaration of war against Japan in July 1937, as the tide of war on the mainland turned against Japan following their defeat in Changsha in 1939, and throughout 1940.

TABLE 3.1. Annual Southeast Asian remittances through private postal exchanges, inns, recruiter-couriers, and banks to Amoy, 1900–1910

Origin(s)	Amount (yuan)	Commodity deposits (yuan)
Singapore	7,500,000	1,700,000
Penang	2,500,000	800,000
Luzon	6,000,000	800,000
Java	3,500,000	2,000,000
Thailand, Vietnam, Burma, and others	2,700,000	1,300,000
Total	22,200,000	6,600,000

Source: George Hicks, ed., Overseas Chinese Remittances from Southeast Asia, 1910–1940 (Singapore: Select Books, 1993), 95.

TABLE 3.2. Annual Southeast Asian remittances through private exchanges, recruiter-couriers, and banks to Swatow

Origin(s)	Amount (yuan)	Commodity deposit (yuan)
Thailand	10,000,000	1,600,000
Singapore	8,500,000	2,500,000
Penang	4,000,000	800,000
Vietnam	2,000,000	1,000,000
Sumatra and Medan	400,000	—
Java, Luzon, and others	3,500,000	200,000
Total	28,400,000	6,100,000

Source: George Hicks, ed., Overseas Chinese Remittances from Southeast Asia, 1910–1940 (Singapore: Select Books, 1993), 99.

These remittances indicate that one of the larger communities of the Southeast Asian Chinese diaspora, the ethnic Chinese in Siam, was, despite problematic citizenship status, active in supporting the Chinese nation in the late nineteenth and early twentieth centuries. The indistinct picture in the Japanese documents is clarified in the many Nationalist wartime documents reporting on financial support for the Republic of China from leading overseas Chinese personalities and associations from the early 1930s until the end of the Second World War. Chinese Ministry of Foreign Affairs

TABLE 3.3. Overseas Chinese remittances to Swatow,
1931–1936

Date	Amount (yuan)
1931	94,200,000
1932	70,700,000
1933	62,800,000
1934	47,000,000
1935	55,000,000
1936	66,000,000

Source: George Hicks, ed., *Overseas Chinese Remittances from Southeast Asia, 1910–1940* (Singapore: Select Books, 1993), 153.

TABLE 3.4. Overseas Chinese remittances to Swatow,
March 1940–February 1941

Date	Amount (yuan)
March 1940	9,629,000
April 1940	9,175,000
May 1940	11,290,000
June 1940	9,877,000
July 1940	13,289,000
August 1940	8,805,000
September 1940	12,581,000
October 1940	13,267,000
November 1940	9,079,000
December 1940	4,570,000
January 1941	9,907,000
February 1941	4,815,000
Total	116,284,000

Source: George Hicks, ed., *Overseas Chinese Remittances from Southeast Asia, 1910–1940* (Singapore: Select Books, 1993), 159.

records of donations from Siam in January 1940 show that the Siamese-Chinese shared generously with the land of their ancestors:

> Yi Guangyan (Chairman of the Chinese Chamber of Commerce), Chen Jingchuan (Chairman of the Chaozhou Association), and Liao Gongpu (Vice Chairman of the Chaozhou Association) have donated 30,000 Nationalist Dollars . . . and have agreed to give a monthly donation toward the Chinese war efforts. . . . Despite mounting pressure and hostility from the authorities, these three have also established a foundation for "monthly donations for national salvation," and donated 7,000,000 yuan as seed money for this new fund-raising campaign.[22]

Immediately following the establishment of this campaign for monthly donations for national salvation, another report from the Chinese Ministry of Foreign Affairs recorded the first month's pledges made through the Chinese Chamber of Commerce in Siam in support of the Nationalist government's war efforts in January 1940 (table 3.5). The same document points out that the Thai government was becoming increasingly concerned about the amount of financial support the ethnic Chinese community was funneling to the Chinese war effort against Japan (which had formally allied with Thailand shortly after the bombing of Pearl Harbor in December 1941). By January 1940, over ¥50,000,000 of ethnic Chinese assets located in Thailand had been frozen.[23]

Siam was a major base of overseas Chinese wealth in Southeast Asia. The Chinese state identified all this as legitimate gains and assets of expatriate Chinese citizens that the state could attempt to claim. The emergence of the Chinese nation-state and the rise of modern Chinese nationalist movements in the early twentieth century had established a sort of loophole through which the Chinese government could manipulate the financial gains of ethnic Chinese communities overseas in the context of the new British and Western-centered world order. Much of this was achieved through the new, powerful, but still vague and malleable concept of citizenship. By insisting on the *jus sanguinis* principle, the Chinese state justified its right to demand nationalist support from the ethnic Chinese. This all-encompassing claim allowed the fledging Chinese nation to benefit from the extraterritorial rights enjoyed by multitudes of ethnic Chinese registered as European subjects throughout Southeast Asia.

The clouded definitions of citizenship in the period unsettle the conventional understanding of the economics of European imperialism in the Far

TABLE 3.5. Pledges made through the Chinese Chamber of Commerce in Siam
in support of the Chinese Nationalist government's war efforts in
January 1940

Donors	Amount pledged (baht)
Rice merchants	50,000
Grain merchants	100,000
Medical industries	1,000 (at least)
Overseas Chinese wholesalers	6,000
Slaughterhouses and pig raisers	9,000
General stores	3,000 (at least)
Dyeing industries	1,000 (at least)
Insurance industries	1,600
Banking industries	500
Tobacco industries	1,000
Others (including laborers and students)	Will donate as much as they can
Pawn shops	200
Gold merchants	200
Timber industries	5,000

Source: Foreign Affairs, 172-1/0703(2)012, "Primary Reports and Suggestions," in *Discussion on Sino-Thai Problems*, January 15, 1940, AH.

East. Britain, France, and the Netherlands could claim to dominate their colonies politically and economically through legally binding unequal treaties bristling with international legal jargon, such as "most favored nation" and "extraterritorial rights." In practice, however, significant portions of the earnings of enterprises owned by Chinese registered as European subjects were being remitted to China in support of Chinese nationalist causes. It appears that European imperialist dominance of Southeast Asia in this roundabout way played a significant role in the early development of the modern Chinese nation-state and its ongoing struggle against Japanese aggression from the early 1930s through the end of the Second World War.

Although Siam would appear to be the losing party in this arrangement, having the Chinese—in the guise of British and other colonial subjects—control most important commodities, including rice, timber, tin, and rubber, benefited the Siamese ruling class. This was a key condition that allowed Siam to be the only state in Southeast Asia and one of the few in the entire

Asian continent to remain marginally independent throughout the height of the colonial period. The close and cordial relations between Chinese entrepreneurs and the Siamese monarchy allowed the intricate ethnic Chinese trade network to continue to function in Siam throughout the colonial period. The Siamese state's willingness to allow extraterritorial rights for colonial subjects in its realm meant that the colonial powers could continue to conduct and expand trade and commerce in Siam without needing to colonize it completely. This also meant that Siam became a gray area in which the ethnic Chinese could enjoy extraterritorial rights in a realm that was not governed by their colonial masters.[24] For example, a Chinese registered as a colonial subject of Britain residing in Siam could enjoy extraterritoriality as a British subject but remain beyond the reach of British colonial administrators in Burma or Malaya. In this respect, Siam became an even more attractive place to reside and conduct business for Chinese colonial subjects in terms of minimizing state interference.

It is important to note that the Kingdom of Siam had neither the power to force nor the money to bribe Chinese entrepreneurs to continue to do business in the realm. The courts of Mongkut, Chulalongkorn, and Vajiravudh had only their friendly history with the Chinese merchant class and the perks of extraterritoriality to use as bargaining chips. These were, in fact, the key conditions that allowed the Siamese economy to remain vibrant and competitive as the only sovereign nation-state in a region of colonial empires from the late nineteenth century through much of the first half of the twentieth century. Moreover, the well-being of the many ethnic Chinese residing and doing business in Siam became a great concern for the Chinese Nationalist government and eventually forced Generalissimo Chiang Kai-shek to support a favorable outcome from the Second World War for Siam despite Siam's depressing record of anti-Chinese policies and persecutions throughout the war period.

NATIONALIZING THE CHINESE-DOMINATED ECONOMY

Only months prior to Vajiravudh's ascension to the throne in 1910, the then crown prince witnessed a spine-tingling display of ethnic Chinese power over the Siamese economy in the Chinese Strike, which brought the kingdom to a virtual standstill for nearly three days to protest Chulalongkorn's last series of tax reforms. Although the state prevailed in the end and the reforms were carried out in full, it became clear to many in the upper echelons of the Siamese ruling class that the rising pride and solidarity among Siam's ethnic Chinese would not be easily controlled.

King Vajiravudh Rama VI was well aware that his regime was judicially hamstrung by extraterritoriality in most matters concerning the ethnic Chinese in Siam. For this reason, he used propaganda and social pressure through media campaigns to both praise and pressure the ethnic Chinese so that they might contribute to the Siamese economy and express their loyalty to the crown through continuous financial support for the king's royal projects. Throughout his fifteen-year reign, not a single law that could be considered discriminatory to the ethnic Chinese was promulgated. Despite the overquoting of the king's notoriously anti-Semitic and anti-Chinese *Jews of the Orient*, the bulk of Vajiravudh's propaganda was not racially based, but rather was intended to address the state's vulnerability resulting from the extraterritorial rights of registered European subjects of Chinese descent. The sixth king penned plenty of economic de-sinification propaganda, which falls roughly into three categories. First, and perhaps most crucially, the king encouraged native Siamese to become more involved in developing their own national economy. While he did not expect his Siamese subjects to completely overtake the ethnic Chinese in trade in the foreseeable future, he warned that the future prospects of the kingdom could be dire should the native Siamese continue to depend on the Chinese to run the economy on their behalf. An example of this type of warning is his newspaper article "Thailand, Wake Up!," penned under the royal pseudonym Atsawaphahu:

Last time there was a Chinese strike in Bangkok, I heard with my own ears some people saying, with all seriousness, that we must starve to death should the Chinese carry on their strike for much longer. It is true that such comments are absolutely senseless. Yet it is an example of how some of us are so dependent upon the Chinese. . . . Should there be a war in our land and all the Chinese leave us, as they have the full right and many reasons to do, what will we do? Where will we find food and supplies? Who will do the work that we have all forgotten how to do ourselves? How will we resolve the situation? Or should we simply lie down and die?[25]

Following this biting opening salvo, Vajiravudh urges his Siamese subjects to become economically independent, to support their compatriots' enterprises, and to rely more upon Siamese labor for the sake of long-term national security, even though, in the short term, it was obvious to all that Chinese goods were of superior quality and Chinese labor was much cheaper and far more productive. Clearly, economic development—rather than racial discrimination—is his main concern.

The second part of Vajiravudh's economic nationalization propaganda carries this line of reasoning farther by proposing to accept ethnic Chinese born in Siam, generally known as *lukchin*, as his own people, with the proviso that they devote themselves wholeheartedly to the Kingdom of Siam and her people and not abandon his realm when tough times arise:

> It is true that *lukchin* are not the same as true Chinese migrants from China. But we can only accept them as truly Thai if they definitely agree to change their citizenship to Thai and abandon all ties with China. That is, they must prove that they are willing to live and die with us. Then we can accept them as one of our own. We must not accept the half-Thai, half-Chinese as Thai (because they will choose to be Chinese or Thai according to their convenience. Such precarious people are much worse than the true Chinese).[26]

Vajiravudh was aware of the precarious nature of citizenship and subjecthood for the ethnic Chinese in Siam and throughout most of the Southeast Asian region. Even if they were registered as European colonial subjects or as Thai citizens, the ethnic Chinese community in Siam preserved ties with their ancestral homeland, and the Chinese state continued to claim them as citizens. China still demanded (and received) patriotic support in the form of regular donations, economic connections, and business loyalty. At times coercing, at times encouraging, but ever with only partial success, Vajiravudh tried to persuade ethnic Chinese to embrace Siam and express their loyalty to the Siamese crown. They were asked to wholeheartedly help develop Siam, to stop supporting the Chinese state, and to refuse to invest in the Chinese Republican government's patriotic fund-raising propaganda. Depending on who complied, the Siamese government decided which Chinese entrepreneurs could be counted as allies and which should be recognized, according to registration records, as European colonial assets.

The final aspect of Vajiravudh's de-sinification propaganda, evident throughout his reign, was the systematic discrediting of the Chinese Revolution and the Republic of China through various editorials and published analyses of current world events. Among the better-known pieces are Atsawaphahu's translation of E. J. Dillon's commentaries on the Xinhai Revolution, published in the *Washington Post* in 1912; Atsawaphahu's comments on Yuan Shikai's presidency, published as a news article in 1915; and the king's memorandum expressing his views concerning the May Fourth Movement in China in 1919.[27] Of all heads of state throughout Thai history, Vajiravudh remains the most prolific commentator on current international affairs related to China. Much of what he wrote, both nonfiction and fiction, was highly critical of political developments in China, especially in matters relating to the revolution and republicanism.

The three documents from 1912, 1915, and 1919 mentioned above are typical examples of Rama VI's attitude toward current affairs in China throughout his reign. He concluded that the Xinhai Revolution was a huge mistake and predicted that neither republicanism nor democracy could ever work in China, or Siam, or anywhere else in Asia. His apparent aim was to discourage the budding Siamese intelligentsia from any unwelcome aspiration to revolution or republicanism in Siam and to convince the ethnic Chinese in Siam that the China of their ancestors no longer existed, because revolution and republicanism had destroyed all that made them so proud. This warning is present in Atsawaphahu's translation of E. J. Dillon's lamentation over the West's failure to prevent the ultimate collapse of the Qing dynasty. Dillon believed that the new regime of inexperienced revolutionaries under the leadership of an authoritarian tyrant like Yuan Shikai could only lead China back to the chaotic era of warring states.[28] In *The New Emperor*, Vajiravudh predicted that even if the postrevolution regime managed to hold the republic in one piece, it would turn out to be not much different from a traditional dynastic government. Yuan Shikai would eventually proclaim himself the new emperor and would establish a new dynasty to succeed the fallen Qing. Those ethnic Chinese who had high hopes for a New China were also doomed to disappointment.[29] Among the most insistent messages presented by Vajiravudh in numerous publications during his reign was that the ethnic Chinese in Siam should abandon their time-honored aspiration to return someday to the land of their ancestors. He was adamant in his belief that the greatness of China was no more, and any hope that it would be reestablished or even exceeded had been destroyed by the revolution. The ethnic Chinese in Siam should therefore embrace their new destiny as complete and devoted citizens of the new Siamese nation.

As fiery as some of Vajirvavudh's anti-Chinese rhetoric was, it did little, in pragmatic terms, to resolve the problem of ethnic Chinese dominance in the Siamese economy. What eventually helped alleviate the crisis of the ambiguous loyalty of the nation's ethnic Chinese was the success of Siamese delegations in revoking certain provisions of unfair treaties, including full autonomy in taxation and an end to extraterritoriality, which began in the latter half of Vajiravudh's reign but did not come into full effect until the late-1930s, after the fall of the absolute monarchy.[30] Those negotiations were made possible through Siam's strategic involvement on the winning side in the First World War. As a result of the changes in old treaties, the options of nationality, citizenship, or subjecthood for the ethnic Chinese in Siam were reduced to two. They could either retain Chinese nationality or fully adopt Thai citizenship. The end of extraterritoriality meant that former ethnic Chinese colonial subjects could no longer claim extraterritorial rights. That category had become obsolete. Some ambiguity did remain, however, in the Chinese state's continuing adherence to the *jus sanguinis* principle and their claim that close to a third of the total Siamese population were in fact citizens of the republic. The issue of Sino-Siamese dual citizenship continued to be a thorn in the side of the Thai government long after the end of Vajiravudh's reign. Even after the end of the absolute monarchy, the post-1932 revolutionary government remained nearly as helpless in truly nationalizing the economy as their royalist predecessors had been.

Gaining more complete control over the economy was among the top priorities of Siam's post-1932 revolutionary government. The worldwide economic depression after the First World War and the crown's inability to resolve the kingdom's financial crisis provided the People's Party with the solid justification it needed for revolution and the establishment of a new constitutional regime. Consequently, two of the six declarations of purpose of the People's Party proclaimed the revolutionary government's determination to improve the nation's dire economic situation and to establish foundations for future economic development.

1) [The revolutionary government will] preserve and enhance all aspects of national independence, including political independence, judicial independence, and economic independence.

. . .

3) [The revolutionary government will] enhance the people's happiness and economic well-being. The new government will allocate employment to all citizens and establish a national economic project that will safeguard the people from famine and starvation.[31]

In reality, there was little the revolutionary government could do to improve or even significantly transform the national economy in any way without embarking upon drastic socialist measures. Despite the transformation of the highest governing body of the kingdom from an absolute monarchy to a constitutional regime, much of Thailand's economy remained, as ever, under the near-absolute control of a minority of ethnic Chinese entrepreneurs. Certain factions within the dominant core of the People's Party did nonetheless anticipate certain left-leaning socialist reforms as part of the revolutionary government's new economic development project. Shortly after the revolution in June 1932, the newly appointed minister of finance, Pridi Banomyong, proposed a National Outline for Economic Development as a guideline for the revolutionary government's economic policies. It was, however, rejected by the parliament, which was apparently unnerved by its socialist tendencies, especially the goals for land reform and public welfare. Many, including King Prajadhipok Rama VII, the kingdom's first constitutional monarch, found Pridi's proposals much too close to Soviet models. Instead of risking a damaging loss of support from the landowning gentry, the new government opted for a more conservative approach to national economic development spearheaded by the People's Party's mentor and chief propagandist, Luang Wichitwathakan.

In its most fundamental aspects, Wichitwathakan's approach to economic development was neither spectacular nor innovative. It followed Vajiravudh's de-sinification rhetoric, encouraging the native population to take control of the economy instead of allowing the ethnic Chinese to dominate trade and services. One not so brilliant twist to Wichitwathakan's credit was the new government's choice of scapegoat. The economic policy widely supported by the revolutionary regime blamed Siam's ethnic Chinese for the country's economic depression and widespread poverty. In Wichitwathakan's analysis, Siamese farmers and the working poor were not industrious enough and did not know how to save part of their earnings. These problems were exacerbated by greedy Chinese middlemen and capitalists, who took advantage of their fellow citizens. To resolve the problem of poverty in Siam, Wichitwathakan proposed a "human revolution," which encouraged Siamese citizens to express patriotism by being industrious in their professions and saving more of their earnings for the sake of national development:[32]

> Economically speaking, nationalism must not interfere with private property. There must be no land reform. The government must not

confiscate the wealth and riches of the rich in order to give to the poor. Instead, [the government] should encourage the poor to develop their own financial status through hard work and solidarity so that they might escape from being enslaved by the wealthy.

. . .

The proletariat should take pride in the glory that they are the driving forces of national production. [They] should consider work as their happiness, their joy of living, and their honor. . . . [T]he well-being of the nation lies in proletarian hands. We do not work only for ourselves. All the work that we do is done for the benefit of the nation."[33]

According to Luang Wichitwathakan, the greed and selfishness of ethnic Chinese capitalists was an important cause of the widespread poverty in Siam. Since the establishment of the Republic of China and the rapid development of various modes of transportation between China and Southeast Asia, the ethnic Chinese appeared to Wichitwathakan increasingly unwilling to assimilate into native Siamese society. In times past, ethnic Chinese often married Siamese women, started new families in Siam, and even offered their services to the Siamese government. He was dismayed to see ethnic Chinese in the twentieth century holding on to their Chinese citizenship, sending their children back to China to be educated, and reserving their greatest loyalty for the Chinese state.

While he strongly opposed Pridi's socialist land reform proposals, Wichitwathakan insisted that the government needed to intervene to protect the Siamese working classes from ethnic Chinese economic dominance. He staunchly advocated the government's campaign to educate Siamese people on the benefits of local cooperative organizations. Wichitwathakan also favored grassroots cooperative organizations as the best way to help Siamese farmers and craftsmen break free from the exploitation of Chinese merchants and moneylenders. Siamese producers had to learn to cooperate in order to eliminate the Chinese middlemen. Furthermore, the government had to provide training and teach organizational techniques that would allow people to compete effectively with the ethnic Chinese in all realms of trade and industry. In the years leading up to the Second World War, Wichitwathakan enthusiastically pushed his nationalist/anti-Chinese plan for economic development. He even compared the "Chinese problem" in Siam to the "Jewish problem" in Europe and suggested that Nazi methods of resolving the Jewish problem might be applicable to Siam's Chinese problem as well.[34]

A strong flavor of Vajiravudh's earlier nationalist rhetoric is apparent in Wichitwathakan's propaganda: a call for citizens to put the greater good of the nation before their own personal gain, for native Siamese to be more industrious and devote themselves wholeheartedly to taking control of their economic history, as well as the negative view of the Chinese in Southeast Asia. What separates Vajiravudh's de-sinification rhetoric from Wichitwathakan's Thai-ification propaganda is their description of the true Siamese patriot. In Vajiravudh's case, where the monarch was presented as the personification of the nation and devotion to the monarch was accepted as a sign of patriotism, writings like *Jews of the Orient* could be interpreted as a public challenge to the ethnic Chinese to prove their loyalty to the Crown, perhaps through a hefty donation to one or more of the king's favorite royal projects. This was a proven tactic for a monarch with depleted royal coffers. When Wichitwathakan employed the same rhetoric, however, it became a war cry and possibly a call for violent extermination of an unwanted minority.[35] The People's Party version of territorial nationalism did not allow transnational business communities with multiple allegiances to maneuver as they had in the old royalist regime.

The new constitutional government had little choice but to view the kingdom's top Chinese entrepreneurial families with even greater suspicion than Vajiravudh had during the absolutist era. This was precisely because of the Chinese community's loyalty and time-honored connections with Siamese royalty. At this difficult moment, the post-1932 People's Party government had to stop the drift of working-class Chinese toward socialist revolution, while guarding against dangerous conspiracies between the kingdom's top Chinese capitalists and their royalist allies from the ancien régime. The new government chose to promote a frankly anti-Chinese nationalist economic policy. They would blame the hardships of the proletariat on rich Chinese capitalists and excuse themselves from having to resolve the plight of either. It was the old strategy of divide and rule.

When the militarist leader of the People's Party and Wichitwathakan's closest political ally, Field Marshal Plaek Phibunsongkhram, came to power as prime minister in 1938, the Siamese government began to understand the potential of its newfound political tools and institutions. The most prominent was a parliament and the right to pass legislation. Without the benefit of the sanctity of absolute monarchism, Phibunsongkhram's government unleashed one of the most intense campaigns of anti-Chinese economic reform in Thai history. At least nine laws and three intervention decrees, all deliberately anti-Chinese, were promulgated within the first twelve months (table 3.6).

The strongest effects of the constitutional government's anti-Chinese economic policies in the pre–Second World War Phibunsongkhram period were felt in the face of, and in concert with, a mighty force of looming foreign aggression. The circumstances more or less replayed an earlier traumatic wave of de-sinification of the Siamese economy during the reign of King Mongkut Rama IV. That is, in 1855, the Siamese ruling class was more or less coerced into abandoning the Chinese tribute system by the intimidating presence of the British governor of Hong Kong, Sir John Bowring. In the late 1930s, Phibunsongkhram's anti-Chinese economic policies were propelled by the awesome power of looming Japanese imperialism in East and Southeast Asia. This time, however, the push back against ethnic Chinese economic dominance was much more violent than what happened with the arrival of British imperialism in the mid-nineteenth century.

By the time Phibunsongkhram came to office as premier in 1938, Japanese troops had occupied parts of Chinese territory for seven years, and a formal declaration of war between China and Japan had been in effect for over a year. The ethnic Chinese entrepreneurs in Siam in the late 1930s were not simply business competitors of the Japanese. For occupying Japanese forces, ethnic Chinese businesses were functionaries of an enemy state. Leading personalities in the Chinese community in Siam had begun organizing boycotts of Japanese goods and businesses in Siam when the Japanese first invaded Manchuria in 1931. If the Thai government were to remain neutral in the Sino-Japanese conflict, it was necessary to at least make a show of keeping the ethnic Chinese in check.

Circumstances only deteriorated for the Chinese in Siam with the arrival of the Greater East Asian Co-Prosperity Sphere in Southeast Asia in 1941.[36] In preparation for seemingly inevitable involvement in the Second World War, Phibunsongkhram's government began declaring prohibited areas in May 1941. These were actually entire provinces deemed by the government to be of strategic importance. For this reason, all alien nationals (mostly that meant Chinese people) residing in these provinces were ordered to evacuate within ninety days. In the course of the Second World War, the Thai government made three such declarations, establishing a total of thirteen provinces as prohibited areas.[37] Most of the prohibited provinces were urban areas and trade centers heavily populated by ethnic Chinese, many of whom still retained their Chinese citizenship at the outbreak of the war. These official declarations were abruptly set forth, and the Thai government made

TABLE 3.6. Anti-Chinese laws and interventions promulgated by the Phibunsongkhram government (December 1938–November 1939)

Anti-Chinese Laws/Interventions	Date	Description
The Thai Rice Company	December 1938	The government established the Thai Rice Company by buying out several ethnic Chinese–owned rice mills in Bangkok. The government owned 51 percent of the company's shares and granted special rates for product transportation via state-owned railways. Cooperative societies for the sale of rice were also established in five localities to support the Thai Rice Company in its attempts to break the ethnic Chinese monopoly of the rice trade.
Revoking of bird's nest concessions	January 1939	Bird's nest concessions were revoked from ethnic Chinese firms and taken over by the government for future development.
Salt Act	March 1939	The Salt Act was promulgated to heighten government control of salt production and to raise tax rates on the commodity. The ethnic Chinese were heavily involved in both the production and export of salt in Siam. Many companies were forced into bankruptcy as a result of this law.
Tobacco Act	March 1939	The Tobacco Act was designed to shake up the tobacco industry just as the Salt Act had done to the salt industry. As a result of the Tobacco Act, three Chinese cigarette factories were sold to the government.
Slaughter of Animals for Food Act	March 1939	The Slaughter of Animals for Food Act offered privileges to Thai butchers and pork merchants to encourage them to break the Chinese dominance in this particular trade.
Revenue Code	March 1939	The new Revenue Code of 1939 increased shop taxes for alien merchants and augmented the licensing fees for the operation of gambling and opium dens, which were known to be traditionally ethnic Chinese trades.
Signboard Act	March 1939	The Signboard Act increased signboard taxes so that boards of which more than half of the letters were non-Thai became ten times more expensive than Thai-language signboards.
Vehicles Act	April 1939	The Vehicles Act denied foreign citizens the right to secure licenses needed for operating taxicabs, a profession tradition-ally heavily dominated by ethnic Chinese.
Vessels Act	April 1939	The Vessels Act mandated that all fishing and trading vessels of more than a certain gross tonnage, in order to operate in Thai waters, must be registered as the property of Thai nationals or of corporations in which at least 70 percent of the operating capital was controlled by Thai nationals.
Liquid Fuels Act	April 1939	The Liquid Fuels Act forced Western firms out of the petroleum business in Thailand by enforcing strict government controls over the importing, distilling, and marketing of petroleum. The ethnic Chinese suffered most from this as they made up the majority of employees and agents of Western petroleum companies in Thailand.
First Cultural Mandate of the State	November 1939	The First Cultural Mandate of the State called for patriotic Thai nationals to consume only Thai food, use only products manufactured by Thai labor, and support only Thai citizens in trade and industry.

Source: G. William Skinner, Chinese Society in Thailand: An Analytical History (Ithaca, NY: Cornell University Press, 1957), 262–64.

no effort to facilitate mass evacuations of neighborhoods, families, or individuals from the prohibited areas. No extra freight trains or cargo services were provided, in spite of repeated requests from various local Chinese associations and the Chinese Chamber of Commerce. To avoid heavy fines for missing the evacuation deadlines, some ethnic Chinese entrusted their assets to friends and relatives with Thai citizenship. Others had to sell most of their belongings to their Thai neighbors at very low prices. Unfortunately for other local people in these areas, the forced evacuation of their ethnic Chinese neighbors made life in prohibited areas suddenly very difficult. Communities immediately experienced a serious lack of essential commodities and services, since nearly all the food peddlers and retailers were Chinese nationals. Unable to manage their daily routines without their Chinese neighbors and tempted by bribes from some Chinese associations, local authorities increasingly failed to press charges when Chinese nationals missed the evacuation deadlines. Many officials turned a blind eye when the evacuees discretely returned to their homes in the prohibited areas a few months after they had been forced out. By the end of 1944, although the government had not officially revoked its declarations, the prohibition was no longer observed in most areas declared prohibited by the government.[38]

Under the Japanese occupation, some policies originally aimed at promoting native Thai competition with the ethnic Chinese in the context of the free market were intensified and transformed into outright anti-Chinese discrimination. In June 1942, the Thai government issued a royal decree reserving twenty-seven occupations for Thai nationals. It is noteworthy that most of the listed occupations not only were among the lower-income professions but also were popular among the lower strata of the ethnic Chinese community. They included, for example, hair-dressing as well as the manufacture and sale of fireworks, bricks, firewood, and lacquer and niello ware. Other occupations on the reserved list appeared to be included out of sentimental nationalism rather than for any practical reason, such as the manufacturing and trade of Buddha images and typesetting with Thai letters.[39] Reports in the Chinese Republican archives from Nationalist government correspondence in Thailand suggest that both the declaration of prohibited areas and the rules on reserved occupations resulted directly in a sharp rise in unemployment within the ethnic Chinese community in Thailand. Increased unemployment not surprisingly led to a rise in criminal activity in the affected areas, which provided an excuse for the Thai government to intensify its anti-Chinese campaigns. The Nationalist government seems to have attempted to appeal these newly promulgated anti-Chinese regulations with the Thai government. However, the Phibunsongkhram regime refused to reconsider and responded simply that the new laws applied to all foreign nationals alike, and that it was not the Thai government's intention to single out the ethnic Chinese for discrimination.[40]

THE BROKEN DREAM OF DISMANTLING THE CROWN
AND THE CAPITALISTS

One of the key conditions that allowed the Chakri dynasty to remain in power in Thailand for more than two centuries is the formidable alliance it formed with the ethnic Chinese business elite starting from the establishment of the dynasty in the late eighteenth century. This alliance was the foundation of an all-encompassing and all-powerful elite that enjoyed near-absolute dominance in both politics and the economy. Both sides of this formidable alliance managed to remain dominant forces within the kingdom despite major external challenges—namely, numerous imperialist threats, such as of unfair treaties and gunboat diplomacy. The Chakri courts of Kings Mongkut, Chulalongkorn, and Vajiravudh quickly adapted to the British colonial standard of international trade, which was the world order of the late nineteenth century, while the Chinese business elite metamorphosed into colonial subjects and continued their economic dominance through the height of the colonial era.

The Siamese Revolution of 1932 was arguably the first time since the establishment of the Chakri dynasty in 1782 that the Crown-capitalist alliance was partially dismantled. For the first time, the court did not enjoy absolute power in government. The cabinet was formed under the new constitution and parliamentary system. Yet the seemingly defunct royalists continued to be a force to be reckoned with, precisely because of what remained of their formidable alliance with the Chinese business elite. The Thai-ification economic policies enacted by the Phibunsongkhram People's Party regime represented a bold attempt to undermine the remaining dominance of the Crown-capitalist alliance. The grand plan started with an attempt to eliminate one of the Chinese business elite's greatest advantages through the revolutionary government's successful negotiation to abolish extraterritoriality. Then the entrepreneurial Chinese were supposed to be bypassed in the economic system when the government helped the agricultural working class establish cooperatives, thus allowing the peasantry to sell their products directly to the consumers without having to go through what state propaganda described as "greedy Chinese middlemen." To seal the fate of the fallen Chinese business elite, the constitutional government switched international alliances from the British imperialists, who had been the traditional allies of the absolute monarchs since the mid-nineteenth century, to the anti-Western imperialist Japanese Empire, whose greatest aspiration was to conquer the Chinese Republic. The Thai-ification of the prewar and wartime Phibunsongkhram regime was designed first and foremost to destroy the economic dominance of the Chinese business elite and therefore bring down the overarching dominance of the Crown-capitalist alliance once and for all.

The alliance of the Crown and the capitalists could have ended with the Siamese Revolution had Japan not been defeated in the Second World War. Both sides of the once-powerful alliance had been systematically neutralized and could have been completely destroyed had the Phibunsongkhram regime not picked the wrong allies in the war and turned against the Western superpower that would dominate postwar Thailand through much of the rest of the twentieth century. Of all the great powers that the constitutional government of Thailand could have aligned itself with, Japan was the only one the ethnic Chinese would not submit to. The seemingly defunct royalists and the badly incapacitated Chinese business elite found themselves drawn again to the same powerful allies—this time, the leading forces of the Allied powers and an organization of patriots in exile known as the Free Thai Movement.

The Far East front of the Second World War—also known as the Greater East Asia War, or the War of Resistance, according to the Chinese nationalist narrative—initially brought hope in the Phibunsongkhram regime. For the first time in the modern history of Thailand, a superpower was willing to support a government of the people against the tyranny of the domineering monarchists and the Chinese business elite. Unfortunately for those who cherished the egalitarian dream of the People's Party, the outcome of this war returned the Crown and the capitalist alliance to their dominant position in both the political and economic realms of the postwar Thai state. The same powerful alliance of the royalists and the Chinese, once again with the support of a Western superpower, would crush the People's Party's dream of an alternative form of nation and any possibility of a nonroyalist democratic state.

CHAPTER FOUR

THE GREATER EAST ASIA WAR

Questioning and Redefining the Thai Nationalist Narrative

THE SECOND WORLD WAR BROUGHT SIAM—OR THAILAND, AS IT was renamed in 1939—full circle in its tumultuous journey into the modern era. Thailand's experience in World War II challenged almost all the old assumptions concerning the kingdom's direction toward modernity since the arrival of Sir John Bowring in 1855. British dominance in East and Southeast Asia in the post–Opium Wars era was being overshadowed by Japan's meteoric rise. The Greater East Asia War also nearly brought an end to the centuries of overseas Chinese domination of the Thai economy. And it almost annihilated what little remained of the conservative, royalist political factions in post-1932 Thailand. However, Japan's catastrophic defeat in the summer of 1945 turned the political tide in Thailand dramatically to the right. The Thai nationalist saga, which leaders of the revolutionary People's Party had so painstakingly attempted to reshape, emerged after the war as a transformed, territorial version of the royalist narrative of the Vajiravudh era. The swift and unwavering support from the ethnic Chinese for the Chinese war effort and for the anti-Japanese royalist underground brought some of those communities back to the forefront of Thailand's postwar economy. The alliance between conservative royalist political forces and overseas Chinese capitalists was strengthened as Thailand adapted to yet another major shift in the global power structure—from the British-dominated colonial era to the bipolar world of the US-USSR Cold War.

Throughout the course of the Greater East Asia War, Thailand, as a minor player in that very international affair, was dominated politically, and to a certain extent economically, by Japan. From the early 1930s to the conclusion of the war, the expansionist Japanese had replaced Britain as the political and trade overlord of East and Southeast Asia. Japan had extended its realm of influence under the banner of the Greater East Asian Co-Prosperity Sphere. Invading Japanese armies were everywhere announcing themselves as the liberators of the Asian peoples from the European imperialist yoke. For the new, modern Thailand, this course of events was compatible with the narrative of the People's Party. That is to say, Japan's replacement of Britain as the overlord of trade and colonial politics in East and Southeast Asia could be seen as legitimizing the replacement of Siam's absolute monarchy by the constitutional regime of the People's Party. The Siamese royalist ruling class had identified closely with British colonial modernity since the end of King Mongkut's reign in the late nineteenth century. The rise of a hypernationalist Asian superpower like Japan in the 1930s reflected badly on Siam's Anglophilic monarchist regime. An anticolonialist, nationalist governing power, much like the one established by the People's Party in 1932, was more in tune with the times. In 1940–41, Japanese support put muscle into Thailand's expedition to reclaim disputed territories along the borders with French-Indochina. Some Thai historians today argue that the Thai government in Bangkok probably had no more legitimacy in claiming sovereignty over the disputed territories than did the French colonial regime, based at the time in Hanoi.[1] But the popular propaganda of the day was that the People's Party had recovered both the nation's territory and its pride, which had fallen to French colonial aggression during the reign of King Chulalongkorn. The rise of Japan in the Far East offered a new standard of modernity for the constitutional regime of the People's Party. There was no longer any nineteenth-century royalist imperative to civilize by anglicizing.

The rise of Japanese political dominance in East and Southeast Asia provided support and legitimacy for the Thai constitutional regime in their handling of ethnic Chinese assimilation and citizenship. This was a dauntingly complex matter, which up to the mid-1930s remained highly problematic for the People's Party government. Without the mystifying allure of a crowned head, that nationalistic emblem on behalf of which Vajiravudh had campaigned so vigorously hardly more than a decade earlier, the nationalism of the People's Party lacked a compelling symbolic center. The government of soldiers and their civilian allies could not produce a culturally convincing compromise to serve as a focus for the required expression of nationalist fervor from its ethnic Chinese citizens. No alternative was forthcoming that would enable the ethnic Chinese to retain their Chinese identity while expressing their loyalty to the Thai state, as they had been able to do under the absolute monarchy. The constitutional regime relied on legislation as their legitimate implement of coercion. However, repressive laws did not effectively discourage Chinese nationalism for many in the ethnic Chinese communities in Thailand, and laws against dual citizenship were not always effective because of the Chinese state's negligence regarding other countries' legal principles vis-à-vis citizenship and subjecthood.

However, when Japan became dominant in the region, Premier Phibunsongkhram's constitutional regime found two major opportunities, in the name of nationalism, to extend its coercive power and control over the problematic ethnic Chinese population. First, any Chinese could be purged who had previously enjoyed extraterritorial rights as a British or French colonial subject and who continued to prosper as an agent of European interests in Siam, even after the unfair treaties had been revised or in part revoked. The anti-European imperialist stance of the Greater East Asian Co-Prosperity Sphere was helpful to the Thai revolutionary regime. Former ethnic Chinese European subjects, even those who might have cultivated a cordial relationship with the Crown, were put in a difficult position. Second, and perhaps even more important, unlike the British, the Japanese were not willing to adopt skillful Chinese agents as colonial subjects. By the time Japanese forces physically arrived in Thailand in 1941, China had openly and officially been at war with Japan for four years. Any Chinese person or friendly supporter of the Republic of China was now, for Japan and her allies, an enemy. In Thailand, since much of the ethnic Chinese population remained sympathetic to their homeland, they were immediately perceived as supporters of an enemy regime and therefore were a threat to the wartime Japanese-Thai alliance. Theoretically, the ethnic Chinese population that chose to remain in occupied Thailand would have no alternative but to sever all ties with their ancestral homeland. The alternative would put transgressors at possibly fatal loggerheads with the government of Japan's most prominent ally in the southern seas. Even so, the revolutionary People's Party government's aspiration to replace Vajiravudh's royalist vision for the kingdom-nation with a new form of territorial nationalism seemed doomed from the outset.

A complete transformation of the modern Thai state's relationship with the modern Chinese state and the ethnic Chinese population in Thailand would have been required had Japan *not* been defeated at the conclusion of the Second World War. On the other hand, Japan's defeat threatened to pull Thailand down with it. Almost immediately after Phibunsongkhram announced his government's fateful decision to enter the war as an ally of

Japan, the largely defunct conservative, royalist political factions started to mobilize in support of the Allied powers. The Thai minister to Washington, DC, M. R. Seni Pramoj, a distant relative of the royal family, mutinied against his own government and established the pro-Allied, anti-Japanese Free Thai Movement from his post in the United States. Exiled members of the royal family—the abdicated King Prajadhipok Rama VII and Queen Rambhai included—along with diplomats and overseas students in Britain followed suit in proclaiming their allegiance to the Allied powers. In the end, it was this small group from the conservative elites and their like-minded confederates in exile, together with the unwavering support for China's war effort from the overseas Chinese community in Thailand, that allowed the kingdom to emerge from the Greater East Asia War as a victor, despite having entered into an official alliance with Japan.

As the tide of the war turned against Japan toward the end of 1942, some factions in the Phibunsongkhram cabinet came to the realization that Japan's defeat would mean not only possible calamity for the nation's economy but also the certain death of the People's Party as a viable political force in Thailand. The royalist conservatives would return to dominate the Thai political arena. With desperate urgency, wartime minister of finance Pridi Banomyong reached out for support from the Republic of China. Altogether, Pridi dispatched four embassies, which he presented as Free Thai missions, in an attempt to gain the recognition and approval of Generalissimo Chiang Kai-shek, supreme commander of the Allied powers in the China war zone. Pridi wanted to show that some factions of the Thai government were in fact also engaged in pro-Allied, anti-Japanese underground movements. Chiang would eventually become the first major Allied leader to endorse the Free Thai Movement and expressed his support for a free and independent Thailand after the conclusion of the war. That announcement was heartily endorsed by US president Franklin Roosevelt soon afterward.

Yet Chiang's endorsement was intended for neither Pridi's Free Thai Mission nor the nationalist ideals of the People's Party's constitutional government, but for the well-being of the overseas Chinese community in Thailand, which had contributed so generously to the Chinese war effort ever since the Japanese invasion of Manchuria in 1931, and who had bravely devoted so much to anti-Japanese activities. Chiang also had reason to anticipate continuing financial support from the Chinese community in Thailand to sustain postwar reconstruction and the future industrialization of the Republic of China. Unfortunately for Pridi and the People's Party, however, China did not contest US support for the return of Seni Pramoj as

Thailand's first postwar prime minister. Nor did Chiang ever contest the ongoing US patronage of royalist military dictators who, throughout the Cold War era, took turns ruling Thailand with an iron fist.

JAPANESE MILITARISM: THE INSPIRATION FOR
THE SIAMESE MODERN NATION

Japan's meteoric transformation from a closed feudal state under the leadership of the Tokugawa Shogunate to a leading world military power at the turn of the twentieth century was a fantastic success story that inspired many Asian political leaders of that era. Thai leaders of nearly all political leanings have been inspired by what was perceived as spectacular success in nation-building on the part of the Meiji Restoration. Despite the numerous differences separating Thai and Japanese circumstances, as well as differences among the political ideologies of the various factions in Thailand, it seemed that both the absolute monarchy and the constitutionalist regime that succeeded it sought at some point in time to emulate different aspects of the Japanese success story. Among the first to suggest Siam's need to emulate Meiji reforms was King Vajiravudh Rama VI, who had himself visited Japan in 1902, on his way home from study in England. Then crown prince Vajiravudh was highly impressed by Japanese military prowess at the dawn of the twentieth century and was convinced of the need to enhance the bonds between monarch and military as the foundation of a strong nation. The king was apparently obsessed with the Prussian military, which was strikingly similar to the Japanese model for military modernization during the Meiji period.

Logically speaking, there was not much in the immediate history of the Siamese monarchy to justify Vajiravudh's aspiration to attain greater control over the military or to substantially invest in modernizing it instead of other sectors.[2] Through the most treacherous periods of European imperialist aggression during the last decade of Chulalongkorn's reign, it was generally apparent that diplomacy, and not military might, had allowed Siam to retain the marginal independence and sovereignty it still enjoyed at the close of the nineteenth century. By the time Vajiravudh ascended the throne in 1910, the worst of European imperialist threats had become a thing of the past. However, much of the Siamese military opposed the new king. In fact, the plotters of the foiled coup of 1912 attested that Vajiravudh needed to be eliminated for Siam to attain the same level of modernization as Japan had achieved through the Meiji Restoration. At first glance, the logic of the coup plotters may appear bizarre, since the major inspiration behind the modernization of the Meiji Restoration was nationalism, which was fundamentally centered on the institution of the monarchy. However, in a strange and twisted way, one might also sympathize with the parallel argument that Vajiravudh, through his fondness for paramilitary organizations and frequent war games, was undermining the military and hampering modernization. That would have been another reason for overthrowing him, just as the Tokugawa Shogunate had to make way for the new and enlightened regime of the Meiji emperor.

The bizarre logic of the 1912 coup plotters in Siam equated Meiji-style modernization and nation-building with a strong, anti-European, military state with or without a monarch. A similar inspiration seemed to move Prime Minister Phibunsongkhram to emulate Japan in his anti-European, imperialist, nationalist campaign in the years leading up to the arrival of the Second World War in Southeast Asia. As the military wing of the People's Party gained dominance in the fledging constitutional regime in Thailand, the Japanese model of a strong expansionist military state became the prevalent theme of the Thai state's nationalist campaigns. Field Marshal Phibunsongkhram, who assumed office as the kingdom's premier in 1938, had expressed soon after he took office that the only way Thailand could escape colonization was for the nation to become an imperialist power in its own right:

> For all nations of the world, there are only two paths. That is, to become a
> great nation or to become a nation of serfs. There is no middle path. . . . I
> believe that at the end of the war, all the small nations in Europe will be
> governed by powers other than their own. There is no other way to escape
> in this day and age. I believe there is no other way for our nation except
> for us to work hard in all walks of life and improve the economy and our
> military might so that we can care for our own people.[3]

Thus the nationalist campaigns of the Thai constitutional regime from the mid-1930s until the conclusion of the Second World War assumed a vehemently anti-European imperialist stance, while adopting Japan's expansionist ultra-nationalist model. Thailand aimed to establish itself as a great nation in its own right. Embracing Japan's "Asia for Asians" propaganda reinforced the Phibunsongkhram regime's presentation of itself as the true nationalist government of the people. The new constitutional government distanced itself from the ancien régime of Siam's absolute monarchy, criticizing the old rulers for investing too much time and energy in negotiating with European imperialists and losing nearly half the kingdom's dominion to British and French colonizers as a result.

Through much of the 1930s, Japanese anti-European, imperialist nationalism came increasingly to replace the British public school model that Vajiravudh had so painstakingly instituted only a decade before.[4] There was a rush toward newly improved and mutually beneficial Thai-Japanese relations. Thailand became one of the first nations to recognize the Japanese puppet state in Manchuria, and by the end of 1938, there was already a proposed trade agreement between the state of Manchukuo and the Thai government.[5] By the end of the 1930s, Phibunsongkhram's brand of pro-Japanese, Pan-Asian, anti-European imperialist nationalism had reached a fever pitch. The new inspiration, infecting much of the cabinet, the armed forces, and the general public, eventually spilled over the borders with calls to liberate Indochina from the yoke of French imperialism and return Lao and Khmer territories to their Thai brethren. The months after France fell to invading German armies and the Vichy government was installed were possibly the most vulnerable period for French colonial forces during the Second World War. Thai armed forces were quick to instigate skirmishes along the Mekong frontier, which ultimately resulted in the outbreak of the Franco-Thai War of 1940–41.[6]

THE FRANCO-THAI WAR/INDOCHINA CONFLICT

The territories at stake in the Franco-Thai War were the same ones France had annexed as part of the French colony in Indochina in 1893 (land between the west bank of the Mekong River and the present Thai-Laos border) and 1903 (areas in eastern Cambodia, namely Siemreap, Battambang, and Sisophon). These problematic territories had never been uncontested parts of the Siamese empire during its recorded history from the thirteenth century CE. They had been governed by local nobles who pledged loyalty and sought protection as tributary states of either Siam (Thailand) or Yuan (Vietnam), depending on which empire was stronger at any given period. The first territorial maps made using modern geographical techniques, which established fixed borders between Thailand and its neighboring states, were produced in the nineteenth century, at a time when France and Britain were challenging Thai sovereignty over certain territories based on established frontiers.[7]

In 1893 and 1903, the territories in question happened to be sending tribute to the Siamese king (Chulalongkorn Rama V). France employed gunboat diplomacy to forcibly remove these tribute states from the Siamese realm of influence. First, in 1893, French gunboats occupied the mouth of the Chaophraya River as far as the Siamese capital in Bangkok and forced Chulalongkorn to forgo sovereignty over most of the territories on the west bank of the Mekong. A decade later, in 1903, France held the eastern sea-board provinces of Trat and Chantaburi until the Siamese government agreed to give up the rest of the west bank as well as the eastern Khmer territories.[8] The geographical boundaries of the Thai nation were thus estab-lished by the French gunboat diplomacy of 1893; as a result, the kingdom gained territories that should have belonged to the Lao or Khmer, accord-ing to modern conventions of culture, language, and ethnicity. Thailand has managed to retain these territories within its sovereignty rights to the present day.[9]

Nonetheless, in the anti-European imperialist, ultra-nationalist view-point of the Phibunsongkhram administration, nearly half the nation's territory had been lost to French imperialist aggression through the unjust means of gunboat diplomacy.[10] According to Wichitwathakan, Phibun-songkhram's top propagandist, there was no doubt that the people residing in those annexed territories were Thai and properly belonged, along with their land, resources, and possessions, with the Thai nation: "Every time I look across the Mekong, I feel as if the water that is rushing through is the tears of the Thai people. We, residing on this side of the river, enjoy freedom. But our brethren on that side are under the yoke of the French imperialists."[11]

The opportunity for the Phibunsongkhram government to reclaim from French Indochina what, according to Wichitwathakan, was rightfully Thai came with the outbreak of the Second World War in Europe. When France fell to German troops in June 1940, the Vichy government requested that the Thai government sign a treaty of nonaggression, which Phibunsong-khram agreed to do under three conditions: (1) that the deep course of the Mekong be used as a natural border between Thailand and Indo-china; (2) that territories on the west bank of the Mekong be returned in their entirety to Thai authority; and (3) that, should France ever forgo its sov-ereign rights over Laos and Cambodia, the two states would become part of the Thai nation.[12] Not surprisingly, these demands were deemed unac-ceptable, even by the Vichy government. Phibunsongkhram brought the matter to public attention, and anti-European imperialist nationalism reached unprecedented levels. For the first time in modern history, univer-sity students in Bangkok took to the streets to demonstrate in support of the government. The provinces also saw numerous public demonstrations in support of Thailand's so-called reclamation of Indochinese territories.

Hostility broke out along the Thai-Indochinese border on November 28, 1940. The Thai government announced that five French aircraft had crossed the border and bombed the province of Nakhon Phanom, leaving six people injured. The Thai Armed Forces promptly responded by invading and capturing all territories in question in less than two months. It should not come as a surprise that, during this period of conflict, agents of the Thai government had come in close contact with and offered a variety of political and military favors to the various local underground independence movements in Indochina in exchange for their support in this expedition to reclaim territory for Thailand.[13]

In December 1940, the Thai government announced it would grant Thai citizenship to the residents of the disputed territories. Thai borders were also opened to Lao and Khmer who desired to enter the country. The Public Relations Department encouraged Indochinese immigrants to take possession and develop the abundant arable land of the northeastern countryside of Thailand. The message was loud and clear: in Thailand, the Lao and Khmer would no longer be treated as colonial subjects. Instead, they would be respected and enjoy equal rights with Thai citizens.[14] The pan–Southeast Asian nationalist rhetoric Phibunsongkhram employed to rally support from neighboring colonies was almost identical to the pan-Asian rhetoric that predominated in Japanese attempts to create a Greater East Asian Co-Prosperity Sphere. Just as Japan pushed "Asia for Asians," Thai propagandists rallied to free the people of "Laemthong" from the imperialist yoke of the French and British.[15] Racial unity became a major theme of the Thai expansionist campaign. The criteria of "Thainess" were stretched far beyond both cultural and linguistic limits as Wichitwathakan repeatedly attempted to include the Khmer and, at times, even the Vietnamese in that mythical race which seemed to expand continuously with the fall of France in Europe and the rise of Phibunsongkhram's influence in mainland Southeast Asia—the "Thai" race.[16]

Japan, whose forces had been stationed on the east coast of French Indochina by the end of 1940, offered to mediate almost as soon as the conflict broke out. While offering to mediate, the Japanese government demonstrated decisive support for the Thai government's nationalist cause by providing up to ten of its own aircraft in place of sixteen American planes that the Thai government had ordered and already paid for, but which the US government refused to deliver in an attempt to discourage the Thais from escalating the violence in the Indochina conflict. Eventually, a cease-fire agreement was signed aboard a Japanese battleship on January 31, 1941, and a formal peace agreement was signed by delegates of the Phibunsong-khram and Vichy governments in Tokyo on May 9. Not surprisingly, all the disputed territories were allotted to Thailand. The news was received joy-ously by the Thai people. Phibunsongkhram's announcement of victory was greeted with a standing ovation from the parliament.[17] Even leaders of the anti-Phibunsongkhram factions—primarily finance minister Pridi Banomyong—spoke with pride of the prime minister's accomplishments in Indochina. The Victory Monument was erected to celebrate this glorious, albeit short-lived, triumph over French imperialism; it is probably, since it stands at the center of the busiest traffic circle in all of Thailand, Bangkok's most prominent landmark.[18]

THE GREATER EAST ASIA WAR IN THAILAND

Multiple competing nationalist forces were at work in Thailand when, in the early morning hours of December 8, 1941, the Second World War arrived on its shores in the form of the Japanese Southern Area Army (SAA). Within the ruling People's Party government, there was already an uneasy rift between the fascist militarist faction, which was the main power base of the prime minister, and the socialist-leaning civilian faction led by Minister of Finance Pridi Banomyong. Though Phibunsongkhram's success in the Indochina conflict had propelled the government toward cooperation with Japan, rival factions, especially Pridi, were wary of allowing Thailand to fol-low Japan down the path of militarism by officially entering the war on the side of the Axis powers. To complicate matters further, supporters of the old regime and more than a few royalists in exile were anxious to return to political dominance. The imminent downfall of the People's Party was highly anticipated by many who had been displaced by the revolution. Bets were on, therefore, as to whether Japan would fail in her mission to replace European imperialist powers as the new overlord in the Asia-Pacific. Hence, in the late evening of December 7, when the message from the Japanese ambassador to Thailand arrived at the prime minister's residence announc-ing that Japan had declared war on the United States and Britain and requested passage through Thailand for the imperial armies, there was an outburst of conflicting reactions from factions within the Thai ruling class.

Strange as it seems, Prime Minister Phibunsongkhram was not home to receive the message. He was touring the territories recently acquired as a result of the Indochina conflict. The historic communiqué was therefore received by the minister of foreign affairs, Direk Jayanama, who would later write a two-volume history, *Thailand and the Second World War*, in which he describes himself as being decidedly in Pridi's pro-Allied camp. Direk unceremoniously declined the Japanese request for passage and alerted the prime minister to the urgent need to return to the capital. Inexplicably, the commander in chief, despite the availability of more rapid means of transport, decided to return to Bangkok by van. Upon his arrival, the prime minister called for an emergency cabinet meeting. A decision was made at 7:30 in the morning not to obstruct the approaching Japanese and to allow the SAA to proceed through Thai territory. Despite more than a few voices of dissent, most of Phibunsongkhram's cabinet agreed that any form of armed resistance would be suicidal.[19]

It was not until midnight that the order to stand down reached the far southern provinces of Songkhla and Pattani, where Japanese troops were making landfall. By the time the order arrived, 141 Japanese military personnel and 183 Thai police and armed forces, including members of the youth militia, had lost their lives in a skirmish at the beachhead.[20] That forlorn little battle was presented by the Phibunsongkhram regime as the result of a most unfortunate miscommunication that resulted in tragic loss of life. Nonetheless, this clash between the Thai armed forces and the Japanese SAA served later as evidence when those who had supported the Allies from the beginning claimed that Thailand had been forced into the war by Japanese aggression. Some even wondered if Phibunsongkhram had not deliberately orchestrated events in a way that would allow Thailand the possibility of later switching to a pro-Allied stance.[21] As soon as news of the cease-fire order and the declaration of Thailand's nonresistance arrived in the United States, the Thai minister to Washington, DC, M. R. Seni Pramoj, in defiance of his own government, declared that the Free Thai supported the Allied powers. Thus came into existence the Free Thai Movement, the most notable pro-Allied movement in mainstream Thai history.

To what degree the Japanese occupation of Thailand affected the resident ethnic Chinese community and how much they contributed to the downfall of the Greater East Asia Co-Prosperity Sphere are among the most problematic and hotly debated matters related to Thailand's involvement in the Second World War. Historians of the Thai nationalist mainstream—Direk Jayanama being the most prominent among them—accord little credit for the ultimate outcome of the war to the ethnic Chinese.[22] He allocates much of the blame for the Thai government's wartime anti-Chinese policies to the overwhelming pressure of the SAA presence and the incompetence of Phi-bunsongkhram's pro-Axis regime. More recent voices disagree with that position, most vocal among them the Japanese historian of Thailand and the overseas Chinese, Eiji Murashima.[23] He argues, to the contrary, that many anti-Japanese activities were carried out by members of the ethnic Chinese community long before the SAA's arrival in Thailand and continued, mostly unimpeded, through the war years. He states furthermore that anti-Chinese sentiments were already overwhelming among members of the Thai ruling cabinet and had been so since the end of the nineteenth century. In other words, Phibunsongkhram's regime was already anti-Chinese, even before entering into the formal alliance with Japan. Documents from the Republican Chinese government provide a slightly more complex and comprehensive perspective. A group of delegates from the ethnic Chinese community in Thailand had been meeting with officers of the Chinese Ministry of Foreign Affairs in the Sino-Thai Problem Discussion Group (Zhong-Tai Wenti Taolun Hui) on almost a monthly basis from the late 1930s to 1943. The minutes of those meetings provide a glimpse into the background and buildup to the Japanese-Thai alliance in a way that most wartime records, focusing solely on events of the war years, do not.

From the perspective of the Chinese authorities, Japan had begun to exert its influence in Thailand since the late 1930s by taking advantage of Thai distaste for Chinese nationalism and by supporting Phibunsongkhram's ambitions to reclaim territories from French Indochina. Japan's calculated approach, backed up by action, made it nearly impossible for the Thai state, virtually abandoned by its British and American allies, to resist the influence of Japanese hegemony.

> Around the same time that the War of Resistance broke out in China [1937], Japan forcefully entered Thailand. [The Japanese] took advantage of the rising nationalist movement in Thailand to undermine Sino-Thai relations and persecuted the overseas Chinese. [They] instigated the Thai-Vietnamese [Indochina] Conflict, weakened American and British influence in Thailand, and were preparing to progress further south. Since the outbreak of the Pacific War, Thailand has become a vassal kingdom of Japan. Her resources, manpower and land have been employed by the Japanese to further their war efforts. . . . If China and Britain had helped put Vietnam [Indochina] in control before the Japanese troops went south, Thailand would never have joined the Japanese and the Japanese southern expedition would never have been so successful.[24]

Records from the meetings of the Sino-Thai Problem Discussion Group may be the first primary documents that suggest a clear parallel between the anti-Chinese sentiments of the Vajiravudh era and the buildup of anti-European imperialist nationalism in the prewar Phibunsongkhram regime. The ethnic Chinese had made themselves unpopular to a certain extent by using their vague and problematic citizenship status to claim extraterritorial rights as registered European subjects in Thailand. Other regional powers, in particular China and the British Empire, failed to intervene on behalf of Thailand in the Indochina conflict. All this made it easier for Japan to win the trust and support of the Thai government. The anti-imperialist nationalist sentiment of the Phibunsongkhram era was not only pointedly anti-Chinese; it also strongly supported Japan's expansion into China and Southeast Asia.[25] Of course, Japan had much more leverage in Thailand after the Indochina conflict. The report from the tenth meeting of the Sino-Thai Problem Discussion Group in 1942 recorded the following: "Following the enemy's [Japan's] envious suggestions for control of [overseas Chinese] national salvation activities, the Thai government attempted to flatter the Japanese by openly discouraging such activities in various ways, such as raiding [Chinese] news publishers and [Chinese] school dormitories, arresting patriotic overseas [Chinese] compatriots, campaigning against the use of their [overseas Chinese produced] goods."[26]

Also included were reports of the signing of the Japanese-Thai Treaty of Alliance and a suggestion that that event was influenced by the successful Japanese mediation of the Indochina conflict and the rise to power of Phibunsongkhram's pro-Japan faction in the Thai cabinet.[27] The next meeting noted that the Thai military had been coerced into supporting the Japanese military expedition in British Malaya and that possibilities for improving Sino-Thai relations would remain grim as long as the Japanese had military control over Thailand.[28] The twelfth meeting mentions the plan for Sino-British joint military operations to counter Japanese attacks on British Burma and the southern Chinese province of Yunnan. It also mentions Thailand's latest diplomatic agreement with Nazi Germany and the Soviet Union's concerns over rising Japanese influence in the Far East, which could lead to further USSR involvement along the Allied powers' East and Southeast Asian battlefronts.[29]

By April 1942, according to the report from the twenty-fourth meeting, Japan had gained so much control over the Thai economy that it had managed to convince the Thai cabinet to devalue the baht, making its exchange rate identical with the yen. By then, the United States had joined the war on the Pacific front, and Japan's advantageous position in the region was increasingly threatened. The twenty-fourth meeting also notes Phibunsong-khram's extreme national security measures, which had direct detrimental effects on the livelihood of many in the ethnic Chinese community. For example, the capital was set to be relocated to the still thickly jungled province of Phetchabun and the implementation of antialien strategic areas, which drove many ethnic Chinese from their homes, had been announced. The same report mentions that Japanese forces had instigated mass arrests and persecution of noncollaborating ethnic Chinese.[30]

While the Thai government appeared to be willing to cooperate with the SAA, reports from the Sino-Thai Problem Discussion Group meetings also reflected, early in the war years, that some factions in the Thai ruling class, including members of Phibunsongkhram's cabinet, were secretly subverting Japanese occupation of Thailand. Some leading figures in the Thai intelligentsia had expressed concern that the state's unjust persecution of the ethnic Chinese might bring serious consequences at the conclusion of the war. As early as the beginning of 1942, there were rumors of an underground pro-Allied movement, possibly led by the minister of finance, Pridi Banomyong, already well known for being anti-Japanese.[31] By the end of 1942, Thailand had recognized the sovereignty of the newly established Japanese puppet state of Manchukuo. The twenty-eighth meeting reported the appointment of the first Manchukuo ambassador to Thailand. Despite all the fanfare in diplomatic circles, the meeting suggested that at the grassroots level, all was not well in the Japanese-Thai alliance:

> There was a devastating flood in Thailand from early this month [October]. Last report on the 22nd stated that the water had not yet begun to recede. The total economic loss from the flood has been estimated at approximately 230,000,000 baht. . . . According to the enemy's [Japan's] broadcast, the enemy had been helping to alleviate the damage due to the flood. . . . However, the enemy is insisting that Thailand transport a large stock of military supplies to the northern borders [despite damages from the flood]. This has been a cause of the Thai resentment toward the Japanese.[32]

The twenty-ninth meeting reported the arrival of a Japanese adviser in trade who hoped to rescue the Thai economy from ethnic Chinese dominance. The report stated that Thailand expected to double its income from trade in 1943, but at least one-third of that increase was assigned to military funding. Moreover, the report suggested that "since the war broke out in Burma, Japan has not been as active in training Thai military personnel. They are worried that the growing sense of patriotism in Thailand may become a disadvantage to their cause."[33]

By the end of 1942, there had been a definite change in the Thai government's attitude toward the Japanese. As circumstances started to favor the Allied powers, Thai authorities moved toward reducing SAA privileges in Thailand. Japanese military matters were no longer of utmost urgency.[34] In January 1943, the thirtieth meeting reported continuing developments in Japanese-Thai relations, in cultural areas (establishment of the Japanese-Thai Cultural Association in Bangkok and a Thai Studies Center in Tokyo, and the exchange of trade officers from both countries) and in political areas (Thai government recognition of three Japanese puppet states—Manchukuo, Mongolia, and the Nanjing regime in China, and a joint military expedition against Allied forces in Burma and Yunnan). The same document, however, also reported that Japan's development aid for Thailand had been aimed largely toward the development of agricultural production, not industrialization.[35] This, of course, became a cause for resentment among the rising anti-Japanese factions in the Thai government.

The thirty-first meeting reported even more severe signs of the growing rift in the Japanese-Thai alliance. The economic situation in Thailand was dire by this point. Supplies were becoming scarce, and inflation was soaring. The meeting concluded that although Thailand had entered the war with great aspirations, the situation had taken a turn for the worse due to rising Japanese demands: "After the outbreak of the Pacific War, Thailand has essentially become a Japanese vassal state. Its resources, manpower, and strategic geographical properties have been exhausted in support of the Japanese war efforts."[36] The same report also commented that Thai troops fighting in Yunnan had made contact with Chinese Nationalist troops requesting a cease-fire.[37]

EMERGENCE OF THE FREE THAI MOVEMENT

By the end of 1942, it had become clear to observers in the Sino-Thai Problem Discussion Group that there were at least two conflicting forces competing for dominance in Phibunsongkhram's wartime cabinet—the pro-Japanese mainstream militarists led by the prime minister, and the underground pro-Allied group led by an elusive yet highly influential member of the cabinet, most likely the minister of finance, Pridi Banomyong, under the code name Ruth. Early in 1943, a third group emerged from the already complicated Thai political scene and reached out for direct contact with the government of the Republic of China, then seated in the southwestern capital of Chongqing. Sometime toward the end of March 1943, a Thai national by the name of Chamkad Balankura and his interpreter, Phaisan Trakunli, crossed the northern border of French Indochina into China and were promptly arrested by customs officers. Chamkad claimed to be an agent of the Free Thai Movement (FTM) sent by Pridi to discuss urgent matters concerning the pro-Allied movement in Thailand with the president of the Chinese Republic, Generalissimo Chiang Kai-shek. According to his diary, Chamkad stated four main objectives of his mission to China:

(1) To convey Pridi's agenda to M. R. Seni Pramoj, leader of the Free Thai Movement in the US, and to have Seni negotiate that agenda with British and American authorities;

(2) To rally support from the Allied powers for future activities of the FTM;

(3) To request intelligence and tactical support from the Allies in order to transport leaders of the pro-Allied faction in Phibunsongkhram's cabinet to establish a government in exile in British India; and

(4) To convince the British to allocate the currently frozen funds of the Thai government in Britain for use by the FTM.[38]

The Free Thai Movement in itself was not new from the point of view of the Chinese authorities. Documents suggest that there had been communications between the Chinese Foreign Ministry and its British and American counterparts concerning the Thai pro-Allied movement since early 1942. Moreover, news of the mutiny of the Thai legation in Washington, DC, and the declaration of support for the Allied powers by the Thai minister to Washington, M. R. Seni Pramoj, had circulated widely among Allied diplomats almost as soon as the war broke out in Southeast Asia in December 1941. In fact, only a matter of months before Chamkad's arrival in Chongqing in February 1943, the generalissimo himself had broadcast his historic statement endorsing the stance of the Free Thai Movement and confirming that the Chinese government perceived Thailand as a victim of Japanese imperialist aggression and not a collaborator.[39] The arrival of Chamkad in China was very curious, however, because neither Seni nor any of the leading members of the British FTM knew of him or his mission to China prior to his arrival in late March 1943. It took the Chinese authorities nearly two weeks to substantiate Chamkad's identity. The Thai legation in Washington confirmed that a Thai student in the United States by the name of Kamhaeng Balankura had come forward to identify Chamkad as his brother. He confirmed that Chamkad had studied philosophy at Oxford but had returned to Thailand before the war and was a close acquaintance of Pridi. Yet Seni Pramoj, who was recognized as the FTM leader, was reluctant to provide Chamkad with financial support or even substantiate his claim that he was a Free Thai agent. Moreover, communications from the British legation that arrived soon after Chamkad's arrival in Chongqing clearly portrayed him as an unreliable and untrustworthy agent: "From the information available, the Foreign Office considers that B. [Chamkad Balankura] has gone off half cocked and has in fact no practical plan which could now profitably be put into effect."[40]

Matters became even more complicated when Chamkad refused to meet with Lieutenant M. L. Khap Kunjara, the FTM liaison, sent to Chongqing by Seni Pramoj himself. The British FTM leader, Prince Subhasvastiwongsesnith Svastivatana, was also unsure of Chamkad's position vis-à-vis the royalist branch of the FTM in Britain. Together with the most confidential reports on Chamkad, the British legation sent background information on Khap and Prince Subhasvastwongsesnith which confirmed Chinese suspicions that the three were not working together in the same movement after all. According to British intelligence, Khap had close personal ties with Phibunsongkhram's family—close enough that Phibun, who was extremely fearful of being poisoned, would willingly ingest food cooked by Khap's wife. Hence, they warned that Khap should not be trusted with any information that could be of use to the Japanese. As for Prince Subhasvastwongsesnith, the British noted that he was the brother-in-law and personal secretary of the former King Prajadhipok (Rama VII) and a staunch supporter of the restoration of absolute monarchy in Thailand—a political stance that would conflict with Pridi's vision of a democratic Thailand in the postwar era.[41]

Despite the confusing circumstances surrounding Chamkad's mission, he managed to convey his message to the generalissimo in person shortly before dying from cancer in Chongqing on October 7, 1943. Even so, he accomplished none of the main objectives of his mission. Pridi dispatched two more missions to China before the conclusion of the war in 1945. The first came soon after it became apparent that Chamkad's negotiations were going nowhere. Sa-nguan Tularak, former member of Parliament and a prominent figure in the ethnic Chinese community in Thailand, was dispatched along with Daeng Khunadilok, a high-ranking officer of the Thai

Ministry of Foreign Affairs, and five other delegates, to Chongqing in August 1943. Sa-nguan and his team were much better equipped than Chamkad to handle the situation. Most of them had been involved in the ethnic Chinese underground anti-Japanese movement for some time, and three of the seven, Sa-nguan included, were fluent in Chinese, English, and Thai. Republican Chinese archival materials documenting this visit suggest that it was much more comprehensive and fruitful. Repeating the same strategic request as Chamkad, Sa-nguan also provided a brief report on the grim circumstances surrounding the ethnic Chinese community in Thailand under the Japanese occupation. Sa-nguan took full advantage of his Chinese ancestry to convince Chinese authorities that it was in China's best interest to support the FTM's efforts to push the Japanese out of Thailand.

Perhaps the most persuasive offer coming from Sa-nguan's team was their apparent willingness to acknowledge Seni as the internationally recognized leader of the Free Thai Movement. With this assurance, the Chinese government was able to provide some support without having to worry too much about the Washington-based FTM or about jeopardizing whatever little support Seni had managed to garner from his American friends. As a direct result of Sa-nguan's negotiations, the Republic of China agreed to provide military resources for the training of FTM agents in certain areas of South China.[42] According to Prasit Rakpracha's memoirs, Free Thai agents were sent from Britain and the United States to train in India and South China from late 1943 until the conclusion of the war.[43] The units trained by the British in India were nicknamed White Elephants, while those trained by the Chinese were known as Red Elephants. After a brief period of training, the agents were sent back with orders to infiltrate through enemy lines into Thailand, either by parachuting or by making amphibious landings.[44]

The achievements of the Sa-nguan mission, albeit more substantial than Chamkad's attempt, were limited to areas that did not challenge Seni's internationally recognized position as leader of the Free Thai Movement. Throughout the war, leading Allied powers continued to refuse Pridi's faction access to frozen Thai government funds in Britain and the United States. Neither were they willing to help smuggle Free Thai political leaders out of Thailand to form a government in exile in India. The best indication of the Allied Powers' preference for Seni over Pridi was the fact that, upon the conclusion of negotiations in Chongqing, Sa-nguan and Daeng were sent to Washington to report to Seni before returning in a roundabout manner to join the Allied powers headquarters in Kandy as representatives of the Free Thai Movement.[45] The leading Allied powers were apparently willing to recognize missions dispatched by Pridi as Free Thai missions only as subordinates of the Washington-based organization founded by Seni at the outbreak of war. Not surprisingly, Pridi resented this treatment and continued to assert that he was the founder and had been the true leader of the FTM throughout the remaining years of the Second World War in the Far East.

The last FTM mission to China during the war years was dispatched in September 1944, with Thawin Udon—former Roi-ed MP and close confidant of Pridi—as the principal envoy. Aside from the primary objective of negotiating postwar Sino-Thai diplomatic relations that would secure Thailand's position among the Allied victors of the war, Thawin also delivered a personal message from Pridi to Chiang:

> Ever since the enemy [Japan] gained dominance over Thai territory,
> Prime Minister Phibunsongkhram's regime had yielded to all its [Japan's]
> demands. Patriotic Thais and the overseas Chinese in Thailand, therefore,
> joined forces to establish the Free Thai Movement to liberate Thailand
> from Japanese occupation. [The FTM] had sent Chamkad and Sa-nguan
> as his agents to negotiate for support from the government of China. In
> the name of the long-standing friendship between our two countries, [the
> third mission] has come to request for your esteemed nation to aid in the
> establishment of a Free Thai government in exile and military and
> organizational support in fighting the enemy and retaining our
> independence.[46]

In his letter to the generalissimo, Pridi clearly spelled out his leadership claims by stating that the Free Thai Movement was established through the joint efforts of "patriotic Thais and the overseas Chinese in Thailand." At no point in this historic communication did he acknowledge Seni's role in founding the FTM, as stipulated in the internally recognized historical narrative at that point in time. In approaching the matter in such a way, Pridi was also reminding Chiang of the continuous support the Republic of China had received from the ethnic Chinese community in Thailand long before the leading Allied powers of the West became actively involved in the Far Eastern war zone. After all, it was Chiang who took the initiative of formally and publicly endorsing Thailand's pro-Allied position, and it was for the sake of Thailand's ethnic Chinese community and their ability to support China's postwar reconstruction that the generalissimo made his landmark decision. This was not only spelled out in Chiang's historic endorsement, broadcast in February 1943,[47] but it was also clearly reflected in the outline for postwar settlements that he negotiated with Thawin:

1. The Free Thai provisional government should be established with China's approval. After the Free Thai Movement successfully seizes power [in Thailand], it should immediately send representatives to discuss a diplomatic treaty and to make plans for the establishment of formal Sino-Thai diplomatic relations between our two nations.

2. After the establishment of formal Sino-Thai diplomatic relations, a Sino-Thai treaty of trade and commerce should be established within six months.

    The treaty of trade and commerce mentioned above should include the following principles,
    (1) Principle of mutual benefits
    (2) "Most-favored nation" clause
    (3) Overseas subjects of both countries would be granted freedom to reside, conduct business, labor, travel, study, and practice religious faith [in both countries]
    (4) Exchange of consul personnel

3. All overseas Chinese who had been unlawfully expelled from Thai territory during the war must be allowed to return [to Thailand] and allowed freedom of association with no interference from the Thai government.

4. The Thai government must compensate for all losses of overseas Chinese lives and property which occurred in Thai territory during the time of [Japanese] occupation.

5. All laws that were promulgated during the war and used to discriminate against or persecute the overseas Chinese must be abolished. The Thai government's control of overseas Chinese education must also be modified accordingly after liberation [from Japanese occupation].[48]

China's endorsement of Thailand's pro-Allied position in the Second World War was crucial in bringing about further endorsement by the United States and eventually a favorable outcome for Thailand upon the conclusion of the war. By his three FTM missions to China, Pridi attempted to gain further support from the Republic of China so as to ensure the survival of the constitutional regime in Thailand, even after the fall of Phibunsong-khram's militarist government with the defeat of Japan. That outcome already appeared inevitable by the end of 1943. Even so, the postwar world order of that era would not allow Pridi's socialist democratic ideals to prevail in Thailand.

The constitutional regime did survive the fall of Phibunsongkhram and the end of Japanese occupation. The United States became the superpower and the dominant force throughout the Asia-Pacific region. Faced with the powerful challenge of the USSR and the rapid expansion of the Communist bloc, the United States chose to back the royalist FTM leader, M. R. Seni Pramoj, who was eventually established as the postwar prime minister of Thailand, while Pridi was forced to accept the prestigious, yet relatively powerless, position of regent to young King Anandamahidol Rama VIII. As for China, all Sino-Thai agreements negotiated by the Sa-nguan and Thawin missions were honored in their entirety. In 1946, a follow-up mission was led by Luang Sitthi Songkhram, an army officer of Chinese descent, to report to the Republic of China on Thailand's postwar reforms, especially concerning government policies toward the ethnic Chinese.[49] Pridi arrived in China later the same year to finalize details of the postwar Sino-Thai diplomatic agenda. Some important issues discussed included the following:

(1) Siam's current policies concerning the Anglo-American supported Marshall Plans
(2) . . . preparations to dispatch [Chinese] personnel to attend to ethnic Chinese matters in Siam
(3) . . . renovation and reestablishment of the Office of the [Chinese] Commercial Commission in Bangkok
(4) . . . 10,000 baht compensation for the damages to [Chinese] Chambers of Commerce [during the war][50]

Needless to say, no part of these agreements conflicted with the postwar US political agenda for either China or Thailand. The Republic of China, devastated by more than a decade of Japanese aggression, was in no position to challenge American hegemony in the immediate aftermath of the war. While China descended into civil war, postwar Thai politics witnessed the deterioration of Pridi's position in the face of rising political conflict between his faction and Seni's dominant conservative royalist faction.

In June 1946, the tragic and yet to be fully explained shooting of eighteen-year-old King Anandhamahidol put tremendous pressure upon Pridi, who was regent and already in a precarious position due to his left-leaning stance in politics and economic matters. It did not take long for the former FTM royalists and their cohort to find themselves in a peculiar alliance with the disgraced and disgruntled militarists of the war years. In November 1947, Seni's conservative faction supported a military coup overthrowing the postwar civilian government. Phibunsongkhram returned to power as prime minister, and Pridi went into exile for the rest of his life, first to Beijing and later to France. The coup of 1947 unleashed a series of violent purges of the remaining Pridi supporters and associates in Thailand. Sa-nguan Tularak, who by then was the Thai ambassador to the Republic of China, went into self-imposed exile in Beijing for a full decade, only to be arrested as a communist sympathizer and imprisoned upon his return to Thailand in 1957. Thawin Udon was assassinated while in police custody, also on communist-related charges, in 1949. The odd alliance between the conservatives and the military dominated the Thai political scene with the blessing of the United States throughout the Cold War years. Once a strong force in the People's Party and a crucial faction in the highly complex diplomacy of the Second World War, the left-leaning civilian constitutionalists were systematically driven from public life, through violent persecution and an inexorable process of elimination in the creation of the mainstream conservative nationalist historical narrative.

RETURNING TO ROYALIST NATIONALISM

Thailand's experience through the Second World War and Japanese occupation can be understood as the culmination of complex political relationships between the Thai state and the ethnic Chinese. Perhaps more importantly, the conclusion of the war also marked the end of Thailand's brief yet significant experiment as a nonroyalist, semirepublican state under the constitutional government of the People's Party following the Revolution of 1932. As the torrential currents of international conflict swept through Southeast Asia from the late 1930s to the end of the Second World War, the newly established constitutional regime had, in a Siamese déjà vu, been forced into a situation where it had to align itself with a superpower as a matter of survival. The People's Party government, under the leadership of the militarist Field Marshal Phibunsongkram, attempted to stabilize and fortify the new constitutional regime by forging friendly ties with Japan—the new Asian superpower of that era. Phibunsongkhram led the Thai state into an anti–European imperialist, nationalist campaign against French Indochina. This strategic move not only gained considerable popular support with Thai reclamation of the nation's lost territories; it also allowed the People's Party government to sideline the crown and the old absolute monarchy, and to present themselves as the true nationalist leaders of the modern Thai nation-state.

Furthermore, subscribing to Japanese Pan-Asian, anti-European, and anti–American imperialist rhetoric also provided the young constitutional regime with an opportunity to reclaim judicial and economic autonomy. They succeeded in revising or revoking unfair treaties that had been forced upon the kingdom since the nineteenth century by Western imperialist powers. The abolition of extraterritoriality allowed the Thai state to distance itself from the political and economic dominance of European imperialist powers, especially Britain. It also allowed the state to gain more control over many in the ethnic Chinese community who had dominated the Thai economy through extraterritorial privileges they had acquired as registered European subjects. The formal alliance with Japan at the outbreak of the Second World War put the ethnic Chinese in Thailand under tremendous pressure to accept naturalization as Thai citizens or risk increasing scrutiny and persecution as citizens of an enemy state. This seemingly heavy-handed policy toward the ethnic Chinese could also be seen as an indirect strategy to weaken the position of the monarch. There were royalist factions that continued to support the Crown, despite the hostile environment of the wartime militarist constitutional state. The monarchy was no longer in a position to grant economic favors to close traditional allies, and Japanese occupation exacerbated the anti-Chinese policies of the Thai regime. The era of the People's Party was indeed exceptionally difficult for the ethnic Chinese in Thailand.

To establish a modern nation-state based on civic nationalism that did not rely on the mythic personage of the monarch was not going to be easy. Switching political allegiance from one superpower to another would not be an automatic fix. Unfortunately for Phibunsongkhram's grand schemes for Thai nationalism, the tides of war started to turn against Japan as early as the end of 1942. Alternative means of national salvation had to be sought. The royalists in the United States and Britain had already declared allegiance to the Allied powers. The only way the constitutional regime of the People's Party was going to survive Japan's defeat was by gaining the support of a leading Allied force influential enough to secure a democratic future for Thailand in the postwar era. Wartime finance minister Pridi Banomyong attempted to achieve this near-impossible feat by dispatching pro-Allied missions to negotiate with the government of the Republic of China in Chongqing. Pridi's approach was not too different from the strategies employed by some of his most successful forebears in Thai politics: he sought the support of a superpower external to the current conflict—in this case, the Republic of China. This powerful ally could provide a balance against the overwhelmingly dominant forces supporting his rival, in this case, the United States and Britain. The Western nations vaguely supported the Free Thai Movement represented by M. R. Seni Pramoj, Thai minister to Washington, DC. The Republic of China was the leading Allied power in the Far East, and it had come into being through an antimonarchist revolution. China also had a commendable anti-imperialist record through much of the early twentieth century. Thus it appeared that China would be Pridi's best bet for regaining political dominance and possibly blocking the triumphant return of the royalists in the postwar era.

There were more than a few obstacles to Pridi's grand scheme. Politically, the Chinese were deeply divided and had been even before the outbreak of the Second World War. Chiang Kai-shek's Nationalist armies had borne the terrible brunt of Japanese military might. Now, following Japan's defeat, the Nationalists would have to struggle for survival in a civil war with China's Communist forces. Although they were willing to support the ethnic Chinese community that Pridi's missions claimed to represent, the Nationalist government was not in a position to argue with the Allies concerning the final outcome of the war. There was also the matter of Pridi's prosocialist history. Chiang's regime tended to prefer their powerful anticommunist American sponsors over a diasporic politician who had been branded more than once a communist sympathizer. Not surprisingly, the outcome of the Second World War for Thailand came in the form of a compromise that allowed the Land of Smiles to stand among the Allied victors. The ethnic Chinese in Thailand, who had bravely supported Chiang's regime, were thereby spared the grim fate of living in a defeated nation. The United States had the last word on postwar arrangements in Thailand, and this outcome clearly paved the way for US dominance in the kingdom throughout the Cold War period, perhaps even to the present day. However, the arrangement also resulted in the royalists' return to power, to the inevitable detriment of Pridi and his political supporters.

The appointment of Seni as the postwar prime minister marked the official return of royalist conservatives to political dominance. Aside from putting Thailand squarely into the anti-Communist camp throughout the Cold War years, this outcome of the Second World War returned the country to the royalist nationalism championed in the eras of Chulalongkorn and Vajiravudh. This turn of events influenced, at the most fundamental levels, relations of the Thai government with Thailand's ethnic Chinese community and the now fragmented Chinese state.[51] The Thai state reverted back to the imperial mentality, tolerating a minimal degree of ethnic and cultural diversity, so long as the royalist ruling class was able to maintain control of what was considered the sociopolitical correctness of the day. The ethnic Chinese were allowed to maintain their cultural identity as long as they clearly expressed undivided loyalty to the Crown and avoided showing support or sympathy for socialist ideals. They were allowed to maintain contact with the nation of their ancestors so long as they acknowledged only "one China," that is, Chiang Kai-shek's Republic of China and not Mao Zedong's People's Republic. The imperial mentality of royalist nationalism and the state's bifurcated policies toward China and the ethnic Chinese soon became even more pronounced.

Royalist politicians soon formed a peculiar but powerful alliance with postwar militarists. After Phibunsongkhram, grown vulnerable and unpopular, was overthrown in 1957 and exiled, the new alliance was virtually invincible, with the added blessing of American Cold War policies. The United States opted to support military dictatorships rather than risking the installation of democratic systems that could allow socialist or communist regimes to come to power. The postwar political scene in Thailand resembled more than ever the client-patron system of the late eighteenth and early nineteenth centuries. In those earlier reigns, the Chakri court had offered protection and patronage to prominent Chinese tycoons, who in turn provided the monarchy with financial support and entrepreneurial skills in various state-owned enterprises. Chinese tycoons of the period following the Second World War once again acquired political protection and a steady flow of lucrative government contracts by cultivating traditional ties with royalist politicians and politically influential generals. It was a formidable alliance of the conservative ruling classes—royalists, militarists, and capitalists—capable of effective repression of the progressive and radical underclasses. The picture matched almost exactly the Cold War tendencies of most pro-American states in Southeast Asia.

At the close of the twentieth century, the ethnic Chinese community was still divided. The urban educated middle and upper classes, which constituted the ethnic Chinese community in the public imagination, appeared to be the most royalist in politics and most capitalist in their way of life. The urban proletariat and rural agricultural working classes, by contrast, produced more radicals and socialists. They were also, when active, the first to be violently suppressed and demonized as grave threats to national security and the sociocultural harmony of Thai society. State support for patriotic, entrepreneurial Thai Chinese was then hailed as Southeast Asia's ethnic assimilation success story. At the same time, the violent suppression of the less affluent ethnic Chinese working class was methodically erased from the mainstream historical narrative and from the public's image of the ethnic Chinese community in Thailand.

CHAPTER FIVE

THE COLD WAR

The Return of Royalist Politics in the Postwar Territorial Nation

THE PERIOD FROM THE CONCLUSION OF THE GREATER EAST ASIA
War to the end of the Cold War in Asia in the late 1970s was a major transition in the history of the Thai nation.[1] During this era, the ethnic Chinese
community and the politics of Sino-Thai relations were of exceptional
importance in shaping what the Thai nation and nationalism were to
become. The royalist faction had returned to dominate Thai politics with
the support of the United States at the conclusion of the war, and in the
context of fighting communist threats in Asia and establishing Thailand as
America's most important ally in the Vietnam War, the Thai monarchy
was further encouraged by the United States. The Thai nation, despite having been redefined as a territorial nation under People's Party rule in the
1930s and 1940s, was transformed once again into a nation symbolized by
the monarchy.

The political structure remained a constitutional monarchy with parliamentary politics and periodic elections. The nation itself, like many new
nation-states emerging after the Greater East Asia War, remained a territorial nation with clearly defined geographical boundaries and a population
of citizens. The most striking change was the significant increase in the
monarch's influence over the political scene both domestically and internationally. King Bhumibol Rama IX (r. 1946–2016) was technically a constitutional monarch. However, with more than a dozen coups taking place
during the Cold War, many of which resulted in redrafting of the constitution, the fact that there was only one monarch who reigned through the
entire period of the Cold War and for more than three decades afterward

attests to the king's political influence in comparison with the constitution in Thailand.

While the position of the monarch was not threatened by any domestic political faction—in the way the People's Party had attempted to systematically decrease the power and influence of the king through much of the 1930s and 1940s when they were in power—the greater challenge was the need to establish a strong and reliable alliance with the correct superpower in the Cold War. In this respect, both the Thai monarchy and the capitalist ethnic Chinese chose to openly side with the United States. For the monarch, this resulted in the forging of a formidable alliance with the military, in which the court often lent support and approval to military regimes through much of the Cold War. For ethnic Chinese entrepreneurs, this proved more of a challenge as the land of their ancestors was overrun by the Chinese Communists, and maintaining any ties with their homeland, ethnic heritage, or even cultural background was, at times, perceived by the strongly pro-US, anti-Communist Thai state as a threat to national security and the capitalist world order. Surviving the politics of Cold War Thailand therefore required delicate negotiations and compromises among all of the conservative royalist capitalists involved—the monarchy, the ethnic Chinese entrepreneurs, the military, and the United States, with its enormous influence and financial support.

FROM BEIJING TO SAIGON: SWITCHING ALLIANCES WITH SUPERPOWERS

Not long after the conclusion of the Greater East Asia War, the first major transition in Thai politics occurred with the return of the wartime premier, Field Marshal Plaek Phibunsongkram, who became prime minister in 1948. Nonetheless, Phibunsongkhram's second term in office would be a very different experience from his prewar term. In 1948, the United States had become the most influential patron superpower of Thailand and had made clear that it would support the Thai monarchy and a government that was willing to work with the monarch in opposition to rising communist threats across Asia. Phibunsongkhram was allowed to return to office only after providing assurance that fighting communism would be the central policy of his regime. He had no choice but to go against the People's Party's ideals and accord paramount importance to King Bhumibol as a highly politically influential symbol of the nation. This peculiar partnership of Phibulsongkhram and Bhumibol, set up under US influence, became the earliest form of what would become the norm in Thai politics throughout the Cold War years and into the twenty-first century—the royalist military dictatorship.

During the first two decades of the Cold War in Asia, the biggest communist threat came from the People's Republic of China. The fact that Phibunsongkhram, the prime minister who had declared war against the Allied powers, was allowed to return to office in 1948 had much to do with Chinese Communist forces gaining ground on the mainland and the rise of ethnic Chinese communist guerrillas in British Malaya. Once Mao Zedong successfully declared the establishment of the People's Republic of China on October 1, 1949, the Thai government was on high alert to the danger that PRC-supported communist groups in Southeast Asia would attempt to carry out communist revolutions in this region as well. Hence, when the Korean War broke out in the following year and China sent volunteer troops to support the communist cause, Thailand became the first Southeast Asian nation to contribute troops to the US-led coalition fighting in support of South Korea on the Korean Peninsula.

Phibunsongkhram's government justified the decision to send troops to Korea as a preemptive move to stop the expansion of Chinese Communist influence, which if allowed to take over the Korean Peninsula, by the Thai government's estimation, would soon reach Southeast Asia. Contributing to the Korean War was also an expression of support for the United States in the Cold War in Asia. This demonstration of loyalty to the US cause occurred again in 1952, shortly after the People's Republic of China hosted the Asia and Pacific Rim Peace Conference in Beijing to protest US intervention in the Korean War.[2] In November of that same year, Thai authorities arrested over a hundred individuals in connection with the Asia and Pacific Rim Peace Conference, jailing anyone who demonstrated support or sympathy for the aims of the Peace Conference or who attended or expressed an intention to attend the conference on the basis of being part of a plot to stage a "Peace Rebellion." The majority of those arrested were ethnic Chinese or people in professions related to China and the Chinese community in Thailand—including ethnic Chinese journalists and journalists at Chinese newspapers, labor activists, and leftist politicians. The best-known among those arrested in the Peace Rebellion case was Poonsuk Banomyong, the wife of the wartime minister of finance, Pridi Banomyong, who was by then in exile in China.

By the mid-1950s, Phibunsongkhram was losing control of domestic politics in Thailand. US support was clearly directed more toward the monarch and the royalist factions in both the government and the armed forces.

When Indonesian president Sukarno proposed to host the Asian-African Conference in 1955, Phibunsongkhram decided to expand his options and reached out to a more inclusive network of foreign allies by sending a delegate to observe the conference in Bandung. The Thai delegate was completely charmed by Chinese premier Zhou Enlai, who was also an observer, and by the end of the year Phibunsongkhram had made a fateful decision to engage in underground diplomacy with the People's Republic of China. By September 1957, Phibunsongkhram was ousted for the last time. His replacement was the self-proclaimed royalist prime minister, Field Marshal Sarit Thanarat, who had no direct connection with the People's Party and proclaimed an unambiguously pro-US stance in his foreign policy.

The People's Republic of China continued to be at the core of the Thai government's anticommunist policies up to the end of the 1960s. The major turning point came with President Richard Nixon's historic meeting with Chairman Mao in 1972. The Thai military government, which by then was under the leadership of prime minister Field Marshal Thanom Kittikhachorn, took the not-so-subtle hint that the PRC was to become Thailand's new partner in fighting the Vietnamese communists in Southeast Asia. Three years later, in 1975, Thailand established formal diplomatic relations with China through a historic handshake between Mao Zedong and the right-wing royalist prime minister M. R. Kukrit Pramoj. All of a sudden, the Thai government's anticommunist propaganda shifted in the 1970s to target Vietnam and the ethnic Vietnamese as the greatest communist threats. Even though the rising leftist student movement of that era continued to draw inspiration from the Maoist ideology of the Chinese Cultural Revolution, by October 6, 1976, when students were massacred by right-wing militia groups on the grounds of Thammasat University, government statements claimed that the student movements had been infiltrated and influenced by Vietnamese elements.

FROM YAOWARAT TO PHLAPPHLACHAI: THE GOOD AND BAD CHINESE DICHOTOMY

Through this complicated switching of national alliances in the Cold War, part of the ethnic Chinese community in Thailand managed to survive and maintain dominance in the Thai economy by forging alliances with the court, royalist political factions, and the armed forces. Once again, the politics of ethnic Chinese assimilation in Thailand seemed to return to the Vajiravudhian narrative of the "good Chinese" siding with the royalist ruling class while the "bad Chinese" sided with local bad elements and became a threat to national security. In other words, the ethnic Chinese position in Thai society was decided more by socioeconomic and political classes than ethnic background. The rich Chinese sided with Thais in positions of political power and cooperated with the state's persecution of the poor Chinese, who allied themselves with working-class rebels. Vajiravudh branded the working-class Chinese activists as secret societies. During the Cold War they had come to be known as communist sympathizers. Yet the political narrative of Thailand during the Cold War remained quite similar to that of the earliest decades of the twentieth century. The ethnic Chinese economic elite survived through its alliance with the conservative/royalist political elite while the working class and revolutionaries of all ethnic backgrounds were violently suppressed for the sake of national security.

THE YAOWARAT INCIDENT OF 1945

Among the first incidents clearly symptomatic of the "Cold War Cycle" in Thailand was the Yaowarat Incident of September 20–21, 1945. That event is known today among only a tiny segment of the general public in Thailand, and it has been virtually invisible in Thai academia. The Yaowarat Incident was the first race riot to take place in Bangkok in the modern history of Thailand. It occurred only a few days before recognized members of the Free Thai Movement were to march through the capital on September 25 in celebration of the Allied victory in the Second World War. Ironically, one of the fundamental causes of violence in the Yaowarat Incident was, in fact, that very celebration. On the evening of September 20, members of the ethnic Chinese community in Bangkok—many of whom had been active in the anti-Japanese underground throughout the war years—gathered on Yaowarat Street, Bangkok Chinatown's main street. They had come together to rehearse a parade honoring the Republic of China's National Day that was set to take place on October 10. After four years of Japanese occupation, the upcoming Chinese national day celebration was expected to be more spectacular than ever. China had emerged victorious after enduring over a decade of Japanese invasion, and Generalissimo Chiang Kai-shek had endorsed the Free Thai Movement, an endorsement that was key to securing Thailand a place among the victors in the most devastating war in human history. However, at around 7:00 p.m., the enthusiastic crowds of Chinatown were confronted by police officers who informed them that it was illegal to display foreign national flags—in this case, the flag of the

Republic of China—without being accompanied by the Thai national flag. As no Thai flags had been prepared for the rehearsal, the officers proceeded to take down the Chinese flags. Not surprisingly, this resulted in an angry scuffle between some people in the crowd and the police. Unable to subdue the frustrated crowds of Chinese nationalist supporters, the police called in military reinforcements.

By 10:00 p.m. all of Bangkok's Chinatown had been cordoned off, and a full-scale shoot-out took place between the authorities and the angry merrymakers-turned-rioters. The shooting died down in the early morning hours of September 21, when the military regained control of the Chinatown area.[3] All the shop houses on Yaowarat Street were subjected to thorough searches, as authorities claimed they had been employed as pillboxes by ethnic Chinese snipers during the shoot-out. The elusive Chinese gunmen were never arrested, but the majority of Chinatown businesses were locked down for much of the rest of September. Residents and local entrepreneurs went into self-imposed exile, fearing violent repercussions not only from military forces but also from the non-Chinese general public. Meanwhile, looting and burglary became prevalent as law enforcement turned a blind eye toward a community that was easy to regard as unpatriotic. There were suggestions in police reports that some military personnel had taken advantage of their position to loot valuable objects from Chinatown shop houses during their search for the purported gunmen.[4]

Among the most intriguing aspects of this ironic and tragic postwar situation was the peculiar management of the situation by Thailand's newly established postwar government. When the Yaowarat Incident erupted, Prime Minister M. R. Seni Pramoj had been in office for barely three days, and the peace agreements ratifying Thailand's part in the wartime victory were not yet final. It was an inauspicious moment for such an outburst of violence to take place in Bangkok's Chinatown, especially because Thailand was at the mercy of Chiang Kai-shek's government, in terms of both the kingdom's ultimate postwar status and its application to the newly established United Nations, where the Republic of China was proudly represented on the Security Council. Anti-Chinese nationalism had been fanned to feverish levels during Phibunsongkhram's wartime regime and remained quite strong among many sectors of the general public. Fear of retaliation for wartime anti-Chinese policies was also widespread. There were rumors that because of Phibunsongkhram's fateful alliance with Japan, Thailand would have to stand among the defeated, and Chinese troops would occupy the kingdom just as American forces would occupy Japan in the immediate postwar years.

The manner in which Seni's government handled this diplomatic tinderbox both on the domestic front and at the international level might be called a model of "iron fist in Thai silk glove" diplomacy. To pacify dissent at the domestic level, state forces acted swiftly and brutally. They brought the riot to a halt and gained control of the Chinatown area. Government reports released in the immediate aftermath of the Yaowarat shoot-out claimed that swift action by state forces was needed to bring the situation under control. Rioters were endangering the public, the reports claimed, especially the ethnic Chinese community, which made up the majority of the residents of Yaowarat shop houses. The Department of Public Relations was also quick to dispel any rumors that the Yaowarat Incident might affect Thailand's postwar status. The following communiqué was released on September 24, 1945: "The authorities wish to stress once more, so that the Chinese people may not be deceived by the sinful rumors that Siam has been defeated in the war. Persons who spread such rumors have impure intentions and desire only to cause public disorder and harmful happenings."[5]

On the following day, September 25, a victory march of the Allied powers took place as planned. It highlighted the participation of the Free Thai Movement (FTM) under the leadership of the wartime Thai minister to Washington, DC, Seni Pramoj. Emphasis was overtly on the support of the US government and the colorful elite personalities who had participated in the British and American branches of the FTM. Handsome scions of the upper classes and well-groomed government scholars, all educated at leading institutions in Britain and America, together with a few distant members of the royal family, marched proudly in celebration of the part played by the kingdom in the victories that ended the Second World War. Thailand's mainstream nationalist historical narrative was destined, from that day on, to erase the fact that the ethnic Chinese ever had anything to do with achieving Allied endorsement for the FTM, or that China, in the person of Generalissimo Chiang Kai-shek, had played a central role in delivering the kingdom from its fate as a defeated nation.[6]

At the international level, however, it was a totally different story. The Thai legation in Washington, DC, published an article on September 30 in the local newspaper, *Democracy*, concluding that the conflicts which had triggered the Yaowarat Incident had been resolved. The story emphasized positive developments in Sino-Thai relations, which were said to be progressing speedily toward the successful establishment of formal diplomatic relations.[7] Later in November, the legation published two more articles in DC-area newspapers eagerly reporting the rapid development of postwar Sino-Thai relations and stressing that conflicts associated with the Yaowarat Incident had been resolved, thereby further benefiting Sino-Thai relations. On November 5, an article appeared in a smaller local paper, which reported in detail Seni's press conference announcing the results of the investigation of "the incident of the Chinese attacking Thai people" on Yaowarat Street earlier that year.[8]

The Seni government's decision to publish such propaganda in local American newspapers indicates the political direction of the ruling class in the postwar era. With the wartime Thai minister to Washington, DC, installed as Thailand's first postwar prime minister, it was clear that the United States had replaced Britain as the overlord of the Thai ruling class in the postwar era. Consequently, all matters relating to international relations and Thailand's standing in regional and global conflicts were properly reported in the United States. As a patron of both Seni's postwar rule and Chiang Kai-shek's republican regime, the United States approved and monitored all "legitimate" Sino-Thai interactions at the state level. Some may suggest that this temporary situation was necessary because no formal diplomatic relations as yet existed between China and Thailand. It might be thought to have been necessary to communicate indirectly, using the United States as an intermediary.[9]

It is important to note, however, that Pridi managed to communicate effectively with Chiang's government during the war years without using the Thai legation in Washington as a go-between. Furthermore, the Chinese Chamber of Commerce had for decades been functioning as the ad hoc Chinese consulate in Siam. That all communications between the Thai and Chinese states in the immediate postwar years had to be conducted through Washington clearly indicates that the Thai state would endorse only Chiang Kai-shek's pro-American regime. Lining up behind the United States, Thailand would not recognize Mao Zedong's Communist China. All matters concerning Sino-Thai relations would from then on be dominated by Seni's conservative royalist faction and not Pridi's progressive socialist clique, regardless of what had been achieved during the war years.

With the rise of communist influence in mainland China and in many areas of still colonized Southeast Asia in the immediate postwar years, Thai conservative leaders took full advantage of their anticommunist American backing to persecute and eliminate political rivals on the domestic front.

The once fine line between the "good Chinese" and "bad Chinese" now became an explicit hard line. Ethnic Chinese leaders and politicians who maintained ties with Communist China or expressed any degree of sympathy for the socialist cause, regardless of their contributions during the war years, were methodically persecuted and eventually eliminated from their positions. Pridi was quickly ousted and forced into exile by the coup of 1947, which brought Phibunsongkhram back to power as the postwar, anti-Communist prime minister. Thawin Udon—along with three other northeastern politicians, all close associates of Pridi—was accused of plotting a communist revolution in the northeastern region of the kingdom and died under suspicious circumstances in police custody in 1949 while awaiting trial. Sa-nguan Tularak, suspecting that a similar misfortune awaited him following the coup of 1947, sought political asylum in China, where he stayed for a full decade before returning in 1957, only to be arrested by the ruling junta and imprisoned for eight years on communist-related charges.

Amid the escalation of the Cold War in Asia, the dominant power that emerged on the Thai political scene was a formidable anticommunist alliance of the royalists and military dictators who received the full backing of the United States in the form of aid for development and military support. The alliance of the royalists and the military became invincible on the domestic front through their brutal anticommunist strategies, which forced ethnic Chinese upper- and middle-class entrepreneurs to clearly express their support for the conservative dictatorship or face the dire misfortunes that had befallen Pridi's associates and many others. By the early 1970s, with the Vietnam War rapidly drawing to a close, the stance of the Thai ruling regime toward the ethnic Chinese increasingly resembled the royalist nationalist attitude encouraged during the reigns of Chulalongkorn and Vajiravudh, but with more brutal consequences for those who did not generously and regularly demonstrate their allegiance to the dictators. The second explosively violent race riot in the modern history of Thailand and the ruling regime's heavy-handed response to that disaster provide tragic evidence of this seemingly unavoidable postwar political tendency in Thailand.

THE PHLAPPHLACHAI RIOT OF 1974

The Yaowarat Incident happened about thirty years before the paroxysm that was the Phlapphlachai Riot. This second convulsive outbreak took place at a time when pro-American Thailand, figuring the odds on the domino theory, was confronted with America's war in neighboring Indochina. To the modern student of Thai history, Phlapphlachai looks like a nasty flash-back, an unpleasant moment of déjà vu in which the ruling Thai regime and Bangkok's ethnic Chinese community appear to act out in 1974 some melodramatic Vajiravudhian nationalist drama.

The Phlapphlachai Riot flared in the evening hours of July 3. The date is significant in many ways. Those who are familiar with the political history of postwar Thailand know that this was barely eight months after the massive prodemocracy student demonstrations of October 14, 1973, which supposedly toppled the regime led by the military triumvirate of Thanom Kittikachorn, Praphas Charusathien, and Narong Kittikachorn. Although the overthrow of these three powerful dictators did not result in immediate democratic elections, the king appointed a caretaker prime minister, and a hopeful sense of freedom prevailed. Heady talk of democracy was heard in the streets of the capital, and student activists began planning to topple bigger and meaner political bullies. On the evening of July 3, 1974, veteran student activists were preparing for a massive July 4 march from the royal grounds at Sanam Luang in front of Thammasat University to the US Embassy on Wireless Road. This was not a parade in honor of American Independence Day, but rather was intended to protest American imperialism. The students were going to demand no less than complete evacuation of all American military bases and withdrawal of all personnel from Thailand. All was not well in Thai politics in the last years of the Vietnam War. Barely three years after the illusory, but still revered, popular victory of October 14, the biggest slaughter of student demonstrators in the history of Thailand would take place on the grounds of Thammasat University on October 6, 1976. After that bloodbath, the kingdom would descend for the next two decades into the familiar pattern of pro-American military dicta-torship. The student activists who went ahead with their program at Thammasat may have entertained a naive optimism that the kingdom's political ruling class had entered a period of enlightenment. However, the violent suppression of the Phlapphlachai Riot should have thrown up a red flag, a clear warning that the government was returning to the despotic practices of prewar Siam.

On the evening of July 3, 1974, while student activists at Thammasat University were preparing for their anti-American march, taxi driver Pun Lamlueprasoet stopped at the curb in front of a bustling cinema in China-town to pick up his next passengers. Instead of a fare, Pun was confronted by two police officers who informed him that it was illegal to park in front of the cinema. Then they demanded that he pay a fine. The area in question was a regular stopping place for taxis. Furthermore, this was going to be Pun's third traffic fine in two days. The cabbie, who was later identified as being of Chinese descent, refused to pay. He was arrested on the spot and dragged away to face formal charges at the Phlapphlachai Police Station. Pun, however, refused to go without a fuss. As he was manhandled by the officers, he screamed accusations of police brutality and extortion to the crowd in front of the theater. By the time Pun disappeared into the Phlapphlachai precinct station, a sizable crowd had accumulated in front of the building, shouting demands for the officers to free the arrested cabbie. The crowd continued to grow as the night wore on.

Close to midnight, they acquired loudspeakers and a student activist faction, making it a legitimate antigovernment demonstration according to the standards of the day. Eventually, people at the scene began to throw sticks and stones at the precinct building. Rubbish bins were set ablaze. These provocations prompted the police to parade Pun out to the front of the precinct in an attempt to appease the crowds by assuring them that he was being treated fairly and no police brutality had been committed. However, this did little to improve the situation. Before long, one side of the building had caught fire and the lights went out inside the Phlapphlachai Police Station.[10] Fire engines arrived to put out the flames, and police reinforcements came from across the capital to help bring the fiasco under control. Shortly after midnight, Pun was released in a last-ditch attempt to appease the demonstrators, but to no avail. Sometime in the early hours of July 4, the police charged out of the building, firing directly into the crowd in an attempt to regain control of the immediate vicinity of the police station. At least seven people died instantly in the first wave of police fire. The crowd fell back, but people came streaming into that part of Bangkok's Chinatown from all directions. The violence escalated. Police vehicles were burned, shots were exchanged, and there were fiery bursts of flame from Molotov cocktails. In the face of this escalating violence, military forces were called in to pacify the crowds. Fielding tanks and soldiers in full battle gear, by daybreak the state had managed to regain control of the district.

The Phlapphlachai Riot was not put down as easily as the disturbances of the Yaowarat Incident some three decades earlier. Caretaker prime minister Sanya Dharmasakti declared a state of emergency at midnight on July 3, as heavily armed military reinforcements flooded the area. However, although a tense peace could be maintained in the daytime, rioters returned to the streets of Chinatown upon nightfall with guns and homemade fire-bombs. Violent clashes between rioters and law enforcement continued for several days. Business went on as usual in daylight hours, but there were full-scale shoot-outs by night. It was not until the evening of July 7 that the government regained complete control of the Chinatown vicinity and declared the area safe from violence. The official tally was 24 killed and 124 injured, with extensive damage to private and public properties in places where the fighting had been most violent.[11]

The government's official explanation of the causes of the riots and their justification for using firearms and heavy artillery in the streets of Bang-kok's Chinatown are recorded in state documents and in the mainstream, state-sanctioned historical narrative. The official statements are intriguing. The secret society trope was mobilized almost immediately. From the first night of the unrest in Chinatown, in declaring the state of emergency, Sanya announced that the protesters in front of Phlapphlachai precinct were "mostly hooligans" and that all peaceful means of control had been employed without success. It was "necessary to employ extreme measures in order to bring this situation, which could endanger people, under control."[12] Even before the riots were brought completely under control on July 6, the government announced that the disturbances were caused mainly by two rival motorcycle gangs in Chinatown—the Eagle Gang and the Dragon Gang. By July 8, the capital's Southern Metropolitan Police Division managed to arrest an ethnic Chinese named Sutham Kueawikphai, also known as di Pheng (Little Brother Pheng), who they claimed was the most notorious of Chinatown's criminals and the ringleader of the Phlapplachai Riots. The description of Sutham's physical appearance, as well as the account published in newspapers the day of his involvement in the Chinatown unrest, sounded more like something from a Vajiravudhian melodrama than anything that might actually have taken place at the intersection in front of the Phlapphlachai precinct:

> Mr. Sutham Kuawikphai or di Pheng has tattoos over most of his body—a dashing tiger on his chest, an eagle on his abdomen, a dragon wrapped around his left arm, and a Spartacus knife on his right arm. On the night of 3 July when the riots broke out, Mr. Sutham or di Pheng took off his shirt and jumped onto the roof of a car parked in front of the Phlapphla-chai Police Station. [He] announced that he was the leader of a gang of thugs operating in the Yaowarat area. [He] had just been released from Ladyao prison and wanted to lead the people in fighting the police.[13]

This was the explanation recorded in state documents concerning the reasons for the outbreak of violence at the Phlapphlachai Precinct in early July 1974. Basically, criminal gangs of Chinatown decided to take advantage of the legitimate arrest of Pun, the cabbie, to take revenge on the upstanding police officers who had long been major obstacles to their criminal enterprises. In short, it was recorded, most of the two dozen victims of the armed force's heavy-handed riot control tactics were pimps and drug runners, and there was really no other way to get such people under control aside from shooting them with live ammunition.

The way various newspapers reported the Phlapphlachai Riot was also intriguing. The majority of Thai-language newspapers, all of which were under strict surveillance and censorship by the state, reported the matter along lines similar to the official version. That is, the rioters of Phlapphlachai were part of a class of criminally inclined ethnic Chinese who had caused periodic unrest in Siam ever since the reign of King Chulalongkorn. Editorial columns abounded with derogatory terms—gangsters, thugs, mixed blood, Chinese brats—used to describe the detestable working-class portion of the ethnic Chinese community in Thailand. One account in particular harkened back to the events of the Yaowarat Incident of 1945:

> Think back to when the World War had just ended. The Chinese in Bangkok caused a riot with a hope that could not be understood in any way aside from their lack of awareness of His Majesty's abundant compassion and [their] desire to rule our land.
>
> The Chinese who caused the riots this time reside in the same area as the Chinese who caused the riots back then.[14]

This columnist appears to have stuck closely to the Seni Pramoj government's interpretations of the significance of the Yaowaraj Incident almost three decades earlier. With an equally conservative interpretation, the writer manages to glimpse similar motives and forces behind the latest uprising. Just as the Chinese of the 1945 Yaowarat Incident had been accused of calling for Republican Chinese troops to occupy Thailand in the immediate postwar period, so the "gangsters" of the Phlapphlachai Riot were said to aspire to overthrow the royally established government and the monarchy to establish in Thailand a socialist republic like the People's Republic of China. The invocation of the secret society trope and the condemnation of those Chinese who "lack awareness of His Majesty's abundant compassion," however, did allow for a discriminating sifting out of the bad

Phlapphlachai rioters from the generally decent citizens of the ethnic Chinese community. Using rhetorical language similar to that of Chulalongkorn's era, government mouthpieces of the 1970s were willing to admit that there were "good Chinese" who were hardworking, law abiding, and abundantly aware of His Majesty's boundless compassion. The same newspapers published heartfelt pleas from leading figures in the various ethnic Chinese organizations—the Chaozhou Association being among the most prominent—for ethnic Chinese parents to keep their children at home during the period of unrest so as to limit the possibility of Chinese youths coming in contact with criminals and rioters and being led into violent acts against the state.

There were dissenting perspectives as to how such extreme violence could erupt in Chinatown over such a seemingly trivial matter as a traffic violation. Not unlike the Yaowarat Incident some three decades earlier, reports published in foreign-language newspapers presented a drastically different story from the accounts in Thai-language media for Thai readers. There was an obvious consensus between the two leading English-language newspapers. The *Bangkok Post* and the *Nation* saw that the riot was an outburst of pent-up frustration in the Chinese working class after long years of intimidation and extortion by generations of corrupt state officials. One of the *Nation*'s most celebrated columnists, M. R. Ayumongkol Sonakul, summed up the root cause of the Phlapphlachai Riot, apparently believing this was common knowledge among the Thai general public: "It is no secret that police, in some areas at least, have been treating people of Chinese descent like dirt. Particularly, they have been victims of extortion: being moneyed but unhonored."[15]

Another matter on which the *Bangkok Post* and the *Nation* appear to agree is the fact that the state's attempts at riot control amounted to extreme brutality and were absolutely unjustifiable, especially considering the lessons in riot control that the state should have learned from the October 14 bloodbath less than a year before. Suthichai Yoon, the *Nation*'s editor, expressed his outrage over the actions of the police in an editorial a week after the violence in Chinatown: "There is incontrovertible proof—'the camera does not lie'—in every newspaper office in the city in the form of huge stacks of photographs that some policemen used unnecessary violence in their somewhat emotional response to the riots of Chinatown last week."[16]

The *Bangkok Post* appeared to be less outspoken about the degree of violence in the state's riot-control efforts, despite the fact that one of their editors, Paisal Sricharatchanya, had been brutally beaten by a group of officers who mistook him for a rioter. Paisal, covering the story on the second night of the disturbances and armed only with his pen and notebook, was camped out in front of the Phlapphlachai Police Station. The beating nearly cost him an eye, and he suffered other serious injuries that left him debilitated for three months. In a later interview, Paisal confirmed that the riot was "a spontaneous display of resentment against the police." He said the working-class Chinese in the area of the Phlapphlachai precinct had been subjected to police intimidation and extortion for as long as they could remember, and that most of them had remained docile toward the corrupt state power for just as long. On the fateful evening of July 3, a slightly intoxicated cabbie lost control and lashed out against the third police extortion he had suffered in two days. That was the spark that lit the fires of the Phlapphlachai Riot.[17]

Some of the most intriguing accounts of the Phlapphlachai Riot were recorded in a handful of Chinese-language newspapers. A casual glance at the front-page headlines of Chinese-language newspapers in Thailand for that week revealed no discussion of any major violence in Bangkok's Chinatown. However, thumbing through to pages 4 and 5, one finds whole collections of chilling images of armed forces with tanks and rifles, numerous people lying dead on the streets, and more of the injured being rushed to the safety of hospital emergency rooms. Though the images were alarming, the tone of the stories remained painfully muted. There were vague suggestions of bad blood between state law enforcement and the residents of Chinatown.[18] The accounts noted many innocent bystanders among the dead in Phlapphlachai.[19] Nonetheless, there was no explicit outcry against corrupt police practices of extortion and intimidation of ethnic Chinese working-class people in Bangkok. There were no outraged demands for investigations into claims of police brutality. There were no claims of compensation owed for the damage done by heavy-handed officials sent in to quell the Phlapphlachai unrest. The restrained tone of the reports in the Chinese-language press suggests a general consensus within the ethnic Chinese community not to fight back against the officers of the state who had been so unjust and brutal. News of the violence would not appear in front-page headlines in their newspapers because it made more sense to move on to more positive and productive matters.

State violence in the Phlapphlachai Riot was destined to be forgotten by the Thai general public. Thai-language newspapers closely adhered to the story line concocted by the state. English-language newspapers had a much smaller readership, mostly expatriates and highly educated technocrats and intellectuals. The ethnic Chinese community seems to have cooperated exceptionally well with the state's subliminal requirement that the incident be forgotten as soon as possible. The reports in Chinese-language newspapers were extremely muted, considering the explosive nature of the riot itself, and very few ethnic Chinese witnesses of the Phlapphlachai Riot were willing to talk about their memories of what they had experienced in those dark days of violence. After their heroic resistance of October 14, student activist groups could reasonably have been expected to speak out against this state oppression of the citizens of Bangkok, but they largely dismissed the rioting as a political diversion staged by the CIA to foil their plans for a July 4 march from Thammasat University to the US Embassy in protest of the stationing of American troops in Thailand. Little did they know that the tide of history was already turning against them. Many leading figures in the student movement were rallying against the United States (which would pull out of Vietnam the following year). They distanced their movement from the violence at Phlapphlachai. Stern criticism of student demonstrations was beginning to appear more often in leading Thai-language mass media. It is chilling in hindsight to note how, in the press, the student activism of October 14 and the riots in Chinatown were lumped together in public perception as pointless antiestablishment movements:

> It is impossible to make the general public accept the actions of the numerous [student] organizations that have recently been established. Anything that is too large in quantity tends to lose its value. Moreover, democracy is not a toy or an experimental tool in forming or clashing within and among various groups. As we have recently heard from the general public, everyone expressed the same feeling that [certain student organizations] are overreacting. Sometimes they try in various ways to act as a "shadow government." This has caused much annoyance to the common people.[20]

The secret society trope was beginning to be successfully applied to student activists. The conservative ruling class was characterizing student protests as yet another unpatriotic, antiestablishment threat to national security. Barely two years later, after the United States had pulled out of Vietnam and communist forces had taken over what was left of the former French Indochina, a gruesome and cold-blooded massacre of student activists took place on the grounds of Thammasat University at the hands of the police and several right-wing militia groups. Like the Phlapphlachai

Riot, the student massacre of October 6, 1976, was painted over in the mainstream, state-sanctioned historical narrative of Thailand of the Cold War era.

POLITICAL AMNESIA AND ALLIANCES OF INTEREST

Students of modern history exploring Bangkok Chinatown's celebrated museum, the Center of Yaowarat History, which is located in the Grand Pavilion of Wat Traimitr, the Temple of the Golden Buddha, will find among the museum's exhibits no memory of state violence toward Thailand's ethnic Chinese. The exhibition is divided into six sections: (1) thriving under royal patronage; (2) origins of the Chinese community in Bangkok; (3) path through the golden era of Chinatown; (4) lives of prominent community leaders; (5) royal patronage of His Majesty, King Bhumibol Rama IX; and (6) Yaowarat today. The general story line of the history of the ethnic Chinese community of Yaowarat exactly follows the official narrative: (1) destitute Chinese migrants fled war and starvation in South China to come to Siam; (2) within the realms of His Majesty's limitless compassion, the Chinese started new lives, worked hard, and prospered; and finally, (3) the Chinese are extremely grateful for His Majesty's patronage and have contributed much to Thai society from their arrival to the present day. There is no mention of violent clashes between state power and members of the Chinese community. It appears to be the history of ethnic Chinese in a parallel universe, an idyllic world in which neither the Yaowarat Incident of 1945 nor the violence of the Phlapphlachai Riot of 1974 ever happened. The Center of Yaowarat History is, without a doubt, one of the most staunchly royalist museums in the country, though it is not state owned. It was created and continues to operate with the financial support of Chinese entrepreneurs in Yaowarat.[21] Outside the grounds of the museum, in the grand scheme of Thai politics in the globalized age, the three districts that encompass Bangkok Chinatown—Pomprap, Bangrak, and Samphanthawong—have become major bastions of political support for the Democrat Party.[22] Such is the evidence of the enduring love-hate relationship between the Bangkok's ethnic Chinese community and the conservative ruling powers of Thailand.

There might have been some degree of truth in Vajiravudh's harsh criticism of the ethnic Chinese, especially in his infamous article *Jews of the Orient*, in which the king asserts that the Chinese are willing to serve any master or be registered as subjects of any empire so long as their business enterprises benefit. From the evidence of the Center of Yaowarat History, it would appear that in addition to being willing to register as European imperial subjects in the late nineteenth and early twentieth centuries, ethnic Chinese entrepreneurs of the twenty-first century are also willing to forget the tragic deaths of their own people at the hands of the state (in both Yaowarat of 1945 and Phlapphlachai of 1974), to express overt loyalty to the conservative ruling classes, and to benefit from that powerful alliance. Stoically pragmatic in their expressed patriotism, the Chinese appear to be equally businesslike in their alliances with the Thai ruling regimes.

Similarly, since the nineteenth century, Thai leaders have seemed willing to ally with whichever world power appeared to be on the winning side, even if that meant breaking a treaty of alliance signed in the Temple of the Emerald Buddha. The flexibility of Bangkok's ethnic Chinese entrepreneurs and Thai political conservatives stems from their unusual capacity for political amnesia and their propensity for alliances of interest and convenience. Their unlikely partnership has endured for more than one hundred years through numerous challenging circumstances. It is a relationship that has been highly effective and formidably tenacious. It is not simply a case of the Chinese being beaten into submission or conservative politicians being bribed into cooperating with their Chinese business associates. Active participation characterizes both sides. Atrocities are ignored and there is much overt praise and mutual support, despite all the bad blood in the past. This formula for cooperation serves their mutual interest in dominating their true common opponents, the masses of the working class and supporters of left-wing socialist politics.

Certainly one key to the formidable vitality of the bond between conservative politicians and ethnic Chinese capitalists in Thailand should be their extreme flexibility in adapting and surviving under constant threat from more powerful entities. Always in the minority, the diaspora communities of ethnic Chinese thrive on the hard-learned wisdom of being flexible and versatile. The ability to adjust and compromise with dominant powers in strange lands helps them survive and makes them more competitive in business. They know how to adapt in neighborhoods, towns, and cities where local people learn to depend on their ingenuity and skill in providing goods and services. At the same time, history has taught them how to quickly pack up and move when circumstances become impossible. By contrast, Thailand's conservative rulers enjoy a measure of stability, influencing and controlling the government of an established territorial state. The government has a degree of security because it controls the armed forces, and it has the international backing of the world's superpowers. Geographically situated at the crossroads of greater powers, Southeast Asia is a politically and economically volatile region, but conservative Thai politicians have managed to survive from one era to the next. They have an aptitude for forging reliable alliances with the winning superpower and for swiftly and seemingly effortlessly switching sides at the first sign of change in regional and global political tides. It is this similarity in their survival tactics that has forged the enduring yet unlikely alliance linking ethnic Chinese capitalists to one conservative political leader of Thailand after another. This is also why what appears to be Chinese assimilation and discrimination in Thailand cannot be understood in the same framework as other Southeast Asian regimes. As fickle as Vajiravudh once deemed the ethnic Chinese to be, the sixth king would be loath to admit that his royal ancestors—from Rama I to Chulalongkorn—always remained, for similar reasons, alert to changes in the wind. His political heirs in the conservative camp, from Seni Pramoj to the leaders of today's Democrat Party, have survived numerous political and economic challenges in tandem with their unlikely bedfellows, Thailand's "good Chinese."

CONCLUSION

IN HIS LANDMARK ESSAY, "STUDIES OF THE THAI STATE: THE State of Thai Studies," Benedict Anderson boldly questioned the validity of one of the most revered axioms of the modern history of Thailand: that Thailand had started down the path of modernization "in the 1850s under Mongkut Rama IV and has continued to do so ever since."[1] He argued convincingly that there was a "stunted and incomplete transition from kingdom to modern nation-state."[2] According to Anderson, absolutism had continued, almost without interruption, through much of the (so-called) modern history of Thailand from the late nineteenth century through the twentieth century. He challenged the mainstream, state-sanctioned historical narratives that portrayed the modernization projects of King Mongkut and King Chulalongkorn as progressive. The Revolution of 1932 did not succeed in transforming the governing powers of the kingdom into a constitutional regime. Anderson's revisionist argument gave rise to new lines of argument by later scholars of history and political science concerning the character of the colonial period in Thailand. Had Thailand been virtually, if not officially, colonized by European powers? Were the "modernization" projects of Mongkut and Chulalongkorn little more than the monarchs' own colonial policies, versions of civilizing missions aimed at the backward masses in their own country? Perhaps late nineteenth-century Siam and early twentieth-century Thailand might be a colonial state after all, considering the history of its interactions with neighboring states and with the ethnic minorities within the realm.

Anderson's arguments inspired revolutionary lines of historical investigation that pushed forward studies in modern Thai history and historiography of much of the post–Cold War era. However, it may be possible to discover more complexity behind the paradigm of impact-response modernization, which Anderson's theory seems basically to be. The phenomenon known as "modernization" has been deeply implicated in the history of Thailand and Southeast Asia since the conclusion of the Second World War. However, whether the reforms of Mongkut and Chulalongkorn meet

Anderson's standards of modernization or whether Vajiravudh and Phibun-songkhram's policies were in fact nation-building projects may be completely beside the point.

It is possible to see other forces besides the arrival of European colonialists at work in the profound transformation that took place across Southeast Asia in the modern era. To imagine that Western colonialism was the pivotal point that brought about modernization in Asia now seems unacceptably Eurocentric and anachronistic, especially for Asian historians in the twenty-first century. The claim that the arrival of Europeans and Americans in Southeast Asia in the mid-nineteenth century brought about all that was novel and progressive in the region simply does not compute. Sociopolitical and economic developments in Siam during the colonial period and up to the conclusion of the Second World War need to be seen in greater detail in the context of Siam's relations with regional Asian powers—especially China and Japan—and not only the well-studied and often overemphasized interactions with the European and American empires. Modernization has been scrutinized from many angles but still has much to reveal. Seen in a new light, the whole landscape of historical development in Thailand and Southeast Asia since the conclusion of the Second World War could look quite different.

Siam's ruling classes reacted to encroaching European—and later Japanese—imperialist forces from the late nineteenth through much of the first half of the twentieth century by resorting to trusted political techniques that had been useful to the dominant powers in the Siamese political scene. From the eighteenth century almost continuously to the present day, with perhaps one exception during the hostilities of the Second World War, it has been understood that to sustain political dominance in Siam, one must (a) acquire and maintain the political approval and support of the appropriate foreign superpower of the current era; and (b) forge a reliable and mutually beneficial alliance with Siam's financially powerful and economically dominant ethnic Chinese capitalist class. These two conditional strategies for political dominance on the domestic scene have been practiced by Siam's ruling powers time and again from the days of Qing dynastic patronage in the eighteenth century, to British colonial dominance from the late nineteenth and early twentieth centuries, and most recently in response to American hegemony through much of the Cold War era.

Regardless of which regional or global superpower happened to be the dominant force in Southeast Asia in each historical period, ethnic Chinese entrepreneurs have continued to maintain stable dominance of the

Siamese economy. In the eighteenth century, they functioned as go-betweens representing the Siamese state's interests in its tribute trade with the celestial court of the Qing dynasty. Later, at the height of European colonial power in Southeast Asia, the ethnic Chinese again dominated the local economies as registered subjects, trade agents, and compradors of European colonial interests in the region. Finally, through much of the Cold War in Southeast Asia, ethnic Chinese entrepreneurs in Thailand were among the most distinguished representatives of the free market ideals of capitalist society—albeit often operating and maneuvering within the context of the political dictatorships of junta regimes. The various sociopolitical developments of the Thai state from the nineteenth century to the present day—the transformation (stunted or not) from kingdom to modern nation-state, and the development (or decline) of the democratic system and rule of law—probably have less to do with the modernization policies (or lack thereof) of Mongkut and Chulalongkorn or the arrival in Siam of European imperialist aggressors than with how much backing could be gained from local Chinese businessmen and what kind of bargains could be struck with which foreign powers.

The complicated relationship between the Thai ruling class and the ethnic Chinese business elite and the special position China held in the history of nation-building in Thailand are perhaps more relevant to the crises of the present day than one might imagine. In post–Cold War Asia, as China transforms from the most fundamentalist Maoist nation into the second largest economy in neoliberal world and expands its influence through wealth and political power down south, the ability to understand Southeast Asia—and Thailand at the heart of things—as the most historically significant home base of the Chinese diaspora is of fundamental importance in the comprehension of crucial developments in current regional and transregional politics. While the central struggles in the post–Cold War era no longer concern political ideology and most definitely not the fear of Communist world domination, similar historical trends could be observed to have carried on across historical periods.

Thailand continues to be the exemplar "success story"[3] of ethnic Chinese assimilation in comparison to neighboring members of ASEAN.[4] The Thai monarchy not only appears to have been consistently fostering close ties with the ethnic Chinese business community from the end of the Cold War to the end of King Bhumibol's long reign in 2016 and beyond; the monarch and the royal family have also led the way in forging a strong alliance with the one Asian nation to emerge as the new superpower of the twenty-first century. From the very beginning of China's new era of reform and openness, when Deng Xiaoping made his first voyage overseas as the new leader of the People's Republic of China in 1978, his first stop was Bangkok and his first meeting with King Bhumibol. In what seemed like a most ironic gesture between a king and the leader of the most populous communist country in the world, Deng Xiaoping was invited to join the ordination ceremony of then crown prince Vajiralongkorn.[5]

In 1980, HRH Maha Chakri Sirindhorn, then second in line to the throne, embarked on her lifelong study of the Chinese language. Princess Sirindhorn went on to visit the People's Republic of China ten times before the end of the century, with all except for her first visit in 1981 taking place after the Chinese government's violent response to demonstrations in Tiananmen Square in 1989. The princess was, in fact, one of only a few state representatives to make repeated official visits to China so soon after the internationally broadcasted Tiananmen tragedy. Sirindhorn's insistence on presenting herself as a friend of China through the 1990s, despite pressure from the international community to express solidarity with the victims of the massacre, earned her a place on the list of "Best Friends of the Chinese People," selected through popular voting by Chinese citizens in commemoration of the sixtieth anniversary of the establishment of the People's Republic of China. The Thai princess was the only person from Southeast Asia to receive this honor. She received the award in person on December 8, 2009, during her twenty-ninth visit to the People's Republic of China.

Aside from the Thai royalist ruling class shifting its closest superpower ally from the United States during the Cold War to China in the post-Cold War, another phenomenon that might be taken as a clear indication of China's ascension to the ranks of world superpower and transregional hegemon is its intensified territorial claims to the South China Sea through the announcement of the Belt and Road Initiative (BRI) by President Xi Jinping in 2013.[6] From at least the eighteenth century on, the South China Sea has always been dominated by the world power that was in control of transregional trade between China, Southeast Asia, and the Indian Ocean, and that same world power has usually been the dominant political force across the East and Southeast Asian regions. The British Empire established its hegemonic control of trade in this area through a colonial empire spread across the Indian Ocean from British India to the Malacca Strait and its control of treaty ports along the coast of South China following China's defeat in the Opium Wars. Japan seized control of the South China Sea and replaced Britain as the overlord of Southeast Asia briefly during the Greater East Asia

War. Throughout the Cold War period the South China Sea was firmly under the control of the United States, which positioned key allies, fleets, and navy bases in the Taiwan Strait, the Philippines, and parts of mainland Southeast Asia up to the conclusion of the Vietnam War in 1975. If there is a world power that could replace the United States' Cold War role in Southeast Asia in the post–Cold War period, it would be the People's Republic of China. If China is to gain the same level of dominance and control over trade and politics in this region, it requires firm control over the South China Sea.

During the more than a century and a half that has passed since King Mongkut signed the Bowring Treaty in 1855, the meaning of the Thai nation-state, the Thai nationalist movement, and Thai citizenship has evolved through numerous crises in the domestic and international arenas. Yet the alliance between the conservative ruling class and the leading capitalists of the realm remains fundamental to the stability of the political structure and economic development in the country. The ethnic Chinese who descended from the labor migrants and sojourners of the nineteenth and early twentieth centuries may have mostly attained Thai citizenship and forgotten the Chinese dialects of their ancestors, thus significantly changing the cultural identity of the Chinese diaspora in Thailand. Nonetheless, the continuous influx of investment capital for the People's Republic of China and of Chinese tourists into mainland Southeast Asia since the turn of the century guaranteed that China and Chineseness would continue to be crucial to Thai socioeconomic and cultural life in the post–Cold War era. The Thai nation in the twenty-first century, as when it was founded in the early twentieth century, has survived and flourished by continuing to include Chinese capital and the network of Chinese trade as an integral part of the national project.

GLOSSARY OF CHINESE TERMS

Romanization of terms follows standard Chinese (Mandarin). Simplified characters are followed by traditional characters in parentheses.

Ai shen 爱神 (愛神) *Love God* (serialized novel)

bao 保 (保) protection
baoguo 保国 (保國) protect the nation
Baohuanghui 保皇会 (保皇會) Society for the Protection of the Emperor
baojiao 保教 (保教) protect Chinese education
baozhong 保种 (保種) protect the race

Chen Shouming 陈守明 (陳守明) Tan Siomeng Wangli
ci shi ci di 此时此地 (此時此地) focusing on the here and now

Datong Xuexiao 大同学校 (大同學校) Great Unity School

geming 革命 (革命) revolution
Guowen Xuetang 国文学堂 (國文學堂) National Culture School

Hongmen 洪门 (洪門) Sons of the Hongwu Emperor (secret society)
Hongzi 洪子 (洪子) Sons of the Hongwu Emperor (secret society)
Huaqiao 华侨 (華僑) Chinese sojourner; ethnic Chinese
Huaqiao ribao 华侨日报 (華僑日報) *Overseas Chinese Daily* (newspaper)
Huaqiao wei geming zhi mu 华侨为革命之母 (華僑為革命之母) Overseas Chinese are the mothers of the revolution
Huaqiao Yinhang 华侨银行 (華僑銀行) Overseas Chinese Bank
Huaxian xinbao 华暹新报 (華暹新報) *Sino-Siam News*
Huayi Xuetang 华裔学堂 (華裔學堂) Ethnic Chinese School

Lafu ge sheng 拉夫歌声 (拉夫歌聲) *Sound of the Love Song* (serialized novel)
Lianqiao bao 联侨报 (聯僑報) *United Sojourners' Newspaper*

mian xiang zu guo 面向祖国 (面向祖國) looking toward the country of origin
Mingming niao 命命鸟 (命命鳥) *The Mingming Bird* (serialized novel)
Minguo ribao 民国日报 (民國日報) *Republican Daily* (newspaper)

Panghuang 彷徨 (徬徨) *Hesitation* (specialized arts and literary edition
Pingwu 平芜 (平蕪) *The Prairie* (specialized arts and literary edition)

Qiaokan 侨刊 (僑刊) *Emigrant Newspaper*
Qiaosheng 桥声 (僑聲) *Sojourners' Voice* (newspaper)
Qinan ribao 起南日报 (起南日報) *Enlightened South Daily* (newspaper)

Sandian Hui 三点会 (三點會) Triad Society (secret society)

Sanminzhuyi 三民主义 (三民主義)
Three Principles of the People

Tan Zhensan 谭振三 (譚振三)
Tam Chinsam

Tiandihui 天地会 (天地會) Heaven and
Earth Society (secret society)

Tianhan bao 天汉报 (天漢報) *Milky Way*
(newspaper)

Tianxia 天下 (天下) China; all under
heaven that is civilized

Tianye 天野 (天野) *The Wild* (specialized
arts and literary edition)

Tongmenghui 同盟会 (同盟會)
Revolutionary Alliance

Xianjing ribao 暹京日报 (暹京日報)
Siamese Capital Daily (newspaper)

Xiao Focheng 萧佛成 (蕭佛成)
Siao Hutseng

Xin Shenghuo Yundong 新生活运动
(新生活運動) New Life Movement
(social campaign)

Xinhai geming 辛亥革命 (辛亥革命)
Chinese Revolution of 1911

Xinmin Xuexiao 新民学校 (新民學校)
New Citizens School

yi 移 (移) migration

Yi Guangyan 蚁光炎 (蟻光炎)
Hia Guang-iam Iamsuri

yü 育 (育) education

Zheng Zhiyong 郑智勇 (鄭智勇)
Tae Ti Ong

zhi 殖 (殖) settlement

Zhonghua minbao 中华民报 (中華民報)
Chinese People's Newspaper

Zhonghua Zongshang Hui 中华总商会
(中華總商會) Chinese Chamber of
Commerce

Zhongyuan bao 中原报 (中原報)
Central Plain Newspaper

Ziyou Taiguo Yundong 自由泰国
运动 (自由泰國運動) Free Thai
Movement

NOTES

Introduction

1   The Chakri dynasty was founded by a Siamese army general with the title of Phraya Chakri, who staged the coup that dethroned the ethnic Chinese King Taksin (r. 1767–82). Taksin had reestablished Siam as an independent state following Burmese attacks and the fall of the old capital in Ayutthaya in 1767. Phraya Chakri established himself as king (later to be named by his descendants King Rama I) and established the Chakri dynasty to rule the kingdom from the newly established capital in Bangkok in 1782. See also Anderson, *Exploration and Irony of Siam Studies over Forty Years.*"

2   *Unfair* is used throughout this book, following the mainstream narrative of Thai and Chinese historiography, which suggests that these treaties (Nanjing, Bowring, etc.) were unfair because European colonial powers violently imposed them on the Asian party. For example, China under the Qing dynasty was forced to accept the conditions of the Treaty of Nanjing after it was defeated by the British in the First Opium War; similarly, King Mongkut of Siam agreed to sign the Bowring Treaty because he knew of China's devastating defeat in the Opium War and was certain that Siam would suffer the same fate if it resisted the demands of the British Empire. Numerous instances demonstrate how this notion of the unfairness of such treaties remains an integral part of national history and public memory in this part of the world. A primary example is the People's Republic of China's stance on Hong Kong and Macau, presented to the UN Decolonization Committee almost as soon as the PRC was seated in the UN: "The questions of Hong Kong and Macau belong to a category of questions resulting from a series of unequal treaties which the imperialists imposed on China" (Ming, *The Hong Kong Reader*, 45).

3   Extraterritoriality or extraterritorial rights in the case of the Bowring Treaty and other unfair treaties meant that subjects of colonial powers were not subjected to the host country's—in this case, Siam's—judicial system. That is, should they commit a crime, they would be tried by the colonial consulate's court. When Siam accords extraterritorial rights to subjects of any foreign state, it relinquishes its judicial sovereignty—the power to prosecute legal offenses committed within her realm—to the colonial powers involved in the unfair treaties.

4   Ethnic Chinese in Siam registered as colonial subjects through various channels. Some were born in other European colonies and subsequently relocated to Siam. Some claimed their ancestors were born in the colonies. Others claimed to

have emigrated through colonial treaty ports or to have been brought to Southeast Asia through the bureaucratic mechanisms of the colonial governments in the region. All in all, having extraterritorial rights facilitated business in many respects, and colonial enterprises that employed ethnic Chinese as agents in various trades and businesses tended to support their employees' claims allowing them to be registered as colonial subjects.

5 Often during Chulalongkorn's reign an ethnic Chinese trader ran into trouble with Siamese authorities and claimed to be a subject of a certain colonial power. If the consulate in Bangkok could not verify such claims but conceded the possibility that the individual had been registered in one of the many colonies neighboring Siam, matters were often dropped. Even if the case was pursued, by the time the claim was verified, the individual was long gone (Ruangsri, "Border Trade and the Transformation of States," 62). Such cases demonstrate how extraterritoriality not only hampered the ability of the Siamese state to exercise judicial control over colonial subjects but allowed colonial subjects residing in Siam to escape the control of their colonial masters.

6 Both Chinese and Japanese government sources published in the early twentieth century conclude that Siam is home to the largest overseas Chinese population in Southeast Asia. The "Survey Study of Overseas Chinese Remittances in Southeast Asia," conducted by the Japanese-controlled Bank of Taiwan in 1914, put the number of Chinese immigrants to Siam at 21 percent of the total population (Hicks, *Overseas Chinese Remittances from Southeast Asia*). While Nationalist sources from the 1930s stated that the total number of overseas Chinese in Siam constituted up to a third of the entire population. Foreign Affairs, 172-1/0654 063.2, *The Thai Government's Anti-Chinese Policies* (Taiguo zhengfu paihua de zhengce), July 31, 1941, Academia Historica, Taipei, Republic of China (hereafter AH). Skinner's *Chinese Society in Thailand* (20–27) also clearly stated that by the early twentieth century up to 25 percent of the royal bloodline of the ruling Chakri dynasty was Chinese. This clearly attests to the intimate connections between the ruling dynasty and leading capitalist Chinese families in the last couple of reigns prior to the collapse of the absolute monarchy.

7 The first version of the Citizenship Act was promulgated in 1913.

8 The Siamese Revolution was instigated by a group of civilians and members of the armed forces who called themselves the People's Party. Most of the ringleaders had been government-sponsored students in France and began plotting when they were still abroad. The revolution itself took place on June 24, 1932. It was essentially a bloodless coup, which ended the absolute monarchy and replaced the royal government of King Prajadhipok Rama VII (r. 1925–35) with a revolutionary government formed from among their ranks. Shortly after the revolution took place, the first constitution was drafted, which allowed the institution of the monarchy to continue on as symbolic figurehead of the nation, albeit with significantly decreased political power. Prajadhipok carried on as constitutional monarch until 1935, when he abdicated, citing irreconcilable political differences with the leaders of the People's Party. He was succeeded by the juvenile King Anandamahidol Rama VIII (r. 1935–46), who spent most of his

reign studying in Europe and only returned to his kingdom at the conclusion of the Second World War.

9 There is considerable controversy over the names for the series of armed conflicts between Japan and the Allied powers in Southeast Asia between 1941 and 1945. This book employs the term Greater East Asia War because the principal conflict in the Asia theater involved Japan and China, a conflict that extends back to Japan's invasion of Manchuria in 1931. The ethnic Chinese in Southeast Asia, especially those in Thailand, had been deeply involved in the anti-Japanese war efforts since the early 1930s. Hence, the part of the war that affected Thailand and the ethnic Chinese in Thailand was directly connected to the Sino-Japanese conflict and would be best described as the Greater East Asia War. To call the war in Southeast Asia the Second World War puts too much emphasis on the colonial connections with European powers and the war in Europe. To call it the Pacific War, on the other hand, overemphasizes the US role and denies the central importance of China in the conflict that came into being nearly a decade before the bombing of Pearl Harbor.

10 While Eurocentric historiography dates the end of the Cold War to the fall of the Berlin Wall in 1989 or the dissolution of the Union of Soviet Socialist Republics (USSR) in 1991, within the geopolitical context of East and Southeast Asia, it makes more sense to date the end of the Cold War to the mid to late 1970s, which saw the conclusion of the Vietnam War (1975), the end of the Great Proletarian Cultural Revolution in China (1976), and the beginning of the Chinese reform era under Deng Xiaoping (1978).

Chapter 1: Educating Citizens

1 The First Opium War (1839–42) was fought between the Chinese and British empires. Armed conflict broke out in response to China's destruction of British property in an attempt to eradicate illegal sales of opium that was transported from South Asia to China mostly by British merchants. The First Opium War ended with a British victory and the signing of the Treaty of Nanjing, which forced China to open five treaty ports along the southeastern coast for free trade—essentially ending the Qing dynasty's monopoly on international trade—secured extraterritorial rights for British subjects, and ceded Hong Kong to Britain for the next century. The Second Opium War (1856–60) was related to the results of the First Opium War. The British claimed that Chinese authorities were not respecting colonial subjects' extraterritorial rights. The French then alleged that the Qing government did not protect freedom of religion, and as a result, both French missionaries and Chinese converts were being regularly discriminated against by the Chinese public and persecuted by Chinese officials. The Second Opium War ended with the victory of the British-French alliance. Postwar negotiations resulted in the signing of the Treaty of Tianjin, which opened ten more treaty ports, allowed foreign vessels to navigate the Yangzi River and foreigners to travel inland freely beyond the treaty port, and established foreign legations in Beijing.

2 Perry made a show of American superior military force with the four battleships
   he brought with him in 1853. Consequently, when he returned the following year,
   the shogun was willing to sign the Treaty of Kanagawa, which should be considered a typical "unfair" treaty with demands similar to those in the treaties of
   Nanjing, Tianjin, and Bowring. Such a political drawback seriously compromised
   the shogun's legitimacy as political overlord of Japan. It resulted in a civil war and
   eventually led to a major transformation in Japanese sociopolitical and economic
   reforms in what has become known as the Meiji Restoration (1868–1912).

3 Gellner, *Nations and Nationalism*.

4 This is the mainstream, state-sanctioned version of Thai history, which portrays
   King Mongkut as a patron of modern science education; King Chulalongkorn as
   the modernizing monarch; and King Vajiravudh as the father of the Thai
   nationalist movement and the first monarch to promulgate and attempt to enforce
   a system of compulsory education.

5 Seventy years, counting from the signing of the Bowring Treaty in 1855 to the
   establishment of compulsory education by orders of Vajiravudh in 1921.

6 Kang Youwei led the Hundred-Day Reform, the colloquial term for Emperor
   Guangxu's ill-fated Wuxu Reform of 1898, which began in early June of that year
   and was intended to have profound and far-reaching effects in all major areas of
   politics and society, modernizing the economy, the military, and the educational
   system, industrializing production systems, and transforming the political system
   into a constitutional monarchy. However, this radical program aroused the
   suspicions of conservative factions in the court and resulted in a violent palace
   coup. Consequently, plans for reform were suspended. The emperor was effectively
   put under house arrest, and the leaders of the reform—Kang and his trusted
   disciples—were forced into exile.

7 Xie, "Overseas Chinese Education and the Development of Overseas Chinese
   Nationalism in Southeast Asia in the Early 20th Century," 26.

8 Qiu, "Concerning the Overseas Chinese Educational Policies of the Late Qing
   Government," 59.

9 Bie, *Change and Initiative*, 230–39.

10 Bie and Tian. "Historical Investigation of Modern Overseas Chinese Education," 34.

11 Prior to the Xinhai Revolution of 1911, Sun Yat-sen traveled to Siam in 1903 (no
   specific dates given); on January 11, 1904; early in 1908; and on November 20, 1908.
   Soon after his last visit, the following Chinese schools were established in
   Bangkok; Huayi Xuetang in 1909; Guowen Xuetang in 1909; Xinmin Xuexiao in
   1910; and Datong Xuexiao in 1910. A library and oratory association was also
   established in 1909. See Xia, *Political Activities of the Overseas Chinese in
   Thailand*, 5–11.

12 Bie, "Modern Overseas Chinese Educational Policies and Measures," 64.

13 Huang, "Umbilical Ties."

14 Anthony D. Smith, *Nationalism: Theory, Ideology, History* (Cambridge: Polity
   Press, 2001), 14–15.

15 It is important to note that Vajiravudh's ascension to crown prince could very
   well be considered an accident. Chulalongkorn had established his firstborn,

Prince Vajirunnahis, as crown prince and started training him in the arts of political management and manipulation in the Chakri court from very early on. Other princes were sent to various European countries to be educated in a wide range of modern subjects in both arts and science. The initial idea was that Vajirunnahis, who had been trained as a career politician, would later rule as absolute monarch, and he would be supported by his technocrat brothers, all of whom had acquired state-of-the-art knowledge and technics from the West. Unfortunately, Vajirunnahis died of typhoid in 1895, and Vajiravudh, who was next in line, despite having spent some time studying abroad in preparation to become a technocrat, was arbitrarily made crown prince. Vajiravudh had to end his military training early and switch to a civilian educational path in preparation for his future role as monarch. This switch would later impede Vajiravudh's ability to rule since he was neither properly trained to be a successful politician of the court, as Vajirunnahis had been, nor had he completed his military training, which made him less credible as a military commander than some of his brothers and half-brothers, who were career soldiers and enjoyed much more respect and cooperation from the armed forces. Boontanonda, *Politics in the Military in the Sixth Reign.*

16 Rama VI, R6 N20.12/23, *The New Emperor by Atsawaphahu,* September 18, 1915, National Archives, Bangkok, Thailand (hereafter NA).

17 The Ang-yi Act of 1897. A detailed explanation of the history and context of this law can be found in the royal chronicles of the fifth reign and the essay collection *Nithanboranakhadi* by Prince Damrong (Prince Damrong, *Nithanboranakhadi,* vol.1 [Bangkok: Khurusabha, 1961]. The criminal offense of being an *ang-yi* remains in the Thai criminal code to the present day, and the latest high-profile case of prosecution occurred in January 2017 (*Prachathai Newspaper,* January 13, 2017). *Ang-yi* is probably a Teochiu (Chaozhou) pronunciation of Hongzi—a derivation of Hongmen, also known as the Heaven and Earth Society or Tiandihui—which was among the largest and most influential secret societies in Southeast Asia in the nineteenth century.

18 Rama VI, R6 N20/11, *Memorandum to Chaophraya Yomarat,* June 4, 1919, NA.

19 Klom-iang, "Rama VI's Policies concerning the Chinese in Thailand," 202.

20 Rama VI, R6 N25/2, *Phraya Ratsadanupradit's Report on Kuomintang Activities in the South of Thailand,* April 6, 1913, NA.

21 *Kekmeng* is the Teochiu pronunciation of *geming* (standard Chinese pronunciation), the most common Chinese word for "revolution." In colloquial Thai and Chinese, *kekmeng* and *geming* could also be used for individuals or groups who supported the revolution or revolutionary ideologies. *Kekmeng* used in the way Phraya Ratsadanupradit wrote in his report to the central government could also be translated as "rebels" or "revolutionaries."

22 Rama VI, R6 N25/65, *Tam Chinsam Ahongzittempts to Establish a Secret Society,* October 26, 1923, NA. Tam Chinsam (Tan Zhensan) originated from Chaozhou. He was a well-known personality in the ethnic Chinese community in Siam during this period. Having many powerful friends as well as enemies and being an active member of the Kuomintang, Tan frequently got into trouble with Thai authorities.

However, being a Dutch subject, he was protected by extraterritorial rights and was not prosecuted by the Thai state through much of the pre-1932 period.

23 Rama VII, Interior R7 MI/17, *List of Documents Found in Yok Eng Hak How Chinese School*, December 10, 1926, NA.

24 In this case, the term *kekmeng* is usually a reference to the Kuomintang (Chinese Nationalist Party).

25 Foreign Affairs, MFA39/18, *Arrest Report of Four Teachers at the Mikang Chinese School*, September 17, 1930, NA.

26 Klom-iang, "Rama VI's Policies concerning the Chinese in Thailand," 204–5.

27 Rama VI, R6 N20/6, *Report from the Assembly of Ministers*, April 3, 1911, NA.

28 Boontananda, "King Vajiravudh and the Making of His Military Image," 28–35.

29 Narong Phuangphit, *Prince Thaniniwat and His Execution of Overseas Chinese Educational Policies while Serving as Minister of Education* (Bangkok: Prachan Publishing House, 1974).

30 The debate over whether the Xinhai Revolution should be considered a failure continues today among historians of modern China. To achieve its goal of overthrowing the Qing dynasty, revolutionary leaders had to rely on the support of a leading general in the Qing army, General Yuan Shikai. Yuan successfully negotiated the abdication of the last emperor in return for the position of president of the Chinese Republic after its establishment in 1912. Yuan then ruled the republic as a military dictatorship, outlawed all political parties including the Chinese Nationalist Party (Kuomintang), and moved to establish a new dynasty with himself as the founding emperor. Yuan died quite suddenly from uremia in 1916. Afterward China declined into a state of warlordism. Sun Yat-sen returned from exile to establish a militarist government in Guangdong in 1921 and called for national unification under the leadership of the Chinese Nationalist Party. Sun died without accomplishing this in 1925. Yet in the following year his supporters embarked on a militarist unification effort known as the Northern Expedition, which brought Chiang Kai-shek to the forefront of the Chinese Nationalist Party. He was able to consolidate power and become the president of the republic and head of the Nationalist government seated in Nanjing in 1927.

31 The revolution that ended the absolute monarchy in Siam had taken place in June 1932, but the monarch was allowed to remain as a figurehead leader of the constitutional regime that was established following the revolution. A large portion of the state bureaucracy from the ancien régime was also left in place under the revolutionary government of the People's Party. In this sense, it was expected that the People's Party government would have a more cordial relationship with the Nationalist government of China since both sides came from revolutionary parties. At the same time, the monarchy and royalist factions in Siam would have seen that the revolution they feared had taken place and there appeared to be no significant move to transform the kingdom into a republic or eradicate the monarchy. Hence, their fears of establishing formal relations with the Chinese revolutionary government that existed back in Vajiravudh's reign would have subsided a bit by the mid-1930s.

32 Foreign Affairs, "Guidelines for Sino-Siamese Nationalist Movement (Secret)," in 172-1/0703(1) 012, *Discussion of Sino-Thai Problem* (Zongtai wenti taolun hui), 1932, AH.

33 Limsaihua and Bamrungsuk, "Nationalism and Territorial Dispute in the Field Marshal Plaek Phibulsongkram Government (1938–1941)."

34 Foreign Affairs, "Reports from the Discussion of Sino-Thai Problem (15th Meeting)," in 172-1/0703(3) 012, *Discussion of Sino-Thai Problem*.

35 Foreign Affairs, "Reports from the Discussion of Sino-Thai Problem (32nd Meeting)," in 172-1/0703(4) 012, *Discussion of Sino-Thai Problem*. The New Life Movement (Xin Shenghuo Yundong) was a sociocultural campaign launched by the Nationalist government in 1934. It was a disorderly mix of Confucian, Christian, nationalist, and authoritarian ideologies aimed primarily at countering the spread of communism. The campaign achieved a degree of success in improving the general population's quality of life during the War of Resistance. Sun, *Powerful Husbands and Virtuous Wives*.

36 Foreign Affairs, "Problem That Should Not Have Occurred," in 172-1/0654 063.2, *Discussion of the Thai Government's Anti-Chinese Policies* (Taiguo paihua de zhengce), 1948–49, AH.

37 This matter is explored more thoroughly in chapter 4.

38 The Six Principles of the First Declaration of the People's Party:
    (1) To preserve all aspects of independence—political independence, judicial independence, economic independence, etc.—to remain firmly established in this country
    (2) To maintain security within the country
    (3) To improve economic livelihood of the people
    (4) To make all people equal in the eyes of the law
    (5) To allow people to enjoy liberty and freedom
    (6) To provide people with full access to education

39 Foreign Affairs, 172-1/0646, *Supporting Overseas Chinese Education in Siam*, 1935, AH.

40 According to the first Primary Education Act of 1921, children of primary school age were those between seven and fifteen years old.

41 Murashima, *Politics of the Overseas Chinese in Siam*, 35–36.

42 Skinner, *Chinese Society in Thailand*, 266.

43 Ibid., 228.

44 Ibid., 229–30.

45 Foreign Affairs, FA39/25, *Report on Raid of Hainanese Library Association*, September 16, 1932, NA.

46 Foreign Affairs, FA39/26, *The Meaning of Encouraging Young Workers*, December 10, 1932, NA

47 Ibid.

48 Murashima, *Politics of the Overseas Chinese in Siam*, 112. Most communist activities that involved students or school-age youths were among the less severe offenses, such as distributing communist propaganda pamphlets or participating in the production and distribution of the young communist newspaper, *Young Siam* (Yuwachon Siam).

49 By the end of the Second World War, only two Chinese schools remained in operation in Thailand (both happened to be located in Bangkok). The rest had either been shut down by the government or forced out of business by the hostile political environment.

50 According to a Thai police report from this period, teachers and journalists were the two professions most likely to become involved in communist movements.

51 Foreign Affairs, "Reports from the Discussion of Sino-Thai Problem (10th Meeting)," in 172-1/0703(3)012, *Discussion of Sino-Thai Problem* (Zhongtai wenti taolun hui), 1941–42, AH.

52 A document issued by the Nationalist Foreign Ministry in 1948 mentioned that "the government of the Republic of China agrees that the Siamese government should consider the CCP and communism as enemies, but not all overseas Chinese residing in Siam should be categorized as such." Foreign Affairs, 172-1/0654 063.2, *The Thai Government's Anti-Chinese Policies* (Taiguo zhengfu paihua de zhengce), July 31, 1941, AH.

53 Hodges, "Western Science in Siam," 95.

Chapter 2: Publishing Nations

1 Anderson, *Imagined Communities*, 46.

2 A powerful summary of the crucial role played by language in the origin of nation-states is given in Elie Kedourie's essay on national self-determination (*Nationalism*, 58): "The world is a world of diversity, and humanity is divided into nations. Language is the external and visible badge of those differences which distinguish one nation from another; it is the most important criteria by which a nation is recognized to exist, and to have the right to form a state on its own."

3 Anderson, *Imagined Communities*, 37–46.

4 Murashima, *Politics of the Overseas Chinese in Siam*; Intarabhirom, *Seaw Hudseng Seeboonreung*. See also Hicks, *Overseas Chinese Remittance from Southeast Asia, 1910–1940*; Ho, *Documentary Collection on Overseas Chinese in Southeast Asia*, vol. 1.

5 Some sources claim that Zheng was a subject of Portugal (Murashima, *Politics of the Overseas Chinese in Siam*, 127), but this contradicts more recent accounts of the official history of the Poh Teck Tung Foundation (Tanprasoet, *Po Tek Tung on the Path of Thai Social History*, 93) and the fact that Zheng later became the founder and chairman of the Sino-French Chamber of Commerce, which was established for the purpose of encouraging association and cooperation among ethnic Chinese merchants who were registered as French subjects and conducting business in Siam (Bisalputra, *Chinese and Mon Diaspora in Siam*, 59). Murashima's misunderstanding might, however, be attributed to the possibility that Zheng, who was Siamese-born, attained colonial subject status when he returned to China as a child. Some suggested that he had been registered in the Portuguese territory of Macau.

6 The grand master of most Chinese secret societies was customarily referred to as "big brother." However, in the numerous cases of secret societies in South China

and in overseas Chinese communities in Europe and America, the existence of this shadowy figure always proved uncertain. Though frequently alluded to, such a person could not be found or arrested. Hence, to be known as "second brother" implies that Zheng Zhiyong must have been very close to the top of the secret society hierarchy, if not the grand master himself.

7   The lottery tax farm was one of the most lucrative tax farms King Nangklao Rama III (r. 1824–51) established in the early nineteenth century and one of the last tax farms to be abolished by the end of King Vajiravudh's reign in the 1920s. Tax farming was a popular method of collecting taxes throughout colonial Southeast Asia. Rama III based the practice on the system used by the Dutch in the Dutch East Indies. Basically, the government would award the tax farm to the highest bidder, usually a very rich and influential entrepreneur and almost always ethnic Chinese. The tax farmer then had the right to collect taxes from everyone trading that specific commodity in the land. In Zheng Zhiyong's case, this would be anyone involved in running lotteries in Siam. Tax farms facilitated the establishment of a monopoly. This was the case for Zheng, who became the biggest name in the lottery business in Siam, until his tax farm was abolished in the last wave of tax reforms under Rama VI.

8   The relationship between the Crown and Zheng's enterprises during the early years of Vajiravudh's reign calls for in-depth research. Skinner and Vella both mention that when Rama VI ascended the throne, he had many suspicions and ambivalent feelings regarding the ethnic Chinese minority due to the Great Chinese Strike of June 1910, which crippled the Siamese capital for three full days. The strike was believed to have been staged by the orders of secret society bosses to protest the last series of reforms in the tax-revenue system of Chulalong-korn's reign. Considering Zheng's prominent position in the secret society hierarchy, it is difficult to imagine that he would not have participated to some degree in the strike. Yet considering this illustrious businessman's highly influential position in the Siamese economy and the court, as well as his royalist stance regarding Chinese politics, it is understandable that Vajiravudh would choose to maintain a cordial relationship with Zheng for at least the first few years of his reign. Skinner, *Chinese Society in Thailand*; Vella, *Chaiyo!*.

9   *Baba* is widely used to refer to descendants of early Chinese immigrants to the British Straits Settlements of Singapore, Malacca, and Penang. The term usually implies a mixture of Chinese and Malay ethnicities. Siao Hutseng reflects the pronunciation in the dialect of Fujian, the ancestral homeland of Xiao's paternal line.

10 Rama V, R5 N8/7, *Views from Chinese Newspapers*, January 12, 1908, NA.

11 For example, reports from the *Sino-Siam News* emphasized how long the revolution-ary forces had been able to hold out against the onslaught of imperial forces instead of simply reporting that a certain revolutionary stronghold had been captured. Rama V, R5 N8/10, *Translation of the Huaxian Xinbao*, March 8, 1908, NA.

12 Intharaphirom, *Seaw Hudseng Seeboonreung*, 19.

13 Ibid., 64 (quoting "Opinions from Revolutionary Newspapers" [Khwamhenk-hongnangsuephimkekmeng], *Chino-Siam Warasap*, November 11, 1910).

14 Ibid., 194 (quoting "News on Parliaments of the East" [Praisanilekarueang parliament naitawan-ok], *Chino-Siam Warasap*, July 1, 1914).

15 Rama VI, R6 N25/31, *Reports from Xiao Focheng*, September 4, 1913, NA.

16 Skinner, *Chinese Society in Thailand*, 170. The CCC was essentially the chamber of commerce for ethnic Chinese merchants and entrepreneurs residing and conducting business mainly in Siam. Members of the CCC were from various backgrounds, but the most influential were British and French colonial subjects. These two groups also established separate smaller chambers exclusively for ethnic Chinese British subjects, who were often in fierce competition with the chamber of commerce for ethnic Chinese French subjects.

17 Rama VI, R6 N25/31, *Reports from Xiao Focheng*, September 4, 1913, NA.

18 Intharaphirom, *Seaw Hudseng Seeboonreung*, 285.

19 Murashima, *Politics of the Overseas Chinese in Siam*, 47.

20 Chen Shouming was better known as Tan Siomeng Wangli, which is a combination of the Chaozhou dialect pronunciation of his name (Tan Siomeng) and Wangli or Wanglee, the trademark of his company, which later became the surname of his descendants.

21 Murashima, *Politics of the Overseas Chinese in Siam*, 31.

22 Better known as Hia Guang-iam Iamsuri, which is a combination of the Chaozhou dialect pronunciation (Hia Guang-iam) and the Thai version of his surname (Iamsuri or Iamsuree).

23 Zhao Zhen, "Historical Overview and Future Tendencies of the New Chinese-Language Literature in Thailand," *Journal of Tangshan Teachers College*, January 1999, 52–61.

24 Zhang Junzhe, "History of Chinese-Language Literature in Thailand and an Outline of Its Current Situation," *Overseas Chinese Historical Research*, April 1998, 39–45.

25 Rama VII, R7 M18/6, *Translation of the Zhonghua Minbao Newspaper*, June 28, 1928, NA.

26 Zhao Zhen, "Historical Overview and Future Tendencies of the New Chinese-Language Literature in Thailand," 52–53.

27 Skinner, *Chinese Society in Thailand*, 235.

28 Tejapira, *Commodifying Marxism*.

29 King Vajiravudh Foundation, *"Jews of the East" and "Thailand, Wake Up!" by Ashvabhahu*, 23.

30 In fact, as will become obvious in chapter 3, Vajiravudh's strong anti-Chinese rhetoric could also be understood as a marketing ploy the king used to persuade or put pressure on rich Chinese entrepreneurs to provide more financial support for his various nationalist projects. To crudely simplify, it would not be incorrect to conclude that the status of a true Thai nationalist during Vajiravudh's reign could be easily bought. If one was upset for being called *Jews of the Orient*, the awkward situation could easily be remedied by a sizable donation to one of the king's favorite royal projects—more rifles for the Wild Tiger Corps or an aircraft for the fledgling army air force. Then not only would one have proof of being a true patriot, but the monarch was also known to publish messages of gratitude in his various publications. Atsawaphahu. "Thanks to My Chinese Friends."

31 Rama VI, R6 N13.1/9, *Letter from Prince Thewawong to King Rama VI*, September 8, 1915, NA.

32 Rama VI, R6 N25/10, *Response from King Rama VI to Prince Thewawong*, September 1915, NA.

33 Vajiravudh's exceptional fondness for literature and drama and his funding of the Wild Tiger Corps and their frequent war games amid the declining economy of the early twentieth century were often cited by his critics as obvious indications that he was unfit for his position.

34 Rama VI, R6 N20.12/23, *The New Emperor by Atsawaphahu*, September 18, 1915, NA.

35 A brilliant PhD thesis by Matthew Phillip Copeland from Australia National University, "Contested Nationalism and the 1932 Overthrow of the Absolute Monarchy in Siam," does a magnificent job of cataloging and analyzing an impressive collection of satirical materials—including caricatures and op-ed articles—published in newspapers, magazines, and other sorts of periodicals during the sixth and seventh reigns. The vast collection presented in this dissertation clearly proves that there were competing voices within the domestic political arena of Siam and that they had—in comparison with later periods—a relatively high level of freedom of the press and freedom of expression through the latter period of the absolutist regime.

36 King Vajiravudh Foundation, *"Jews of the East" and "Thailand, Wake Up!" by Ashvabhahu.*

37 See Vella, *Chaiyo!*, xiv; and Anderson, *Imagined Communities*, 100.

38 Reid, *Imperial Alchemy*, 36–37.

39 Hell, *Siam and World War I.*

40 Vella, *Chaiyo!*, 256.

41 This refers to an incident during which British colonial police force opened fire on a crowd of Chinese labor and anti-imperialist demonstrators in Shanghai's international settlement on May 30, 1925. Vajiravudh died on November 25 of that year, and Xiao's *Sino-Siam Daily* was shut down almost immediately following the sixth reign. Leading the Siamese authorities in this closure were members of the same group that had earlier urged Vajiravudh to deport Xiao for his bold stance in carrying on the public newspaper debate with the monarch. This later, more repressive course of events clearly indicates Vajiravudh's position as protector and patron of Xiao Focheng's problematic media enterprise.

42 Skinner, *Chinese Society in Thailand*, 235.

43 Intarabhirom, *Seaw Hudseng Seeboonreung*, 300–13.

44 Vella, *Chaiyo!*, 256.

45 Skinner, *Chinese Society in Thailand*, 273.

46 Sattayanurak, *The Thai Nation and Thainess by Luang Vichitvatakarn*, 4.

47 Skinner, *Chinese Society in Thailand*, 261.

48 Neighboring kingdoms here refers to Burma, which became part of British India in 1886, and Laos and Cambodia, which were annexed by French Indochina in 1893.

49 Copeland, "Contested Nationalism and the 1932 Overthrow of the Absolute Monarchy in Siam."

Chapter 3: Economic Thai-ification

1   Skinner, *Chinese Society in Thailand*, 360.
2   The first Phibunsongkhram administration refers to the period 1938–44, when Field Marshal Plaek Phibunsongkhram became the third prime minister of Thailand under the constitutional regime. This was the administration that changed the nation's official name from Siam to Thailand in 1939, engaged in the Franco-Thai War (also known as the Indochina conflict) in that same year, and led Thailand into the Second World War as a formal ally of Japan.
3   G. William Skinner, "Chinese Assimilation and Thai Politics."
4   The Chinese tribute system came into being during the Tang dynasty (618–907) and reached the height of its influence in the eighteenth century during the Qing dynasty (1644–1911). It is essentially a dynastic monopoly of international trade with China in which foreign states wishing to trade with China must pay tribute to the Chinese emperor. Once the emperor has accepted the tribute, the foreigners are allowed to trade through agents of the court, who collect appropriate tariffs and ensure that each foreign state trades within the quota set by the imperial government according to the level of that state's relationship with China and the amount and frequency of their tribute-bearing missions. Foreign states tended to perceive the tribute trade as a form of commercial tax and cooperated due to the high value of Chinese goods in foreign markets, but for the Chinese imperial government this was viewed as evidence of China's superior civilization, supporting her ethnocentric claim of being the "middle kingdom."
5   The reign of the Qianlong emperor is generally considered the apex of the Qing dynasty's power and influence. This was the period during which the Chinese Empire expanded to its farthest frontiers, incorporating Xinjiang, Tibet, and Mongolia. Nonetheless, problems appeared by the closing years of Qianlong's reign. Most notable were problems related to trade with the West, especially the Chinese government's inability to control the opium trade, which was beginning to take a toll on the Chinese economy from the last decade of the eighteenth century.
6   Lysa Hong, "The Tax Farming System in the Early Bangkok Period."
7   Skinner, *Chinese Society in Thailand*, 118–25.
8   Wyatt, *Thailand*, 169.
9   This spectacular shift in the perspective on international politics is alluded to in what were reported to be the deathbed remarks of Jessadabodindra: "There will be no more wars with Vietnam and Burma. We will have them only with the West. Take care, and do not lose any opportunities to them. Anything that they propose should be held up to close scrutiny before accepting it: Do not blindly trust them." Wyatt, *Thailand*, 180.
10 Ethnic Chinese dominance of the Siamese economy evolved gradually through the development of both the Chinese tribute system and the Siamese corvée-labor system. It is difficult to pinpoint exactly when this dominance started, but definitely by the early eighteenth century—in the latter half of the Ayutthayan period—trade with China had become the most important foreign trade and source of revenue for the Siamese ruling class.

11   The centralization of regional governing power under the rule of the emperor in the Meiji Restoration is a favorite among historians and political analysts, who like to compare the different degrees of success or failure of the modernization projects of Meiji Japan and Siam in the reign of King Chulalongkorn. It is important, however, to be aware that the success of the Meiji Restoration was partly due to a change in the ruling regime from the Tokugawa Shogunate to a national government under the emperor. In the Siamese case, by contrast, ruling power continued to be passed in the Chakri dynasty from Mongkut Rama IV to his son, Chulalongkorn Rama V. In this, Chulalongkorn did not have the privilege of blaming the problems and imperfections of premodern Siam on the evils of the old regime in the way that the modernizers of the Meiji Restoration blamed the backwardness and tyranny of the Tokugawa Shogunate.

12   Lysa Hong, "The Tax Farming System in the Early Bangkok Period."

13   Ruangsilp, *Thai Economic History, 2352–2453 B.E.*, 290–92.

14   Bualek, *Characteristics of Thai Capitalist, 2457–2482 B.E.*, 67–69.

15   Brown, "British Financial Advisers in Siam in the Reign of King Chulalongkorn."

16   Skinner, *Chinese Society in Thailand*, 213–25.

17   Foreign Affairs; 172-1/0703(4)012 "Report from the 13th meeting of the Sino-Thai Problem Discussion," in *Discussion of Sino-Thai Problem Problem* [Zhongtai wenti taolun hui], January 25, 1943, AH.

18   In the xenophobic world of Chinese politics of the late nineteenth and early twentieth centuries, Zhang Bizhi's idea of relying on overseas Chinese financial support appealed to the Qing government because it provided a way for them to have their cake and eat it too. That is, China could acquire financial support for modernization from sources outside its geographical boundaries without having to rely on the mercy of foreign imperialist powers. This allowed them to remain marginally independent while catching up with the West. Godley. *The Mandarin-Capitalists from Nanyang*, 93.

19   The yuan of late Qing China was valued on par with the Spanish dollar or Mexican peso, which were the main currencies used in the transpacific trade between the Americas and East Asia. Hicks, *Overseas Chinese Remittances from Southeast Asia 1910–1940*, 146.

20   Despite all its shortcomings, the early Republican era witnessed a significant improvement in the system of overseas Chinese remittances from Southeast Asia in the Overseas Chinese Bank (Huaqiao Yinhang), which was established in 1919. This development encouraged the flow of remittances from Singapore, Malaya, and Burma back to the mainland branch in Fujian. Tong-an xian difangzhi bianzuan weiyuanhui, *Tong-an Xian Zhi*, 1262.

21   Hicks, *Overseas Chinese Remittances from Southeast Asia 1910–1940*, 153.

22   Foreign Affairs, 172-1/0703(2)012, "Primary Reports and Suggestions," in *Discussion on Sino-Thai Problems*, January 15, 1940, AH. By the time this report came out in January 1940, Yi had been assassinated. His title as chairman of the Chinese Chamber of Commerce was possibly given as the most prestigious position he had occupied during his lifetime. Current positions are cited for other donors mentioned in this excerpt.

23 Ibid.

24 Ruangsri, "Border Trade and the Transformation of States in the Hinterland of Peninsular Southeast Asia," 100–106.

25 King Vajiravudh Foundation, *"Jews of the East" and "Thailand, Wake Up!" by Ashvabhahu*, 41–42.

26 Ibid., 50.

27 Dillon, *The Disintegration of China*; Rama VI, R6 N20.12/23, *The New Emperor by Atsawaphahu*, September 18, 1915, NA; Rama VI, R6 N20/11, *Memorandum to Chaophraya Yomarat*, June 4, 1919, NA.

28 Dillon, *The Disintegration of China*.

29 Rama VI, R6 N20.12/23, *The New Emperor by Atsawaphahu*.

30 Wyatt, *Thailand*, 231.

31 The remaining four of the six declarations include: (2) preserve national security, (4) provide equal rights to all citizens, (5) provide liberty to citizens within the limits of the four declarations already mentioned, and (6) provide education for all the people as much as possible. Kasetsiri, *Political History of Thailand, 1932–1957*, 74.

32 This represents an intriguing aspect of conservative political discourse in Thailand, which has consistently argued that it is the responsibility of the citizen to bring himself or herself out of poverty through the virtues of industriousness, trustworthiness, and frugality. If every citizen could achieve the capitalist dream of becoming rich and educated, the kingdom would truly become a prosperous and developed nation in accordance with the Eurocentric standards of a successful nation of the twentieth century.

33 Sattayanurak, *The Thai Nation and Thainess by Luang Vichitvatakarn*, 87–88.

34 Skinner, *Chinese Society in Thailand*, 261. Wichitwathakan's Jewish-Chinese comparison came up in a speech he gave at the Department of Fine Arts, where he served as director in 1938.

35 In his speech before the parliament on July 25, 1938, Luang Wichitwathakan clearly spelled out his concerns over the possibility that the ethnic Chinese would take over electoral politics in Siam, and he proposed that the government might explore the possibility of employing the methods used by the German government to deal with the "Jewish problem" to handle the "Chinese problem" in Siam as well. Skinner, *Chinese Society in Thailand*, 261–70.

36 Foreign Affairs, 172-1/0703(4) 012, "Reports from the 31st Meeting of the Sino-Thai Problem Discussion," in *Discussion of Sino-Thai Problem* (Zhongtai wenti taolun hui), February 1943, AH.

37 The following provinces were declared prohibited areas: Lopburi, Prachinburi, and Chonburi in May 1941; Nakhonratchasima, Ubonratchathani, and Kanchanaburi in December 1941; and Chiang Mai, Lamphun, Chiang Rai, Phrae, and Uttaradit in January 1943 (Skinner, *Chinese Society in Thailand*, 270–78).

38 Ibid., 278.

39 Ibid., 276.

40 Foreign Affairs, 172-1/0703(4), "Reports from the 31st Meeting of the Sino-Thai Problem Discussion."

Chapter 4: The Greater East Asia War

1 Winichakul, *Siam Mapped*.

2 For a highly detailed study and brilliant analysis of Vajiravudh's aspiration to establish a convincing military image and to build lasting bonds of chivalry and loyalty between the Crown and the armed forces and how that strongly influenced the consolidation of the Crown-military alliance in the post–Second World War period, see Boontanondha, "King Vajiravudh and the Making of His Military Image."

3 Foreign Affairs, FA73.5, *Premier's Interview Given to Newspaper Reporters*, 1940, NA. Interestingly, Phibunsongkhram's vision of the world after the Second World War seemed to resonate with midnineteenth-century German nationalists who believed in the "threshold principle," which proposed that only states that were geographically and demographically large enough could become nations. Economically speaking, a world of great nations should be the next best thing to the as yet unattainable completely unified world. However, the "threshold principle" also encouraged expansionism, allowing big states to become even bigger while small states were continually swallowed up. In this respect, Phibunsongkhram came to the same conclusion: a state could survive in a world of nations only if it succeeded in becoming a great nation in its own right. Hobsbawm, *Nations and Nationalism since 1780*, 30–35. See also Sattayanurak, *The Thai Nation and Thainess by Luang Vichitvatakarn*, 127–28.

4 It is amazing that Phibunsongkhram's Japanese-leaning nationalism succeeded in disassociating itself so completely from the by tradition awesomely sacred Thai monarchs, when Japanese nationalism of the 1930s was fundamentally linked with divine reverence for the emperor.

5 Foreign Office, 371/22215, *Proposed Trade Agreement between Siam and Manchukuo*, 1938, Public Records Office (hereafter PRO).

6 More commonly known in mainstream Thai history as the Indochina conflict.

7 Winichakul, *Siam Mapped*.

8 Kasetsiri, *Political History of Thailand, 1932–1957*, 261.

9 Thongchai Winichakul, "Maps and the Foundation of the Geo-Body of Siam," in Tønnesson and Antlöv, *Asian Forms of the Nation*, 67–91.

10 France employed force five times between 1867 and 1903 in annexing areas that Siam claimed as tributary states. These amounted to a total area of 481,600 sq. km., leaving the Thai nation at its current size of 513,000 sq. km.

11 This is an excerpt from "The Loss of Thai Territories to France," a speech Wichitwathakan gave to teachers and students of the Institution of Military Strategy on October 17, 1940. Sattayanurak, *The Thai Nation and Thainess by Luang Vichitvatakarn*, 64.

12 Kasetsiri, *Political History of Thailand, 1932–1957*, 265. See also Foreign Office; 371/24750, *Report from British Minister Joshua Crosby*. This proposal reversed the previous settlement made during the Franco-Siam crisis at the end of Chulalongkorn's reign, which turned over every island in the Mekong (seventy-seven in total) to the colonial authorities of Indochina.

13 The three major underground anti-French movements were Lao Issara in Laos, Khmere Issarak in Cambodia, and Vietminh in Vietnam.

14 Murashima, "Opposing French Colonialism."

15 *Laemthong* literally means "golden peninsula," a term widely employed in Thai expansionist propaganda to denote the entire area of mainland Southeast Asia.

16 Murashima, "Opposing French Colonialism," 338–42.

17 Kasetsiri, *Political History of Thailand, 1932–1957*, 271–73.

18 After the conclusion of the Second World War, France demanded that Thailand relinquish all rights over territories gained during the Indochina conflict in return for a place in the United Nations, on whose Security Council the French have a permanent seat.

19 Wyatt, *Thailand*, 256–57.

20 Murashima, "The Commemorative Character of Thai Historiography."

21 Chinese documents present a cynical description of that fateful night of December 7:
"At 10 p.m. on 7th December 1941, the Japanese Ambassador TSUBOKAMI called on the Minister of Foreign Affairs, NAI DIREK JAYANAM to ask for the right of transit of Japanese troops though Siam into Burma. Immediately after the interview, NAI DIREK visited the Prime Minister PIBUL SONGGRAM, but he refused to see him, merely sending him a message, 'Carry on as you see fit.' Pibul then fled into hiding." Foreign Affairs, 172-1/0737(1)001, "Most Confidential on Balankura, from British legation," in *The Free Thai Movement (1)*, May 13, 1943, AH.

22 Jayanama, *Thailand and the Second World War*.

23 Murashima, *Politics of the Overseas Chinese in Siam*.

24 Foreign Affairs, 172-1/0703(4)012, "Report from the 31st Meeting of the Sino-Thai Problem Discussion," in *Discussion of Sino-Thai Problem* (Zhongtai wenti taolun hui), February 1943, AH.

25 Murashima, "The Commemorative Character of Thai Historiography."

26 Foreign Affairs, 172-1/0703(2)012, "Report on Overseas Chinese Affairs in Thailand, Sino-Thai Relations, and Suggestions for Further Developments by Li Qiyong," in *Discussion of Sino-Thai Problem*, 1940, AH.

27 Foreign Affairs, 172-1/0703(3)012, "Report from the 10th Meeting of the Sino-Thai Problem Discussion," in *Discussion of Sino-Thai Problem*, January 30, 1941, AH.

28 Foreign Affairs, 172-1/0703(3)012, "Report from the 11th Meeting of the Sino-Thai Problem Discussion," in *Discussion of Sino-Thai Problem*, February 28, 1941, AH.

29 Foreign Affairs, 172-1/0703(3)012, "Report from the 12th Meeting of the Sino-Thai Problem Discussion," in *Discussion of Sino-Thai Problem*, March 28, 1941, AH.

30 Foreign Affairs; 172-1/0703(3)012 "Report from the 24th Meeting of the Sino-Thai Problem Discussion," in *Discussion of Sino-Thai Problem*, April 28, 1942, AH.

31 Ibid.

32 Foreign Affairs; 172-1/0703(4)012, "Report from the 28th Meeting of the Sino-Thai Problem Discussion," in *Discussion of Sino-Thai Problem*, October 27, 1942, AH.

33 Foreign Affairs, 172-1/0703(4)012, "Report from the 29th Meeting of the Sino-Thai Problem Discussion," in *Discussion of Sino-Thai Problem*, November 21, 1942, AH.

34 A formal letter from the Thai secretary of the cabinet to the minister of interior, dated April 20, 1942, stated, "All matters concerning the Japanese, whether requiring support or cooperation, need not be responded to with great urgency. [Thai officials] should attempt to deal with such matters according to strict protocol. Should Japanese personnel fail to operate accordingly, they should be duly reported." Interior, IN2.2.6/4, *Office of the Secretary of the Cabinet informing the Minister of Interior of Matters concerning Japanese Cooperation*, 1942, NA.

35 Foreign Affairs, 172-1/0703(4)012, "Report from the 13th Meeting of the Sino-Thai Problem Discussion," in *Discussion of Sino-Thai Problem*, January 25, 1943, AH.

36 Foreign Affairs, 172-1/0703(4)012, "Report from the 31st Meeting of the Sino-Thai Problem Discussion," in *Discussion of Sino-Thai Problem*, 1943, AH.

37 In *Thailand's Secret War*, E. Bruce Reynolds suggests that due to the decline in performance of the Axis powers as early as January 1943, Phibunsongkhram had instructed the two divisional commanders of the Thai forces confronting the Chinese 93rd Division at the Chinese border in Yunnan to "make a gesture of friendship toward the Chinese side," by returning a group of Chinese prisoners of war. Reynolds interprets this as part of Phibunsongkhram's attempt to distance himself from Japan's failing troops and gain favors from the Allied powers, who seemed to be gaining the upper hand at that point in the war.

38 Srisuka, "Patibatkan Chamkad Balankura," in *Free Thai Movement*.

39 Foreign Affairs, 172-1/0703(4)012, "Report from the 31st Meeting of the Sino-Thai Problem Discussion." See also Foreign Office, 371/35983, *Chiang Kai-shek's Broadcast to Siam*, 1943, PRO.

40 Foreign Affairs, 172-1/0737(1)001, "Most Confidential on Balankura, from British Legation."

41 Ibid.

42 Panthumsen, *Memorial Publication for the Funeral of Mr. Sa-nguan Tularaks*, 112–15.

43 Prasit Rakpracha or Pan Ziming was a third-generation ethnic Chinese born in the suburbs of Bangkok in the early twentieth century. When the War of Resistance broke out in China, he became one of the hundred-odd Thai ethnic Chinese to graduate from Whampoa Academy and served in the Nationalist Army throughout the war. When Sa-nguan's mission arrived in Chongqing, Prasit was assigned as the group's primary interpreter and guardian. He later became deeply involved in other FTM activities in China, including the last FTM mission led by Thawin Udon and the postwar negotiations. Rakpracha, *My Involvement in the Free Thai Movement in China*; Pan Ziming, *Storm of Blood and Iron*.

44 The first group was composed of Free Thai agents from America who arrived for training in Simao, South China, on January 14, 1944. Panthumsen, *Memorial Publication for the Funeral of Mr. Sa-nguan Tularaks*, 115.

45 Ibid., 114.

46 Foreign Affairs, 172-1/0737(2)001, "Letter from Representative of Free Thai Leader, Thawin Udon," in *The Free Thai Movement (2)*, September 1944, AH.

47 Foreign Affairs, 172-1/0703(4)012, "Report from the 32nd meeting of the Sino-Thai Problem Discussion," in *Discussion of Sino-Thai Problem*, April 5,

1943, AH. See also Foreign Office, 371/35983, *Chiang Kai-shek's Broadcast to Siam.*

48 Foreign Affairs, 172-1/0737(2)001, "Principles of Political Negotiations with Thailand," in *The Free Thai Movement (2)*, December 1944, AH.

49 Foreign Affairs, 172-1/0695 012.22, *Siamese Delegates to China*, February–August 1946, AH.

50 Foreign Affairs, 172-1/0696 012.22, "Report of Secretary Sun Binglong's Negotiations," in *Siamese Delegates to China*, August 1946, AH.

51 Soon after the conclusion of the Greater East Asia War, China was plunged into civil war between the Chinese Nationalist Party and the Chinese Communist Party. Mao Zedong led the Chinese Communists to take over the mainland and established the People's Republic of China in 1949 while Chiang Kai-shek established a government in exile, the Republic of China, on Formosa Island. Thailand established formal diplomatic relations with the Republic of China (Taiwan) shortly after the end of the Greater East Asia War but reverted to formalizing relations with the People's Republic of China in 1975.

Chapter 5: The Cold War

1 As mentioned in the introduction, from the perspective of Greater East Asia, the Cold War in Asia ended much earlier than the Eurocentric textbook ending of the Cold War, which is usually marked by either the fall of the Berlin Wall in 1989 or the dissolution of the Soviet Union in 1991. Almost all significant historical markers for the Cold War in Asia happened in the late 1970s. These include the end of the Vietnam War in 1975, the end of the Great Proletarian Cultural Revolution and the death of Chairman Mao in 1976, the beginning of the People's Republic of China's reform era under Deng Xiaoping in 1978, and the end of the Khmer Rouge rule in Cambodia in 1979.

2 The Asia and Pacific Rim Peace Conference (October 2–12, 1952) in Beijing was a gathering of delegates from socialist states, communist sympathizers, and political activists who perceived the United States as an obstacle to peace on the Korean Peninsula. The Peace Conference called for world powers to respect the sovereignty of smaller nations and refrain from interfering in their domestic affairs. Mao's statement at the conference suggested that the Korean War was a civil war and should be sorted out among the Koreans. US intervention in support of one side of the conflict was not only an infringement on Korean sovereignty, but it also might not represent the will of the majority of Koreans.

3 [2] Office of the Prime Minister, 0201.77/16, *Report to the Prime Minister concerning the Unrest on the Night of September 20th 2488 B.E.*, September 22, 1945, NA.

4 [2] Office of the Prime Minister, 0201.77/16, *Letter from Minister of Interior to the Prime Minister concerning Allegations of a Robbery Committed by Military and Police Officers*, November 15, 1945, NA.

5 [2] Office of the Prime Minister, 0201.77/16, *Communiqué from Department of Public Relations*, September 24, 1945, NA.

6   Direk Jayanama's epic *Thailand and the Second World War* devotes less than 10 of
    the work's 643 pages to the role and contributions of China and the Chinese.
    Direk concludes that they were more problematic than helpful to Siam in the
    Second World War. There is no mention of Pridi's Free Thai missions to China.

7   [2] Office of the Prime Minister, 0201.77/16, *Letter from Minister of Interior to the
    Prime Minister concerning Sino-Thai Conflict in Bangkok Chinatown*, October 30,
    1945, NA.

8   [2] Office of the Prime Minister, 0201.77/16, *Letter from Minister of Interior to the
    Prime Minister concerning Sino-Thai Conflict in Bangkok Chinatown*.

9   Wasana Wongsurawat. "From Yaowaraj to Plabplachai: The Thai State and Ethnic
    Chinese in Thailand during the Cold War," in Vu and Wongsurawa, *Dynamics of
    the Cold War in Asia*, 284–316.

10 This was once the mansion of the secret society mafia-turned-tax farmer, Zheng
    Zhiyong, mentioned in chapter 2.

11 *The Nation*, July 8, 1974.

12 News case 7/2517/4 folder 1, *Thairath Newspaper*, July 5, 1974, NA.

13 News case 7/2517/4 folder 2, *Siamrath Newspaper*, July 8, 1974, NA.

14 News case 7/2517/4 folder 1, "Mix-Match by SathianPhantharangsi," *Chao Thai
    Newspaper*, July 8, 1974, NA.

15 *The Nation*, July 7, 1974.

16 *The Nation*, July 9, 1974.

17 From an interview with Paisal Sricharatchanya on December 7, 2007, at the Polo
    Club, Bangkok.

18 *Shijieribao*, July 8, 1974.

19 News case 7/2517/4 folder 1, "Chinese Newspaper Express Opinions," *Thairath*,
    July 7, 1974, NA.

20 News case 7/ 2517/ 4 folder 2, "Be Careful of the Second Drop of Honey," *Daily
    News*, July 9, 1974, NA.

21 The Center of Yaowarat History was constructed as part of the Grand Pavilion of
    the Golden Buddha, which was completed in 2010 to honor King Bhumibol's
    Diamond Jubilee (2006) and his eightieth birthday (2007).

22 Established in 1946 and with M. R. Seni Pramoj among its founders, the Democrat
    Party is not only the oldest functioning political party in Thailand but also the
    most consistently right-wing conservative force in the country's party politics up
    to the present.

Conclusion

1   Anderson, "Studies of the Thai State: The State of Thai Studies," in *Exploration
    and Irony in Studies of Siam over Forty Years*.

2   Ibid.

3   *Success story* should be put in quotation marks when it concerns the story of the
    ethnic Chinese in Thailand. One aspect of the history of the Chinese in Thailand
    that has been a theme throughout this book is the fact that Thai society is not

more open to the assimilation of foreign migrants than other Southeast Asian countries. It was because the ethnic Chinese established an alliance with the monarchy and the royalist elite that they eventually became part of the elite and therefore have not suffered the same sorts of discrimination the Chinese diaspora in other parts of Southeast Asia have had to endure for much of the twentieth century.

4   The Association of Southeast Asian Nations (ASEAN) is a regional intergovernmental organization founded in 1961. It currently has ten members—Thailand, Malaysia, Indonesia, Philippines, Singapore, Brunei, Vietnam, Laos, Cambodia, and Myanmar.

5   Now King Vajiralongkorn Rama X.

6   *Belt* and *road* refer to the Silk Road Economic Belt and the twenty-first-century Maritime Silk Road. These are two super-megaprojects to improve infrastructure connecting China with Central and West Asia and Europe through the belt, and linking by sea to Southeast Asia, the Indian Ocean, the Middle East, East Africa, and Europe through the road. The plan is intended to sustain high rates of growth of the Chinese economy and reestablish China as the center of world trade as it was at the height of the tribute trade in the eighteenth century.

BIBLIOGRAPHY

Archives

Academia Historica, Taipei, Republic of China (AH)
National Archives, Bangkok, Thailand (NA)
Public Record Office, London, United Kingdom (PRO)

Other Sources

Althusser, Louis. *Lenin and Philosophy and Other Essays*. Translated by Ben Brewster. London: NLB, 1971.

Anderson, Benedict. *Exploration and Irony in Studies of Siam over Forty Years*. Ithaca, NY: Cornell University Press, 2014.

———. *Imagined Communities: Reflections on the Origin and Spread of Nationalism*. London: Verso, 1998.

Atsawaphahu. "Thanks to My Chinese Friends" (Khobkhun puan Chin). *Samutthasan* 1 (January 1914): 93–95.

Bedeski, Robert E. *State-Building in Modern China: The Kuomintang in the Prewar Period*. Berkeley: Center for Chinese Studies, University of California, 1981.

Bergère, Marie-Claire. *Sun Yat-sen*. Translated by Janet Lloyd. Stanford, CA: Stanford University Press, 1998.

Bie Biliang. *Change and Initiative: A Research on Modern Overseas Chinese Education* (Chengchuan yü chuangxin: Jindai huaqiao jiaoyü yanjiu). Shijiazhuang: Hebei Educational Press, 2001.

———. "Modern Overseas Chinese Educational Policies and Measures" (Jindai huaqiao jiaoyü zhengce yü cuoshi). *Historical Studies Monthly* (Shi xue yue kan) 5 (2001).

Bie Biliang and Tian Zhenping. "Historical Investigation of Modern Overseas Chinese Education" (Jindai huaqiao jiaoyü de lishi kaocha). *Journal of Hangzhou University* 27, no. 4 (1997)

Bisalputra, Pimpraphai. *Chinese and Mon Diaspora in Siam*. Bangkok: Sarakhadi, 2004.

Bisalputra, Pimpraphai, and Jeffery Sng. *A History of the Thai-Chinese*. Singapore: EDM, 2015.

Boontananda, Thep. "King Vajiravudh and the Making of His Military Image." MA diss., Chulalongkorn University, 2013.

———. *Politics in the Military in the Sixth Reign* (Kanmuang nai kanthahan samai rachakan thi hok). Bangkok: Matichon, 2016.

Brailey, Nigel, et al. *Japan-Thailand Relations*. London: Suntory-Toyota International Centre for Economics and Related Disciplines, 1991.

Brown, Ian. "British Financial Advisers in Siam in the Reign of King Chulalongkorn." *Modern Asian Studies* 12, no. 2 (1978): 193–215.

Bualek, Phanni. *Characteristics of Thai Capitalist, 2457–2482 B.E.* (Laksana naithun Thai nai rawang poso 2457–2482). Bangkok: Phanthakit, 2002.

Chang, C. Y. "Overseas Chinese in China's Policy." *China Quarterly* 82 (June 1980): 281–303.

Chen Chin-chin. *Pre-war Educational Policies of ROC: 1928–1937*. Taipei: Historical Commission, Central Committee of the Kuomintang, 1997.

Chen Xiao-er. "Concerning the Overseas Chinese Contributions towards Thai Society" (Lun Taiguo huaqiao dui Taiguo shehui de gongxian). *Journal of Yunnan Institute for Education*, April 1995.

Copeland, Matthew Phillip. "Contested Nationalism and the 1932 Overthrow of the Absolute Monarchy in Siam." PhD diss., Australia National University, 1993.

Coughlin, R. J. *Double Identity: The Chinese in Modern Thailand*. Hong Kong: Hong Kong University Press, 1960.

Dillon, Emile Joseph. *The Disintegration of China* (Khwam krachatkrachai haeng mueang Chin). Translated by Atsawaphahu. Bangkok: Nangsuephimthai Press, 1912.

Duan Yunzhang. "Sun Yat-sen and the Overseas Chinese in the First United Front" (Di yi ci guo gong hezuo de qi de sun zhongshan yu huaqiao). *Journal of Zhongshan University*, March 1997.

Duara, Prasenjit. *Rescuing History from the Nation: Questioning Narratives of Modern China*. Chicago: University of Chicago Press, 1995.

———. *Sovereignty and Authenticity: Manchukuo and the East Asian Modern*. Oxford: Roman & Littlefield, 2003.

———. "Transnationalism and the Predicament of Sovereignty." *American Historical Review* 102, no. 4 (1997): 1030–51.

Elliott, John E. *Marx and Engels on Economics, Politics, and Society*. Santa Monica: Goodyear, 1981.

Fairbank, John K., and Merle Goldman. *China: A New History*. Cambridge, MA: Harvard University Press, 1998.

Faure, David. *The Rural Economy of Pre-Liberation China Trade Expansion and Peasant Livelihood in Jiangsu and Guangdong, 1870–1937*. Oxford: Oxford University Press, 1989.

Foucault, Michel. *Discipline and Punish: The Birth of the Prison*. Translated by Alan Sheridan. Harmondsworth: Penguin, 1991.

Gellner, Ernest. *Nations and Nationalism*. Malden: Blackwell, 2006.

Gerth, Karl. *China Made: Consumer Culture and the Creation of the Nation*. London: Harvard University Press, 2003.

Godley, Michael R. *The Mandarin-Capitalists from Nanyang: Overseas Chinese Enterprise in the Modernization of China (1893–1911)*. Cambridge: Cambridge University Press, 1981.

Hell, Stefan. *Siam and World War I: An International History*. Bangkok: River Books, 2017.

Hicks, George, ed. *Overseas Chinese Remittances from Southeast Asia, 1910–1940.* Singapore: Select Books, 1993.

Ho Fang-jiau, ed. *Documentary Collection on Overseas Chinese in Southeast Asia.* Vol. 1. Taipei: Academia Historica, 1999.

———. *Documentary Collection on Overseas Chinese in Southeast Asia.* Vol. 2. Taipei: Academia Historica, 2003.

Hoare, Quintin, and Geoffrey Nowell Smith, eds. *Selections from the Prison Notebooks of Antonio Gramsci.* London: Lawrence and Wishart, 2003.

Hobsbawm, Eric J. *Nations and Nationalism since 1780: Programme, Myth, Reality.* Cambridge: Cambridge University Press, 1997.

Hodges, Ian. "Western Science in Siam: A Tale of Two Kings." *Osiris*, n.s., 13 (1998): 80–95.

Hong, Lysa. "The Tax Farming System in the Early Bangkok Period." *Journal of Southeast Asian Studies* 14, no. 2 (September 1983): 379–99.

Hong Lin. "Outline of the Forty Years of Thai-Overseas Chinese Literature" (Tai hua wenxue 40 nian gailun). *Southeast Asian Journal*, April 1994).

Hsu, Madeline. *Dreaming of Gold, Dreaming of Home: Transnationalism and Migration between the United States and South China, 1882–1943.* Stanford, CA: Stanford University Press, 2000.

Huang Jianli. "Umbilical Ties: The Framing of Overseas Chinese as the Mother of Revolution." In *Sun Yatsen, Nanyang and the 1911 Revolution,* edited by Lee Lai To and Lee Hock Guan, 75–129. Singapore: ISEAS, 2011.

Huang Jiwen. "Overseas Chaozhou Chinese and the War of Resistance in China" (Haiwai chaoqiao yü zuguo Kangzhan). *Journal of Shantou University*, March 1995.

Huang Weiyang and Ma Songlin, eds. *Bao-an Xian Zhi.* Guangdong: Guangdong Renmin Chubanshe, 1997.

Hutchinson, John, and Anthony D. Smith, eds. *Nationalism.* Oxford: Oxford University Press, 1994.

Iaw-sriwong, Nithi. "Nation and Democracy" (Chat prachathipatai). *Matichon Weekly*, February 18, 2005.

Intarabhirom, Penspisut. *Seaw Hudseng Seeboonreung: Views and Roles of the Overseas Chinese in Thai Society* (Seaw Hudseng Seeboonreung: Thatsana lae botbat kong Jeen Siam nai sangkom Thai). Bangkok: Institute of Thai-Asian Relations History, Chulalongkorn University, 2004.

Jayanama, Direk. *Thailand and the Second World War* (Thai kap songkhram lok khrang ti song). Bangkok: Prae Pittaya, 1967.

Kasetsiri, Charnvit. *Political History of Thailand, 1932–1957.* Bangkok: Thammasat University Press, 2001.

Kay, Geoffrey. *Development and Underdevelopment: A Marxist Analysis.* London: Macmillan, 1975.

Kedourie, Elie. *Nationalism.* Oxford: Blackwell, 2000.

King Vajiravudh Foundation. *"Jews of the East" and "Thailand, Wake Up!" by Ashvabhahu* (Puak yew haeng buraphatis lae muang Thai chong tuen terd doy Ashvabhahu). Bangkok: Chuanpim, 1985.

Klom-iang, Puang-roi. "Rama VI's Policies concerning the Chinese in Thailand." MA diss., Srinakarindhraviroj University, 1973.

Landon, K. P. *The Chinese in Thailand*. London: Oxford University Press, 1941.

Limsaihua, Daorai, and Surachart Bamrungsuk. "Nationalism and Territorial Dispute in the Field Marshal Plaek Phibulsongkram Government (1938–1941)." *Journal of Politics and Governance* 1, no. 6 (September 2015–February 2016): 459–83.

Ming, K. Chan, and Gerard A. Postiglione. *The Hong Kong Reader: Passage to Chinese Sovereignty*. London: M. E. Sharpe, 1996.

Moolsilpa, Witdichai, and Ladawan Puang-nil. *Development of Private Education* (Pattanakarn khong karnsueksa ekachon). Bangkok: National Committee of Education, 1989.

Murashima, Eiji. "The Commemorative Character of Thai Historiography: The 1942–43 Thai Military Campaign in the Shan States Depicted as a Story of National Salvation and the Restoration of Thai Independence." *Modern Asian Studies* 40, no. 4 (October 2006): 1053–96.

———. "Opposing French Colonialism: Thailand and the Independence Movements in Indochina in the Early 1940s." *South East Asia Research* 13, no. 3 (November 2005): 333–83.

———. *Politics of the Overseas Chinese in Siam* (Kan muang Jeen Siam). Bangkok: Center for Chinese Studies, Chulalongkorn University, 1996.

Na Pombhejara, Vichitvong. *The FREETHAI Legend* (Tamnan Seri Thai). Bangkok: Saengdao Publishing House, 2003.

Nakamura Aketo. *Memoirs of General Nagamura* (Kwam songcham kong naipol Nagamura). Translated by Eiji Murashima and Nakarindr Mektrairatanas. Bangkok: Matichon, 2003.

Noomnandha, Thaemsuk. *The First Young Turks: Rebels of 1912* (Young Turk run raek: Kabot ro so nueng roi samsip). Bangkok: Saitan, 2002.

———. *Thailand during the Second World War* (Muang thai samai songkram lok krang tee song). Bangkok: Saitan, 2005.

Ong, Aihwa. *Flexible Citizenship: The Cultural Logics of Transnationality*. Durham: Duke University Press, 1999.

Ong, Aihwa, and Donald Nonini, eds. *Ungrounded Empires: The Cultural Politics of Modern Chinese Transnationalism*. London: Routledge, 1997.

Pan, Lynn. *The Encyclopedia of the Overseas Chinese*. Richmond: Curzon, 1999.

———. *Sons of the Yellow Emperor: The Story of the Overseas Chinese*. London: Mandarin, 1991.

Pan Ziming, ed. *Storm of Blood and Iron: Records of Thai Overseas Chinese Anti-Japanese Resistance* (Tie xue xiong feng: Taiguo huaqiao kang ri shilu). Bangkok: Thai Whampoa Alumni Association, 1991.

Panthumsen, Tos. *Memorial Publication for the Funeral of Mr. Sa-nguan Tularaks* (Anusorn ngan phrarajatan plerng sop nai Sa-nguan Tularaks). N.p., 1995.

Peake, Cyrus H. *Nationalism and Education in Modern China*. New York: Columbia University Press, 1932.

Possony, Stefan T. *Lenin Reader*. Chicago: Henry Regnery, 1966.

Pramoj, Seni. "Thailand and Japan." *Far Eastern Survey* 12, no. 21 (1943).

Puangpis, Narong. *Prince Thaniniwat and His Execution of Overseas Chinese Educational Policies while Serving as Minister of Education* (Phraworawongther

Krommuen Pityalab Pruettiyakorn lae kan damnern nayobai keaw kab rongrien jeen nai prathet thai mua krang song damrong tamnaeng senabodi Krasuang Thammakan). Bangkok: Prachan Publishing House, 1974.

Purcell, Victor. *The Chinese in Southeast Asia*. London: Oxford University Press, 1965.

———. *Problems of Chinese Education*. London: Kegan Paul, Trench, Trubner, 1936.

Qiu Jianzhang. "Concerning the Overseas Chinese Educational Policies of the Late Qing Government" (Lun wan Qing zhengfu de huaqiao jiaoyü zhengce). *Journal of Henan University* (Henan daxue xuebao) 42, no. 4 (2002).

Rakpracha, Prasit. *My Involvement in the Free Thai Movement in China* (Kapachao kab Seri Thai sai Jeen). Bangkok: P. Watin, 1997.

Reid, Anthony. *Imperial Alchemy: Nationalism and Political Identity in Southeast Asia*. Cambridge: Cambridge University Press, 2013.

Ren Guiyang. "Analyzing the Overseas Chinese Activism in Support of the May Fourth Movement" (Jianshu huaqiao dui Wusi Yundong de shenghuan huodong). *Guangdong Social Science* (Guangdong shehui kexue), March 1999.

Reynolds, Bruce E. *Thailand's Secret War*. Cambridge: Cambridge University Press, 2005.

Ruangsilp, Chai. *Thai Economic History, 2352–2453 B.E.* (Prawattisat thai samai poso 2352–2453 dan setthakit). Bangkok: Thaiwatthanapanit, 1998.

Ruangsri, Waraporn. "Border Trade and the Transformation of States in the Hinterland of Peninsular Southeast Asia from the Nineteenth Century to the Early Twentieth Century." PhD diss., Chulalongkorn University, 2013.

Sattayanurak, Saichol. *The Thai Nation and Thainess by Luang Vichitvatakarn* (Chat Thai lae kwam pen thai doy Luang Vichitvatakarn). Bangkok: Matichon, 2002.

Sen, Amartya. *The Argumentative Indian: Writings on Indian Culture, History, and Identity*. London: Penguin Books, 2006.

Shi Weiyou. "The Reasons of Overseas Chinese Having Been Employed at High Levels by Siamese Royal Family in the Monopoly Trade" (Xianluo wangshi zai longduan maoyi zhong zhongyong huaqiao de yuanyin). *Around Southeast Asia*, May 2004.

Skinner, G. William. "Chinese Assimilation and Thai Politics." *Journal of Asian Studies* 16, no. 2 (1957): 237–50.

———. *Chinese Society in Thailand: An Analytical History*. Ithaca, NY: Cornell University Press, 1957.

Srisuka, Sawat. *Free Thai Movement: Observations on the "Chamkad Balankura Mission" and Certain Military Operations (Funerary Memorial of Dr. Sawat Srisuka)* (Seri thai: Ko sangket "pathibatkan Chamkad Balankura" lae pathibatkan tang tahan bang ruang [anusorn ngan phrarajatan plerng sop dr. Sawat Srisuka]) Bangkok: n.p., 1995.

Stowe, Judith A. *Siam Becomes Thailand*. London: Hurst, 1991.

Sukagasem, Thani. "Thai-Japanese Relations during World War II." MA diss., Srinakarindraviroj University, 1979.

Sun Xiaoping. *Powerful Husbands and Virtuous Wives: The Familial Structure and the Leadership of the New Life Movement, 1934–1938*. Los Angeles: UCLA Center for the Study of Women, 2007.

Tanprasoet, Kannika. *Po Tek Tung on the Path of Thai Social History* (Po Tek Tung bon senthang prawattisat sangkhom Thai). Bangkok: Matichon, 2002.

Tejapira, Kasian. *Commodifying Marxism: The Formation of Modern Thai Radical Culture, 1927–1958*. Kyoto: Kyoto University Press, 2001.

Tien Hungmao. *Government and Politics in Kuomintang China (1927–1937)*. Stanford, CA: Stanford University Press, 1972.

Tong-an xian difangzhi bianzuan weiyuanhui. *Tong-an Xian Zhi*. Beijing: Zhonghua shuju, 2000.

Tønnesson, Stein, and Hans Antlöv, eds. *Asian Forms of the Nation*. Richmond: Curzon Press, 1996.

Tularaks, Kraisri. *Life of a Free Thai Agent (Funerary Memorial of Sa-nguan Tularaks)* (Cheewit Seri Thai [Anusorn ngan phrarajatan plerng sop nai Sa-nguan Tularaks]). Bangkok: n.p., 1995.

Turner, Bryan S. *Marx and the End of Orientalism*. London: George Allen & Unwin, 1978.

Van de Ven, Hans J. *War and Nationalism in China, 1925–1945*. London: Routledge Curzon, 2003.

Vandenbosch, Amry. "The Chinese in Southeast Asia." *Journal of Politics* 9, no. 1 (1947).

Vella, Walter F. *Chaiyo! King Vajiravudh and the Development of Thai Nationalism*. Honolulu: University Press of Hawai'i, 1978.

Vu, Tuong, and Wasana Wongsurawat, eds. *Dynamics of the Cold War in Asia: Ideology, Identity and Culture*. New York: Palgrave Macmillan, 2009.

Wang Gungwu. *China and the Overseas Chinese*. Singapore: Times Academic Press, 1991.

Winichakul, Thongchai. *Siam Mapped: A History of a Geobody of a Nation*. Honolulu: University of Hawai'i Press, 1994.

Wyatt, David K. *Thailand: A Short History*. New Haven, CT: Yale University Press, 1984.

Xia Guang. *Political Activities of the Overseas Chinese in Thailand 1906–1939* (Taiguo huaqiao de zhengzhi huodong 1906–1939). Bangkok: Center for Chinese Studies, Chulalongkorn University, 2003.

Xie Meihua. "Overseas Chinese Education and the Development of Overseas Chinese Nationalism in Southeast Asia in the Early Twentieth Century" (Huaqiao jiaoyü yu 20 shiji chu Dongnanya huaqiao minzu zhuyi de chansheng). *Overseas Chinese History Studies* 1 (Huaqiao huaren lishi yanjiu) (1997).

Xu Yang-an, ed. *Thai Overseas Chinese Personalities* (Taiguo huaqiao wuzhi). Bangkok: Ziyou Wenhua Shiye Chubanshe, 1956.

Yan Yongguang. "Coastal Education: A Bright Page in the History of Overseas Chinese Education" (Haijiang jiaoyü: Huaqiao jiaoyü shi shang de guanghui pianzhang). *Journal of Guangdong School of Education* (Guangdong jiaoyü xueyuan xuebao), no. 2 (2000).

Yong, C. F. *Tan Kah-kee: The Making of an Overseas Chinese Legend*. Oxford: Oxford University Press, 1989.

Yuan Sulian. "Reasons for the Overseas Chinese to Be Actively Involved in Anti-Japanese and National Salvation Movements" (Haiwai huaqiao jiji canjia kangri jiuwang yundong de yuanyin). *Eastern Forum* (Dongfang luntan), December 1995.

Yue Ziyun. "Mr. Yi Guangyan and the Thai Overseas Chinese Anti-Japanese and National Salvation Movements" (Yi Guangyan xiansheng yu Taiguo huaqiao de kangri jiuwang yundong). *At Home and Overseas*, December 2003.

Zhang Junzhe. "History of Chinese-Language Literature in Thailand and an Outline of Its Current Situation" (Taiguo huawen wenxue de lishi yu xianzhuang gailüe). *Overseas Chinese Historical Research* (Huaqiao huaren lishi yanjiu), April 1998.

Zhao Zhen. "Historical Overview and Future Tendencies of the New Chinese-Language Literature in Thailand" (Taiguo huawen xin wenxue de lishi saomiao yu qianzhan). *Journal of Tangshan Teachers College* (Tangshan shizhuan xuebao), January 1999.

Zhao Ziyun. "Mr. Yi Guangyan and the Thai Overseas Chinese Anti-Japanese and National Salvation Movements" (Yi Guangyan xiansheng yü Taiguo huaqiao de kangri jiuwang yundong). *Home and Overseas*, December 2003.

INDEX

A

absolute monarchy: Chinese capitalists under, 43, 112–13, 164n6; competing ideologies, 50, 70; criticism of, 17, 71; and European imperialism, 9, 24–25, 35, 112, 116–17; and extraterritoriality, 9, 45; freedom and flexibility under, 79, 173n35; and the Japanese model, 115; overseas Chinese educational policies under, 24–33; public education under, 16; restorationists, 127; transition to constitutional regime, 7, 103, 156. *See also* antimonarchism; constitutional monarchy; royalist nationalism; Siamese Revolution of 1932

agriculture, 13, 82, 109, 125, 135

Allied Powers: Allied victory celebration in Bangkok, 141, 143; and the Free Thai Movement, 38, 114, 125–30, 143; Thailand's place among, 11, 38, 129, 130, 134, 141

Anandamahidol Rama VIII, King, 131, 164–65n8

Anderson, Benedict: "imagined communities," 47, 48–49, 71, 78; "Studies of the Thai State," 156–57

Ang-yi Act of 1897, 26, 90, 167n17

anti-alien strategic areas, 77, 80, 106–8, 176n37

anti-Chinese policies, 43, 44–45, 67–68, 77–78, 90, 104–9, 113, 123, 142, 172n30. *See also under* Vajiravudh Rama VI, King

anticommunist policies, 41, 43, 140, 144–45

anti-Japanese activities, 62, 63, 65, 106, 114, 121–22, 124

anti-Manchu sentiment, 55, 56–57

antimonarchism, 17, 18, 29, 31, 34, 45, 134

ASEAN countries, 158, 182n4

Asia and Pacific Rim Peace Conference (Beijing, 1952), 139, 180n2

Asian-African Conference (Bandung, 1955), 140

Association for the Protection of the Emperor (Baohuanghui), 19

Association of Chinese Students, 26

Association of Young Workers of Siam, 42

Atsawapahu (pseud.), 56–57, 68, 69, 75, 101, 172n30; "Thailand, Wake Up!" 99–100

Ayumongkol Sonakul, M. R., 150

Ayutthaya, 12, 83, 86, 163n1

B

baba, 55, 171n9

Bangkok: Allied victory celebration, 141, 143; Chinese community in, 49; Chinese schools in, 166n11; consulates in, 164n5; established as capital, 163n1; modernization of, 16; race riots, 11, 141–45, 145–53, 154; Techawanit Road, 53. *See also* Chinatown

Bangkok Post, 150

Bangkok Recorder, 48

Bank of Taiwan, 164n6

Belt and Road Initiative, 159, 182n6

Berlin Wall, 165n10, 180n1

Bhumibol Rama IX, King: and the Center of Yaowarat History, 153, 181n21; as Cold War monarch, 137; meeting with Deng Xiaoping, 158; partnership with Phibunsongkhram, 138

bird's nest concessions, 107

black markets, 88, 89

Bowring, Sir John, 4, 13, 44, 86, 106

Bowring Treaty, 4–5, 8, 81, 86–87, 163nn2–3, 166n5

Boxer Rebellion, 92

Bradley, Rev. Dan Beach, 48

www.ingramcontent.com/pod-product-compliance
Lightning Source LLC
Chambersburg PA
CBHW031132270326
41929CB00011B/1599